Flashpoints
Studies in public disorder

David Waddington, Karen Jones,
and Chas Critcher

Routledge
London and New York

First published 1989
by Routledge
11 New Fetter Lane, London EC4P 4EE
29 West 35th Street, New York, NY 10001

Data Conversion by Columns of Reading
Printed and bound in Great Britain by
Biddles Ltd, Guildford and King's Lynn

British Library Cataloguing in Publication Data

Waddington, David P.
  Flashpoints in public disorder.
  1. Great Britain. Public disorder
  I. Title II. Jones, Karen III. Critcher, Chas
  363.3′0941

  ISBN 0–415–01238–4
       0–415–01239–2 pbk

Library of Congress Cataloging in Publication Data

also available

Contents

Contents

Tables and figures

Tables

Figures

Acknowledgements

During the course of this study we have accumulated a large number of debts which its publication will only partly repay. Our chief debt is to those citizens of South Yorkshire who as participants or witnesses in our case studies gave us their accounts on trust. Thanks are also due to senior officers of the South Yorkshire police who, at a time when the police are often antagonistic to academic research, took our project seriously and within limits gave us frank interviews.

Staff of the Department of Communication Studies at Sheffield City Polytechnic contributed in various ways, especially Guy Fielding, who was heavily involved in the early stages of the project. Secretarial support was excellent, as always, and technical staff gave sound and calm advice to forestall word-processing panic. Past and present students of the department, too numerous to name, helped with various data collection and processing, especially of a survey of a demonstrating crowd.

This book is a joint project for which we take collective responsibility, but the whole enterprise would have been impossible without the fieldwork and research of David Wadding-ton, the only researcher employed on the project. The research was made possible by a grant from the Economic and Social Research Council (Grant no. G0 225 0004) which has since funded a follow-up study of local mining communities in the aftermath of the strike.

Our partners in life, Debbie, Pete and Margaret, sustained and tolerated us throughout the five years from instigation of the research to delivery of the manuscript.

Introduction

The approach

The flashpoints model

The origins of our research on 'flashpoints' of public disorder lie in December 1981 within the research programme initiated by what was then the Social Science Research Council. The Council invited research proposals from a range of social science disciplines into the broad area of crowd behaviour and, more specifically, crowd disorder. This initiative arose in the aftermath of the widespread disorder in the inner cities which occurred during 1981, and was clearly intended to generate research findings which might contribute to policy formation in the area of public disorder.

The focus on flashpoints which was central to our research project arose as a result of its use as an explanatory concept in media and other authoritative accounts of disorder. Whether or not the term was used, a common explanation for the occurrence of disorder cited a pre existent situation of tension or conflict which could be 'sparked off', to use a common metaphor, by an ostensibly trivial incident which became the catalyst for widespread disorder. Such an explanation was mobilized by the highly influential Scarman report on the Brixton disturbances.

> The incident which *sparked off* the disorder on Saturday was nothing unusual on the streets of Brixton. . . . Why, on this occasion, did the incident escalate into major disorder culminating in arson and a full-scale battle with the police? . . . The tinder for a major conflagration was there: the arrest outside the S & M car hire office was undoubtedly *the spark which set it ablaze*. . . . Deeper causes undoubtedly existed, and must be probed; but the immediate cause of Saturday's events was a *spontaneous combustion set off by the spark of a single incident*.   (Scarman 1981, 37, our emphasis)

1

Similar explanations have been invoked in American studies of the ghetto riots of the 1960s, with this type of incident described as 'the match which lighted the powder keg' (Bowen and Masotti 1968, Mitchell 1970). Frequently the actual flashpoint incident is only the latest one in a series of similar incidents, but to the extent that it crystallizes current feelings of discontent, it comes to be regarded as the 'final straw' (Lieberson and Silverman 1965, 888). Such metaphors implicitly recognize the existence of latent hostility based on a profound sense of grievance.

This was the point of departure for our research project on public disorder. We were concerned to establish whether the notion of 'flashpoint' was merely a metaphor or whether it in fact constituted an explanation of the genesis of public disorder which our research could substantiate and elaborate.

Other reasons for our interest in this concept stemmed from our own commitment to interdisciplinary study within the broad framework of communication studies. As we shall see in our brief review of existing theories of disorder, social scientific approaches have suffered greatly from a failure to recognize that such a complex phenomenon cannot be contained within the boundaries of a single discipline. The model of a flashpoint combines reference to antecedent conditions (the 'tinder') with a highlighting of interpersonal interaction (the 'spark'), thus involving both psychological and sociological perspectives.

The inherent interdisciplinarity of the study of flashpoints was reinforced for us, as members of a Department of Communication Studies, by the implied role of various kinds of communicative processes. Such processes may assume importance in the initial formation of a crowd and during its subsequent interaction with others, especially the police. The context in which the crowd appears may be defined by prior communications, particularly those emanating from the mass media. Such considerations give communication a central role in the analysis.

The study of communication necessarily requires analysis of wider cultural processes. Hence a study using the notion of flashpoint would also involve consideration of the meanings attributed to disorderly acts by those present. Crowds assume a corporate identity and collectively interpret their own and others' actions. This invites forms of analysis which stress the symbolic aspects of human action. Moreover, this does not have to involve, as analysis of symbolic behaviour so often does, the sacrifice of any notion of a 'rationale' for such behaviour.

Yet, despite its immediate attractiveness, the notion of a flashpoint remains elusive. The term is habitually used only for those events which do in fact produce major disorder. While there may indeed be good reason to study the common characteristics of such events, the crucial comparison needs to be with those events which superficially have all the attributes of a flashpoint but which never materialize as such. To find out why and how an event becomes a flashpoint, one ideally needs to compare it with an apparently similar event which remains relatively orderly, which, to use the relevant metaphor, does not 'spark off' disorder.

Though desirable, such comparisons were to prove generally unviable since it would have been impossible to monitor all events which might have given rise to disorder. Thus we were led to concentrate mainly on events where disorder did occur. We felt, from the beginning, that our conclusions would almost certainly take us through and beyond the flashpoints model of disorder. It was in part our consciousness of this which led us to consider existing theories of disorder in the widest sense, not just those which used the notion of flashpoint.

Theories of disorder

In his introduction to the second edition of his classic textbook on social psychology, Roger Brown explains his decision to drop the chapter on crowd behaviour which had appeared in the first edition by suggesting that it was one of a number of topics which 'while they were interesting though little developed scientifically in 1965, 1985 finds them still interesting though not much more developed' (Brown 1985, xi). Why this should be so is a matter for speculation. One reason may be that it requires an interdisciplinary approach which conventional academic disciplines cannot easily incorporate. As a result, like the social scientific analysis of other social problems such as crime, the study of crowd or public disorder seems to have been bedevilled by the search for some single cause. Whether psychological, sociological, or political, such causes tend to be extracted and presented in isolation from other variables. The tendency has been for such explanations to become reductive. The activities of a crowd are reduced to a reflection of some underlying psychologically generated disposition, sociologically defined situation, or politically motivated struggle.

Examples of psychological reductionism are to be found in the work of early theorists such as Tarde and Le Bon. Here the assertion is that collective phenomena such as public disorder can be explained by the 'contagion' of emotion which grips a crowd.

The first assumption made is that crowd behaviour exhibits a lower level of morality than individual behaviour; the second, that the behaviour of the crowd or 'mob' is fundamentally irrational and governed by extreme emotionality. The following quotation from Le Bon makes this clear.

> Whatever be the ideas suggested to crowds they can only exercise effective influence on condition that they assume a very absolute, uncompromising and simple shape . . . it cannot be said absolutely that crowds do not reason and are not influenced by reasoning. However, the arguments they employ and those which are capable of influencing them are, from a logical point of view, of such an inferior kind that it is only by way of analogy that they can be described as reasoning.
>
> (Le Bon 1952, 61–2)

The theories of Tarde and Le Bon share the premise that the nature of the crowd and its activities can be explained in terms of the internal dynamics of its psychological processes, without reference to the social context. Tarde did emphasize the links between public opinion, collective action and the emergent mass media (Tarde 1901), but this line of enquiry was not subsequently pursued.

Cruder ideas about crowds were taken up again after the First World War. Works on mass psychology attempted to account for the apparently wanton savagery manifested by the combatants, at least by those of the enemy. In some cases, this explanation was buttressed by notions of the innate character of different races, some of whom were seen to have an inherent tendency towards pack-formation and other animalistic behaviour (Giner 1976).

It is of course but a small step from here to the theoretical premises of sociobiology (Ardrey 1967). This is a form of biological reductionism which sees an analogy between human aggression and animal behaviour based on instincts such as territoriality. Such theories deny the attribution of meaning and its communication, which largely distinguishes the human from the animal world. They represent an attempt to give scientific respectability to common-sense ideas about the primitive nature of disorderly behaviour. The tenacity of such beliefs in the biological explanation of human aggressive behaviour is evident in the selection of leading biologists to advise the National Commission on the Causes and Prevention of Violence set up in the United States after the ghetto riots of 1968.

A much more sophisticated version of this thesis is represented in the work of the ethological school, represented in Britain by the work of Peter Marsh (Marsh *et al.* 1978, Marsh 1978, Marsh and Campbell eds. 1982). Here what appears still to be an innate tendency to aggression, at least in the male, is overlain by the cultural controls of civilization. Where they are ineffective, stylized aggression – 'aggro' – remains. It is not anarchic, since it produces its own rules and structures. But unless it is tolerated or given alternative outlets, symbolic displays can develop into actual violence. The application of this approach to football hooliganism reveals its strengths and weaknesses. Marsh's appreciation of the meanings which hooligans attribute to their activity devalues any attempt at social explanation. We are left with an historical variant of a universal tendency of human males towards aggressive and occasionally violent behaviour.

If Marsh and others draw on the models of anthropology to provide a framework for analysis, others have pursued an interest in the psychology of groups. Zimbardo's (1969) theory of de-individuation posits that membership of, or 'submergence' in a crowd and its anonymity causes a weakening of the individual's sense of responsibility and self-control. The frustration–aggression hypothesis (Berkowitz 1972, Gurr 1970) sees rioting as an impulsive reaction to the frustration engendered by either 'blocked goals' or feelings of relative deprivation. A variation of this approach, drawing on Festinger's cognitive dissonance model, interprets riots as 'dissonance-reducing' activities, induced by the failure of economic, social, or political systems to meet specific expectations (Geschwender 1968).

Such explanations all rest on the central assumption that rioting occurs when members of a crowd respond collectively in ways which reflect a shared state of psychological arousal (Billig 1976, Tajfel 1978). By contrast, economic models (Olsen 1965) or game-theory approaches (Berk 1974) assume that individuals take a calculative attitude towards possible actions. They weigh up the benefits to be gained from looting or taking their revenge on the police against the costs of being caught.

Thus psychological approaches offer two mutually exclusive models of the rioting crowd. One is of a group who have taken on a collective mentality which allows and encourages them to forsake normal controls on behaviour. The other is of a group who take rational decisions about what they may get out of choosing to riot. What both accounts seem to omit is any consideration that collective behaviour does not have to be either irrational or rational but may be both.

One of the few psychologists to have grasped this point is Moscovici (1985). He insists on the expressive dimensions of crowd behaviour, on shared ideals and feelings, which he uses to explain in particular some features of political behaviour and the hold of leaders over their followers. The difficulty here seems to be that of recognizing both the instrumental and expressive aspects of crowd behaviour and revealing their underlying processes, whilst allowing for the specific features of any particular context. Hence Moscovici's theory of 'social representations' links social-psychological to sociological processes. The activity of the group is explicable in terms of their collective understandings of the situation which in turn relate to the wider social and ideological context. Sociologists might suggest that Moscovici has merely arrived at the point from which Durkheim started. We return to this approach in chapter ten. It certainly seems preferable to other social-psychological theories such as attribution theory (Kelley 1973). Heavily reliant on models of information processing, this does scant justice to both the psychological processes involved and the context in which they operate.

Conventional psychological approaches to the problem of crowd behaviour often find that the dynamics of crowds are not amenable to analysis in the terms established for the study of small groups. One investigation of riot behaviour revealed it as composed of 'complex behaviour processes engaged in by different groups, interwoven with varied and shifting motivations, and transmitted or blocked by a variety of formal and informal mechanisms and structures' (Stark *et al.* 1974, 893). Such inconclusiveness occurs because primacy is given to the prior states and motivations of individuals, at the expense of social and cultural influences.

This is not to claim that a sociological approach is sufficient in itself. Indeed, current sociological explanations of major public disorder as a response to social deprivation or as an index of political alienation (Downes 1970a, 1970b, Evans 1975, New Society 1982) seem hardly more convincing. Field and Southgate (1982) point out that such explanations appear to be unable to explain why unemployment and deprivation should lead to rioting at some times and places but not others. Lacking is any sense of the political context in which such riots occur and of the particular events and processes which precede them. As Reiner (1985) amongst others has remarked, the relative decline of black urban riots in the United States can be explained by such political and economic changes as the general lessening of inter-racial tensions, the limited opening of economic opportunities for an emergent black middle class, and the increased power of black communities in urban politics, not least over police forces.

The immediate history of black–police conflict is an intervening factor between experience of deprivation and resentment against law-enforcement agencies. In their account of the British urban riots of 1980–1, Kettle and Hodges (1982) stress the critical role of black–police relations, especially the way policing practices contributed directly to the disaffection of inner-city, mainly black, youth. Tuck and Southgate were prepared, prophetically as it turned out, to suggest how such a context made all interaction between police and black youth volatile:

> for whatever reasons, a small number of difficult encounters do occur and these can easily form the basis for a collective community suspicion of the police (or, indeed, spark off disorder) . . . once this happens, bad relations can become self-perpetuating. (Tuck and Southgate 1981, 44)

Even the best of these sociological explanations are limited in scope. Whilst inner-city rioting has attracted some substantive studies, emphasis on its specific causes have rather precluded comparison with other types of public disorder.

One attempt to overcome this problem of constructing a general sociological model of disorder stemmed from the interest of the structural–functionalist school of sociology in the challenge to the social order posed by individual and collective deviance. Given particular impetus by racial conflict in post-war America, this concern was translated into the attempt to construct a general theory of collective behaviour. The best known exponent of this theory is Smelser. He insists that collective behaviour is no different in principle from that of the individual. 'Collective behaviour is analyzable by the same categories as conventional behaviour' (1962, 23). Smelser bases his analysis on the four components of social action assumed by the structural–functionalist framework: values, norms, social roles, and what he calls 'situational facilities', which enable role performance in line with norms and values. Each of these components is broken down into seven levels of analysis, from the most general to the most specific. Collective behaviour of all kinds is seen as an attempt to reduce system strain in the relations between the different components of social action. Such effects are initially felt at the lower or 'operative' levels and collective behaviour signals the need to make adjustments at the higher levels of the system.

The difficulty with this theory is that it is shot through with the questionable assumptions of structural–functionalism, notably that society is a self-regulating and balancing system, that there exists an integrative and coherent value-consensus, that deviant behaviour is a reflection of flaws in the socialization and social control mechanisms of society rather than a type of motivated action, and, perhaps most questionably of all, that order is the normal state of society, disorder being atypical and exceptional. Despite the development of disorderly conduct through identifiable stages, Smelser portrays it as an irrational response, in which 'generalized hostile beliefs' serve to 'distort' reality and 'short-circuit' the normal mechanisms for redressing grievances. Hostility is frequently directed at groups, especially the police, who in Smelser's view are not responsible for the state of affairs. The basic assumption that there is a single category of collective behaviour serves to reinforce the theory's lack of a comparative or historical perspective. However, since this theory lays the greatest claim to being a comprehensive explanation of disorder, we shall discuss it in more detail in chapter ten.

Thus sociological theories seem to vary between those which are excessively particular in their concern with inner-city riots and those pitched at such a level of generality that the specifics of any individual piece of disorderly conduct are reduced to those elements which can be incorporated within a general theory of collective behaviour. One possible resolution of this difficulty is to adopt an historical perspective, which allows some grasp of the variability in the forms and occurrence of public disorder.

Historians are generally less prepared to have their agendas prescribed by the urgencies of social policy or channel their use of evidence in the interests of a grand sociological theory. Rudé's (1980) comparative study of the role of political and ideological factors in a number of historical instances of mass political mobilization is well known and avoids the reductionism of some more orthodox Marxist explanations of such phenomena.

However, a focus on those types of mass action which can be seen as actually or potentially revolutionary in portent leads to a tendency to overlook other types of collective action less easily assimilated into the categories of political analysis. One of the achievements of E.P. Thompson in his studies of pre-industrial protest (1963, 1975) was to show how collective action otherwise regarded as apolitical or even reactionary was motivated by a common sense of grievance, rooted in popular conceptions of justice:

> It is possible to detect in almost every eighteenth century crowd action some legitimising notion. By the notion of

legitimation I mean that the men and women in the crowd were informed by the belief that they were defending traditional rights and customs and that, in general, they were supported by the wider community.

(quoted in Stevenson 1979, 310)

In a detailed review of evidence about public disorder in the eighteenth and nineteenth centuries, John Stevenson has drawn attention to a number of its general features. The context for such disorders was frequently economic, but there was no direct correspondence between economic hardship and public disorder. The relationship was mediated by a felt sense of relative deprivation rather than absolute hardship. Participants in public disorder were more representative of the communities from which they sprung than has often been imagined. Historical evidence, argues Stevenson, ought to 'dispel the customary associations of riots with the criminal, the unemployed and the marginal' since 'disturbances have been recognised as involving fairly typical cross-sections of the local population' (Stevenson 1979, 301). The dynamics of events were by no means pre-determined. Much depended upon the reactions of authorities:

in studying any particular disturbance it is often possible to pinpoint a moment when things might have turned out differently. There were many occasions when crowds assembled or milled about, rumours circulated, and a kind of 'pre-riot' situation developed. At this stage a great deal depended on relatively fortuitous factors: time and again disturbances were averted by the intervention of magistrates or by a judicious show of force, and leaders of agitations themselves often took decisive actions to urge their followers to disperse when it appeared events might pass beyond their control. But inevitably in many of these situations, an inexperienced troop commander, an over-zealous policeman, a particularly determined section of the crowd, or some other event could tip the balance one way or the other. Often it was the reaction of the authorities which ultimately decided what occurred.

(Stevenson 1979, 304)

The forms of public disorder were often more controlled than they at first appeared. There was discrimination in the choice of targets for attack and restraint in the degree of violence used. Rioters were themselves injured or killed more often than they killed or injured others. Disorder was often ritualized through the use of ceremonies and symbols drawn from the wider popular culture. Not that any of this was recognized by the authorities. As Stevenson wryly notes, 'the word most frequently used to describe popular disturbances was not a description of events but of the people involved' (1979, 7). That word was 'mob'. Towards the end of the nineteenth century, such mobs were increasingly seen as being drawn from the 'dangerous classes'. According to this interpretation favoured by the Victorians, violent behaviour was rooted in marginal groups, such as the Irish, who had yet to be civilized.

The analysis offered by Stevenson and other historians of the contexts, participants, dynamics, motivation, forms of, and reaction to, public disorder has more than historical relevance. As we shall see, there are sufficient resemblances to contemporary disturbances to identify a 'tradition' of popular disorderly protest. Equally important are the explanatory emphases on the defensive nature of disorder, its relationship to a felt sense of deprivation and injustice, the political marginalization of the protestors and institutional reaction defining them as a permanent threat of anarchy.

But such perceived threats were becoming fewer. Stevenson argues that by the 1870s there had been a decline in incidents of public disorder. This he attributes less to more effective means of social control exerted by the state than to its successful absorption of dissent into the process of democratization. This is similar to the argument advanced by Geary (1985) to explain the historical decline in violent picketing, except that Geary argues this did not take place until well into the twentieth century. Clearly, there is some historical work to be done to clarify the precise timing and form of this institutionalization of conflict, some of which is being undertaken at Leicester University (Dunning *et al.* in Gaskell and Benewick 1987). We need a fuller portrait of public disorder in the first half of the twentieth century than has yet been composed. Historians cannot yet deliver a clear portrait of the historical development of disorder, but their work does allow comparison between contemporary forms of disorder and their historical counterparts.

Conceptualizing disorder

This brief review of some of the more obvious and established approaches to public disorder is intended to clarify some of the main problems which any theory of disorder must seek to resolve. Our evaluations have been mainly theoretical in nature, but there are some simple empirical tests to be made of any theory of disorder. As various reviews of the field (Wright 1978, Field and Southgate 1982, Joshua *et al.* 1983, Reicher 1984) have noted, many theoretical approaches have overlooked some fairly basic propositions. Some of the most important are the following:

1 Most crowds remain orderly
2 Disorders most commonly occur in specific types of economic, political, and ideological contexts
3 Disorders often involve ordinary members of the public who do not otherwise commit criminal acts
4 Not all the members of a crowd or community participate in disorder but those who do often have the tacit or open support of the rest
5 Disorder is frequently spontaneous but there are identifiable patterns of communication prior to and during the disorder
6 Disorder is frequently purposive, selective, and limited in its nature and form
7 Far from being innocent bystanders or victims, the police usually play a significant role in forestalling or provoking disorder.

The question which arose for us from our consideration of existing theories was what kinds of conceptual problems a theory of disorder ought at least to attempt to resolve. At the risk of over-simplification, we came to see these problems as four-fold. Firstly, any theory must recognize the collective nature of disorder. It has to be accepted that group activity has a qualitatively different logic from that of the individual, without assuming that it is necessarily of an inferior kind. Secondly and relatedly, there is the problem of meaning. Initially, this has to require concern with the meanings attributed to disorderly behaviour by those involved and by those who are witnesses. Yet we also need to understand such behaviour as a form of social action, the meaning of which is not necessarily recognized by participants or observers. Thus we need to allow for the 'expressive' aspects of disorderly behaviour, in which the expression of a felt sense of grievance may be itself the purpose of the activity. Thirdly, any theory of disorder must fairly clearly define the boundaries of the types of behaviour with which it is concerned. It must in particular avoid the extremes of either generalizing about disorder from the basis of only one type, or reducing different types of conduct to a single category of 'collective' behaviour. Finally, any theory needs to be able to indicate, even if it can never fully explain, the relationship

11

between disorder and its various political, economic, and cultural contexts, without implying disorder to be a simple reflection of strains or contradictions in the social structure as a whole.

Over the period of our research these four concerns became the criteria we felt a theory of disorder would have to meet. While it always seemed improbable that our own work could ever hope to meet all of these criteria, our research effort was directed to meeting as many of them as possible.

Research procedures

Aims

Our research had two major aims, developed in the light of the above considerations. Firstly, to study public disorder as the outcome of both predisposing factors and triggering events. Secondly, to compare and contrast the explanatory accounts of these events offered by different groups of social actors and to establish how and why they differ.

The first aim led us to look specifically at the communication processes occurring before, during, and after the event. To begin with, we felt it was necessary to establish the prior communication context within which events occur. For example, information and rumour concerning similar incidents within the locality, or extensive media coverage of public disorder elsewhere, may sensitize those involved in a potential flashpoint to the imminent possibility of disorder, thus affecting their perception of the likely reactions of others to specific actions. Clearly the communication processes which take place during the actual incident assume a crucial importance. Who says what to whom in which form may determine whether conflict escalates or is defused, as well as being a means by which collective understandings and interpretations of events are formulated and disseminated. The final stage of communication is that which takes place after the original incident. Those involved will give their version of events which will be given credence or not by others. Informally or institutionally communicated, such interpretations form the basis for the reactions of those not immediately involved.

Such communication processes do not occur within a social or political vacuum but have to be situated in a societal context. Pre-existent relations between groups in conflict, their relation to the general contours of political and economic power, and the ideologies available to validate or discredit the actions of those involved, must all be understood as the active context of the event; not just composing its background, but formative of the immediate pattern of interaction.

The second aim involved focusing not so much on the events themselves as on the accounts and explanations of those events given by different groups of social actors. In the early stages of the research, it seemed that we would be studying events which had happened in the past. Accounts would therefore be all the data we had. As it turned out, we were able to get much closer to events as they happened, so that consideration of accounts became less the ends than the means of analysis. Thus, for example, the role of media accounts in our analysis is important, but detailed analysis of the ways in which the media attribute meaning or the lack of it to disorder is to be discussed elsewhere (Brunt *et al.* forthcoming).

Selection of case studies

We began by looking for events which appeared to be or to contain flashpoints, confining ourselves to local events since the research was based in Sheffield. Indeed, we hoped that one original feature of our study would be precisely its emphasis on the role of local factors in explaining the presence or absence of disorder. When the study began in 1983, Sheffield, unlike other major British cities, had experienced no recent inner-city rioting, violent demonstrations or police–picket confrontations.

This had two implications for our research. Firstly, it meant that we had to account for this relative absence of disorder. This had the important effect, reflected throughout this book, of leading us to pay attention to what sustains order as well as to what provokes disorder. Secondly, since we could not rely on any major incidents of disorder occurring during our two-year research period, we undertook a retrospective study of past events which either had or might have produced disorder. In the process, we used various means of identifying such incidents. For example, we carried out a content analysis of a sample of the local press, especially the *Sheffield Star*, for the years 1971–83. We identified all the incidents involving public disorder, with a view to selecting incidents for retrospective study, and found that the incidents reported fell into six major categories, namely:

1 industrial picketing
2 political demonstrations
3 racial incidents

4 violence in pubs and clubs
5 street disorders often involving youth
6 football violence.

We initially explored the possibility of studying a representative range of these events, then decided to confine ourselves to relatively few types of event.

We decided at an early stage not to include football violence, since major research had been going on elsewhere and we did not have the resources to undertake the kind of detailed study necessary to complement them. We were also dissuaded by the relatively low level of football hooliganism amongst Sheffield soccer supporters, though on another occasion this would have been worthy of study in itself.

The category of pub violence, by far the largest type of event appearing in the local press, was also rejected. While it often was collective disorder, it was generally brief, small-scale, and circumscribed.

Racial violence is relatively rare in Sheffield, which has a relatively small Afro-Caribbean or Asian population and a limited history of interracial conflict. The only major incident occurring during the period we monitored was a fracas at an Asian restaurant. This was *sub judice* during the initial period of the investigation. Those accused and the police were therefore reluctant to co-operate with us and we did not pursue our investigations.

Street disorder involving youth was an interesting issue in view of Sheffield's relative freedom from such disorder during the summer of 1981, when comparable major cities experienced extensive rioting. Two incidents suggested themselves to us. In one, a protest march by skinhead youths against alleged police harassment resulted in damage to shop windows and subsequent arrests. In the other, police and black youths became involved in a fracas in the Haymarket shopping precinct in the centre of town. We eventually required only one such incident and alighted upon the Haymarket incident, since it had generated more evidence and was in principle more comparable with incidents elsewhere.

One incident which had assumed national importance but also had distinctive local implications was the picketing of the private steel firm, Hadfields, during the steel strike of 1980. This had been largely peaceful with only one serious outbreak of disorder. It thus contained instances of both the maintenance and disruption of order within an industrial context.

Thus far we had identified one instance of street disorder and one of industrial disorder. One other major form of potential disorder was that of a political demonstration. It was fortuitous that local Labour leaders organized a demonstration against a visit by Mrs Thatcher to attend the annual Cutlers' Feast in Sheffield in April 1983. We were able to do for this example what we could not for the others and follow the development of the demonstration from its initial stages through to observation of the actual event and its aftermath.

The whole course of our research was transformed by the miners' strike, which appeared likely long before it eventually began in March 1984. It seemed inevitable that there would be mass action centred on Sheffield, where the National Union of Mineworkers (NUM) had its headquarters in a traditionally militant region. We were thus able to monitor in some detail the occurrence of disorder. In April 1984, two consecutive rallies of miners supporting the strike were held to lobby members of the NUM's national executive meeting in Sheffield. Various incidents of disorder occurred during and after them. A month later, a coking plant at Orgreave on the outskirts of Sheffield was the focus of a mass picket which turned into a pitched battle between police and pickets. In Maltby and Grimethorpe, mining villages close to Sheffield, there were incidents in June and October 1984 respectively involving widespread community resistance to the presence of the police. Thus we came to have six case studies, three from the miners' strike and three from outside it, all based in or near Sheffield.

One reason for giving such a detailed account of how our case studies emerged is to emphasize that research of this kind is largely improvised. To present findings as if they were discovered in the integrated form in which they are published is to mislead the audience. We would agree that generally

> what really went on in getting some piece of research done is not fully reported in the articles or books published and . . . hence other intending researchers and/or naive readers may develop false impressions about the processes of doing research.   (Atkinson in Bell and Newby 1977, 31)

We did not begin our research with a model of the ideal set of case studies. They emerged from our own explorations and from a momentous political event. If we have therefore succeeded in imposing some sort of logic on our case studies, this should be understood as an outcome of the research process not an integral part of the initial research design. Though not exactly an accident, the pattern of case studies which emerged was contingent upon factors not within our control as researchers, such as the instigation of a miners' strike during the period we happened to be studying public disorder in Sheffield. What we could and did do, was to drop much of our initial general exploration of disorder in order to concentrate on the miners' strike. We were later able to see that it was possible to pair each event outside the miners' strike with one inside it, under generic categories of disorder. This gave the pattern indicated in table 0.1.

Table 0.1   Selection of case studies

Category	Outside miners' strike	Inside miners' strike
Political demonstrations	'Thatcher Unwelcoming' (April 1983)	NUM rallies (April 1984)
Picketing	Hadfields (February–March 1980)	Orgreave (May–June 1984)
Community disorders	Haymarket (August 1981)	Maltby/Grimethorpe (June–October 1984)

Only when we had arrived at this classification did it become clear that a series of early pragmatic decisions could now be endorsed as having an underlying principle. We had in fact dropped what Smith (1983, 159) terms 'issue-less' riots – in our case pub violence and football hooliganism – in favour of what he terms 'issue-oriented' riots, in our case demonstrations, industrial picketing, and community disorder. From this point on, our use of the term disorder ceased to refer generally to those events which disrupt public order but to those in which disorder can be seen as motivated by a conscious issue. According to Smith, issue-oriented riots show the presence of a legitimating belief, stemming from a social structural problem which justifies and explains the actions of the rioters. By contrast issue-less riots are a reaction to social conditions, but the form of the riot behaviour and its targets do not reveal what is being protested against. While not wishing to endorse the use of the term riot or ignore the role of the police (Smith's main aim is to construct a model applicable to sport), the general distinction is one we have come to use in the process of selecting our case studies and offering explanations of disorder.

The problem of defining what constitutes public disorder we solved pragmatically, but in presenting our findings there is an obligation to delimit more precisely the behaviour with which we are concerned. As we discuss in the conclusion, legal definitions, such as 'affray' or 'riot', are apparently defined quite closely but in practice subject to a great deal of interpretative discretion. The criminal charges laid against those involved in the disorders we came to study also included much more diffuse offences, such as threatening behaviour or obstruction. The status of public disorder as a social science concept is even less established, there being no definition of it in social science dictionaries. We can therefore only offer the following definition which came to guide our research, though we claim no great epistemological status for it. Public disorder has been defined for the purposes of our research as action which:

1 happens in a public place
2 involves relatively large numbers of people
3 has an ascertainable purpose related to a specific issue
4 results in violence against persons or property.

Methodology

The process of collecting data was going on all the time we were selecting our case studies and sifting through the relevant literature. With the limited resources of just one, albeit energetic, fieldworker, there was a limit to the amount which could be collected about any one incident. We therefore simply specified the goal of obtaining as many accounts of what had happened as could be collected in the time available. The overall profile of the sources of evidence is presented in table 0.2. The introductions to each of parts one to three of the book give a more detailed picture of the evidence available about that pairing of case studies. Altogether, there were five main data sources.

Table 0.2 Data sources for case studies

Case study	Crowd members	Senior police	Local media	National media	Legal sources	Field observation
'Thatcher Unwelcoming'	√	√	√	√	x	√
NUM rallies	√	√	√	√	√	√
Hadfields	√	√	√	x	x	x
Orgreave	√	√	√	√	√	√
Haymarket	√	x	√	√	√	x
Maltby/Grimethorpe	√	√	√	√	√	x

Introduction

1 Crowd members

In most cases, members of the crowd were interviewed after the event and asked to give their explanations for what had happened. Occasionally, especially when miners had been involved, such material was gained from group discussions. Only in one instance, that of the 'Thatcher Unwelcoming' demonstration, were we able to conduct a survey of the crowd. Otherwise, it was simply a question of talking to as many different kinds of participants as possible. We were generally more successful in gaining the views of ordinary participants than those of political leaders who for various reasons were unable or unwilling to talk to us.

2 The police

For all except one of the incidents, that of the Haymarket fracas, senior police officers from the South Yorkshire force gave us full and frank interviews about their own role in the proceedings. We were not, however, able to obtain interviews with rank-and-file police officers, especially those in the Police Support Units who were most actively involved in the policing of some of the incidents studied. Thus there was a rather peculiar imbalance in the kinds of evidence gathered from what were occasionally the two sides of the conflict. From the crowd, we generally had views of the rank-and-file rather than those of the leadership, whereas the reverse was true of the police. Hence when we compare accounts we are not always comparing like with like, since crowd members were often literally in the front line, while senior police were directing operations, largely from behind the police lines. These 'missing' accounts would have been worthwhile. Later we suggest that two of the many variables likely to affect the likelihood of order are the attitudes of crowd organizers and the nature of the control exercised over front-line police but we were not able to examine such factors in practice as much as we would have liked.

3 Media coverage

We found it possible to use media accounts as a particular kind of evidence about incidents of disorder. This was so despite the considerable controversy surrounding alleged inaccuracies and bias in media coverage of public disorder, especially during the miners' strike. That we felt able to do this was largely due to the quality of reporting in the two local Sheffield newspapers, especially the *Sheffield Star*. We have discussed elsewhere (Brunt *et al.* forthcoming) why and how the attitude of this paper to any incident occurring in or around Sheffield requires it to seek both sides of the story, effectively that of the police and that of the crowd. This practice was helped by the fact that the crowd frequently contained leading local politicians, whose version of events had an inherent legitimacy. This balance was less scrupulously maintained in the now-defunct *Sheffield Morning Telegraph*, though this was a useful source for accounts of local court proceedings. Local radio, especially Radio Sheffield, was another useful source both on matters of fact and for interview material. It is perhaps worth stressing that in research of this kind the quality of the local media is an important factor. As we know from our own and others' experiences in different cities, the local press cannot always be given even the limited trust we were able to give to their accounts. Indeed, we found during our own study that some of the local weekly papers were not always trustworthy.

4 Personal observation

For three of the events our fieldworker was there in person. Thus we were able to draw on his extensive notes as an account in itself and as a cross-check on matters of detail. This was especially valuable for the two demonstration studies, where physical layout assumed critical importance. His notes also provided first-hand observation of an incident after an NUM rally which resulted in fighting between police and miners.

5 Other sources

At various times in the research we obtained interviews with those who had special access to relevant information, for example journalists present at incidents and solicitors conducting subsequent court cases. There were also some documentary sources, including various police reports about disturbances and of course the voluminous literature on the whole course of the miners' strike, in so far as it bore on the incidents which interested us.

The results of this approach were several hundred hours of taped interviews, boxes full of newspaper cuttings, notebooks of observational material, as well as more or less detailed summaries of other relevant studies. We have used these sources mainly for their content. We are aware, particularly from our involvement in communication studies, that the form in which accounts are offered structures the content. A group of miners sitting round a table in the local Miners' Welfare, a police officer giving an interview to a polytechnic researcher, or a witness giving a statement to a solicitor, all use different codes of communication. Not merely how they express themselves but what they feel able and willing to express are determined by the situation and its established modes of discourse. The problem is compounded in media accounts, since they have already been filtered by journalists into the codes of newspapers, radio, or television. We have not been able in our analysis of events to pay the attention to these variations in codes which might otherwise be expected from a communications perspective. This is largely the result of the expanding scale of the research and its eventual orientation. Had the focus been as limited as we originally thought, such considerations would have been more to the fore. A side-product of this research has been at least one study which concentrates on the linguistic and visual codes of press coverage of Orgreave (Brunt *et al.* forthcoming).

These are the kinds of materials and the ways we have chosen to use them in constructing our case studies. We have written them up in the three pairs of demonstrations (part one), picketing (part two), and community disorder (part three). This not only follows the logic of our typology of disorder, it also allows those with a particular interest in one type of disorder to focus on that initially. Thus though there are some cross-references, it is not essential to read the pairs of studies in the order in which they are presented.

Each of the three parts begins with a brief introduction outlining our approach to the material. For each of the two case studies, we present a chapter organized into background, overview, analysis, and summary. In the third chapter of each section we compare the two case studies, consider other comparable documented incidents and offer some general propositions about this type of disorder. The conclusion of the whole book falls into chapters ten and eleven. We first outline our own model of disorder and compare it with other major theories. Finally, we assess the likely effectiveness of current legal and policy initiatives, and their constitutional implications.

A preliminary model

To those interested in such matters, our approach to research could be categorized in terms familiar to social scientists as 'inductive', involving the 'triangulation' of methods and close in some ways to 'grounded theory'. For us, these strategies have been less matters of epistemological principle than pragmatic solutions to the exigencies of research. Problems persisted in the writing up of the research, which we wanted to reflect as far as possible the process of the research itself. Thus, in initial drafts of this book, we held back our own theory of public order and disorder until the penultimate chapter, since it did not logically precede but actually evolved out of our discussion of case study material. Elsewhere (Waddington *et al.* 1987), we have presented our findings in a condensed form, so that the theory was outlined before using case study material as exemplification. This is the more orthodox way of writing up social science research. Our departure from this procedure in our initial draft puzzled and disappointed whose who read it, since they expected our own model to be presented early in the proceedings. We still think that holding it back is a correct and logical way of presenting our research. But any book is an act of communication and indications of difficulty in decoding require some adjustment in the message.

Thus, while a full account of our theory remains delayed until chapter ten, it seems that it would be useful to offer some preliminary outline of the general ideas which guided our analysis of empirical material. We present this, as it was originally formulated for an early presentation of our work, in figure 0.1. Its design, as a series of concentric rings, is both crude and arbitrary. Nevertheless, it does reveal how we initially concep-tualized the research problem, as we reviewed the literature and our own preliminary findings.

We began with the notion of a *flashpoint* and sought to set it in a number of ever-widening contexts. We assumed that a flashpoint was a dramatic break in a pattern of *interaction* which might itself help to explain why and where disorder broke out. Such interaction would take place in a defined *situation*. Essentially, this would be that of a demonstration, picket, or street confrontation, but significant variation might be expected in the characteristics of any situation, including its precise physical location. A particular incident would also have its own pre-history – incidents of a similar nature in the recent past which would be common knowledge amongst all those present. This we termed the *contextual* level. But how this context, and indeed the situation and its interactions, might be understood seemed likely to vary amongst participants according to their preconceptions. This *cultural* element might well incorporate definitions of the situation, leading to one or both sides perceiving their interests to be threatened by the presence or actions of the other.

This idea of threat and conflict was likely to have previously

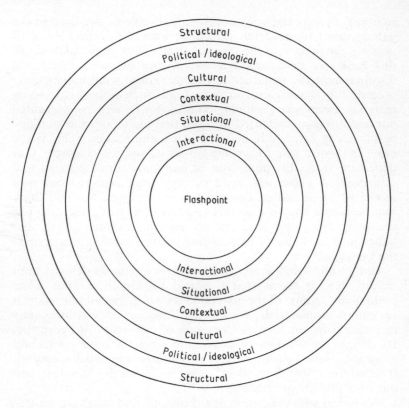

Figure 0.1 Levels of structuration in public order situations

entered the *political/ideological* arena, so that members of political elites would have debated the rights and wrongs of the issue and its manifestations, especially through the media. This was most likely where broader questions of political and economic power were at stake, so that the whole incident would be related to underlying *structural* conflicts of interest in the society as a whole.

We were attempting to represent different levels of influence in a way which avoided two ways of reducing the complexity of flashpoints. The first, most typical of the psychological perspectives reviewed earlier, confines itself to the dynamics of the interaction in its immediate situation, so that the only wider context considered is that of the mentality of the crowd. The second, most prevalent amongst sociologists, sees flashpoints as the inevitable outcome of racial, political, or industrial conflict, with little attention to what actually happens on the ground. We were seeking a pattern or configuration of factors which cumulatively and in interrelation would explain why some incidents became disorderly and others did not.

The precise details of the number and complexity of the factors identified as salient at each level are given in chapter ten, where we draw on examples from our case studies. It was as a way of testing out the development of this initial model that we decided to supplement our own case studies with others of a similar kind for which we could find adequate documentation. Only by considering both our own data and that from others could we progressively redefine the model to the point where we felt that we had encompassed all the relevant variables. So we have maintained our strategy of delivering the model at the point and in the form in which it appeared in the progress of the research. Here we have simply given some indication of the preliminary considerations which guided our analysis.

Part one

Demonstrations and disorder

Introduction

Our first set of case studies focuses on political demonstrations. The first example quite clearly comes into that category. In April 1983, local political and trade union leaders organized a demonstration against a visit to Sheffield by Mrs Thatcher. The outcome was almost entirely orderly. This took place during the period of our fieldwork, so we were able to study the whole event in some detail. Our account is therefore based on a multiplicity of sources. Our fieldworker observed the meetings of organizers and the demonstration itself. Documents of various kinds relating to the demonstration, such as leaflets and circulars, were collected. Local and national media coverage of the event was carefully monitored. A survey of a crude sample of just over 300 of the 4,000 to 5,000 demonstrators present was conducted by a team of polytechnic undergraduates using a standardized questionnaire. The principal organizers of the protest were interviewed, as were the Chief and Deputy Chief Constable of South Yorkshire.

This example of an orderly demonstration is in this section compared with what were strictly speaking rallies. During the early part of the miners' strike in April 1984, two rallies were held by members of the NUM in Sheffield within a week of each other. Incidents of disorder occurred both during and after the first rally, held to lobby a meeting of the union executive. The main part of the second rally to lobby a conference of national delegates remained largely orderly but there was a serious incident of disorder shortly afterwards. Both of the main rallies were observed. The same two senior police officers were again interviewed. Twelve members of the Yorkshire area NUM gave us interviews and we had access to sworn statements and court evidence given by witnesses and participants about events after the second rally. Media coverage was more extensive than that for the 'Thatcher Unwelcoming' demonstration, including detailed eye-witness accounts from journalists.

Description and analysis of the 'Thatcher Unwelcoming' demonstration is the subject of chapter one. The equivalent for the NUM rallies is provided in chapter two. In chapter three the case studies are compared with each other and with other major studies of disorder at demonstrations. These include the accounts by Halloran *et al.* (1970) of the 1968 Anti-Vietnam war demonstration, the National Council for Civil Liberties (NCCL) inquiry (1980) into events around a National Front election meeting held in Southall in 1979, and the Report of the Independent Inquiry Panel (1985) to Manchester City Council about a visit to the city's university by Home Secretary Leon Brittan in 1985. A model is then developed of the factors which predispose political demonstrations to greater or lesser degrees of order or disorder.

1
The Cutlers' Feast demonstration, April 1983

Background

The Cutlers' Feast is an annual Sheffield event, with origins in the fifteenth century as a celebration of the trade. Originally, the Feast lasted for three days and was the excuse for a local holiday. A tradition was established for the Master Cutler to invite a principal guest to show gratitude for some favour extended to the cutlery industry, or in anticipation of future benevolence (De Gorde Peach 1960).

At various times in its history, the Feast, as a symbol of wealth and prestige, has been the occasion for political protest. As late as 1868, a local Liberal MP was threatened with violence should he attend the Feast. In the twentieth century, controversy has been less frequent, though in 1971 the Conservative Prime Minister, Edward Heath, attended the Feast during conflict over his Industrial Relations Bill. As he stepped from his car at the entrance to the Cutlers' Hall, an apple was thrown at him by one of the 300 demonstrators present. Fighting broke out as police moved in and eleven people were arrested.

James Callaghan, Labour Prime Minister, fared no better in 1979 when he was invited to receive the freedom of the city during the 'Winter of Discontent', when the Trade Union movement opposed his government's counter inflationary policy. Callaghan was met outside the City Hall by 200 demonstrators campaigning against low pay. The demonstration itself was peaceful, though his acceptance speech was heckled.

The decision was taken in 1983 to invite Mrs Thatcher to be the guest of honour at the Feast. During the previous two years, the Prime Minister had become a regular target for angry protestors. Various incidents had occurred during her visits to Warminster and Bristol in 1981; Grantham, Glasgow, and Aberdeen in 1982; Bingley, Lancashire, and Cambridge early in

1983. Eggs, flour, and tomatoes had occasionally been thrown at Mrs Thatcher's car with some arrests as a result. A hostile reception seemed likely when she visited a city whose industry had virtually collapsed, governed by a left-wing council opposed to rate-capping. Predictably, local political leaders announced their intention to organize a demonstration.

The impetus for the demonstration was provided at a steelworkers' rally in Sheffield on 29 January 1983, the day after her acceptance of the invitation was disclosed in the *Sheffield Star*. At the rally, speakers advocated some form of protest. A local political activist approached two speakers from the Iron and Steel Trades Confederation (ISTC) and expressed his willingness to organize and publicize a demonstration if they would act as figureheads. This they agreed to do.

A 'Thatcher Reception Committee' was formed and expanded around this nucleus. Approaching the Labour group on Sheffield City Council, the committee discovered that the local Trades Council and District Labour Party were forming an 'Unwelcoming Committee' of their own. The Reception Committee were invited to merge with this 'official' body. Whilst suspicious of the motives of the Labour group in view of impending local elections, they agreed.

Major disagreements about strategy threatened this alliance. The Reception Committee advocated industrial action to bring Sheffield to a standstill but the Unwelcoming Committee favoured an orderly demonstration. These differences were never satisfactorily resolved. As leader of the Unwelcoming Committee, Roger Barton took the view that the impact of the demonstration would occur as much in the build-up to the event, as during and after it. Consequently the Unwelcoming Committee distributed in shopping centres, factories, and unemployment benefit offices leaflets including supportive statements from a range of local political groups. Letters and posters were sent out to various organizations requesting their support.

The Reception Committee favoured a mass appeal. The Socialist Workers' Party produced and distributed thousands of posters and leaflets bearing a huge head-and-shoulders portrait of the Prime Minister captioned: 'Stop Thatcher! Demonstrate April 28th'. Such differences, manifestly of style and latently of objectives, produced a deterioration in relations between the two groups, culminating in an acrimonious meeting early in March when a permanent split occurred. This division did not radically affect the outcome of the demonstration, since the Unwelcoming Committee soon established a dominant position.

This dominance was especially evident in their use of the local media to put across their hopes and intentions for the demonstration. One example of the sophistication of their strategy was to promise a spectacular finale to the demonstration which would be talked about for years to come. This transpired to be a minute's silence for the unemployed, not a wholly original gesture, but one which served to whet the media's appetite. Local radio gave airtime to the organizers, though avoiding any implicit endorsement of the demonstration. Thus coverage included an allegation that the City Council had threatened to blacklist the firm with the contract to ferry the Cutlers' Feast guests to and from the hall.

Press coverage was more partisan. The pre-demonstration editorials in the local evening *Sheffield Star* tended to express approval for the demonstration as defined by the Unwelcoming Committee. On 27 April, its editorial saw the demonstration as 'a welcome chance for Sheffield to state its case and express its feelings' which 'should not be wasted'. The following evening's edition carried an open letter to Mrs Thatcher, appealing to her to recognize the protest as 'a human cry of distress from a community that is suffering and full of fear for the future'. By contrast, the daily *Morning Telegraph* projected the views of its business readers, some of whom would be attending the Feast. Its leader writer on 28 April considered it 'shameful' that a guest of the city should be treated to such a reception. It forecast that 'the whole squalid, shabby business' would be all too predictable, 'the converted yelling shoulder to shoulder with the converted'. 'Rent-a-mob' protestors and their 'exhibitionism' would only damage Sheffield's reputation. Even here, however, there was no direct suggestion that any disorder would occur. The objection was to the lack of courtesy involved rather than to any threat to public order. Since the police also expressed their hope that order would prevail, the immediate context of the demonstration betrayed no hint of potential disorder.

Overview

To understand the outcome of the demonstration, it is important to establish a sense of what the crowd was like. Our survey of the demonstrators, which was random in the literal rather than the scientific sense, provided a rough profile of the demonstrators. Of the 4,000 to 5,000 people attending the demonstration, 58 per cent were male and 42 per cent female. Eleven per cent of the demonstrators were under 18 years of age; 38 per cent were between 18 and 24; 34 per cent between 25 and 34; and the remainder (17 per cent) were over 35 years old. Ninety-one per cent of our respondents were residents of Sheffield.

Approximately one third of the demonstrators belonged to the Labour Party, just under a quarter to CND, and one sixth to trade unions. Also present, though fewer, were members of women's groups, the Communist Party, the Socialist Workers' Party, ethnic and anti-racist organizations, and tenants' and pensioners' action groups. But a third of those present belonged to no such organization (table 1.1).

Table 1.1 Political affiliation of demonstrators at the 'Thatcher Unwelcoming'

Political group	%
Labour Party	34
CND	23
Trade union	17
Women's group	8
Socialist Workers' Party	3
Ethnic organization	3
Communist party	3
SDP Liberal Alliance	2
None	33
Others	1

N = 314
Multiple responses allowed

Of every ten demonstrators, two were unemployed, four were students, three were employed in non-manual and one in manual occupations (table 1.2). The young and the actually or potentially middle-class therefore provided the mainspring of dissent.

Table 1.2 Occupational status of demonstrators at the 'Thatcher Unwelcoming'

Occupational status	%
Non-manual, employed	28
Manual, employed	9
Self-employed	3
In full-time education	35
Housewife	2
Old age pensioner	2
Unemployed	21
Total	100

N = 314

Table 1.3 What people were protesting about

Issue	%
Unemployment	46
All Tory policies	35
Government defence policy	29
Public spending cuts	17
Cheap fares in South Yorkshire	13
Steel closures	13
Racism/immigration laws	12
Police powers	9
Northern Ireland	7
Employment legislation·	6
Old age pensions	6
Others	11

N = 314
Multiple responses allowed

Given the relative prominence of Labour Party supporters, CND activists, trade unionists, and the unemployed, it was not surprising that 'all Tory policies', 'government defence policy', and 'unemployment' were the issues most protested against. Some diversity was evident in less prominent issues, which included such national matters as 'public spending cuts', 'racism', and 'trade union rights', and more local ones, such as 'steel closures' and 'cheap fares in South Yorkshire' (table 1.3).

Activities during the demonstration reflected the diversity and energy of the demonstrators' political commitments. Leaflets were circulated imploring the demonstrators to 'Stop This Missile Madness' and join the Campaign for Nuclear Disarmament (CND), 'Oppose the Police Bill', 'Remember Bobby Sands', or support the occupation of the Firth Derihon factory where eighty workers were resisting compulsory redundancies. An official souvenir programme was distributed on behalf of the Socialist Society which contained details of the seven courses that were on the menu for those not invited to the Feast. 'Whitehall Leak Soup, strips of national assets (doused in North Sea Oil), red herrings (freshly manufactured), steel workers (locally butchered), sliced welfare steaks (with austerity sauce), profit rolls and, to end it all, bombe surprise.'

This combination of the serious and the satirical was accentuated by street and Caribbean bands, effigies of the Prime Minister, street theatre players, and a National Association of Local Government Officers (NALGO) Victorian Soup Kitchen. The crowd watched with amusement and discussed the issues. Most could and did listen to a succession of speakers.

Local ISTC official, Keith Jones, stressed that the demonstration was not aimed at the Prime Minister herself but what she stood for. The leader of the South Yorkshire County Council took local unemployment for his theme, one reiterated by a representative of The People's March For Jobs, which had reached nearby Huddersfield. A CND speaker opposed nuclear arms and power. David Blunkett, leader of the City Council, argued that those outside the hall were more representative of the people of Sheffield than those inside it. Arthur Scargill felt the demonstration heralded the start of a mass campaign to remove the present government.

Part of Scargill's speech was drowned by a storm of booing as the first coach bearing guests for the feast drew up. Whenever this happened, the crowd set up a chant of 'Scum! Scum!'. One coach was hit by an apple, some eggs, and a bag of flour. These sudden eruptions remained sporadic and did not increase in intensity or duration.

By the time of Mrs Thatcher's arrival, the police were standing four deep in front of the crowd with a row of mounted police behind them. This made it difficult for the demonstrators to see what was happening in front of the hall. When the Prime Minister did arrive and stepped out of her car, a chain reaction was set off by people booing, jeering, and shaking their fists in the air, but not all realized that Mrs Thatcher had arrived.

Her arrival was the moment when a flashpoint might have developed but little happened. An egg hit one mounted police officer, momentarily unsettling horse and rider. In a separate incident, a police horse panicked, lost its footing and banged its head against a police car, shattering the windscreen. The horse bolted and threw its rider but was soon retrieved. Neither this incident nor the general noise seemed to affect Mrs Thatcher as she walked quickly into the hall.

That many demonstrators did not even know she had arrived was evident from various rumours circulating amongst the crowd, to the effect that she had sneaked in through a back way or had been hidden amongst the guests on one of the coaches. Another version was that the horse had been frightened by a brick being thrown and that the perpetrator had been arrested. The crowd were confused and a little puzzled but their concern was in no way angry or resentful.

There was a sense of anti-climax, relieved when David Blunkett reappeared on the platform to congratulate the crowd and ask for their participation in a minute's silence, which was for the most part observed by the crowd. Blunkett then thanked the crowd, invited them to the Alternative Feast and asked them to join with the Caribbean band in a rendition of 'Give Peace a Chance'.

Shortly afterwards, the demonstrators began to disperse, some going to the Alternative Feast, others homeward. Altogether thirteen people were arrested during the demonstration, two for assaulting a police officer, three for throwing eggs, eight for threatening behaviour. Six more were arrested later as drunk and disorderly, making a grand total of nineteen arrests. As one local councillor remarked, this was fewer than might be expected at a local football match.

Analysis

After the demonstration, both the police and the organizers provided their own explanations for the order which prevailed. The organizers referred to such factors as the careful organization beforehand, the rapport built up between themselves and senior police officers, and the responsible attitude of the crowd. The police similarly paid tribute to the good behaviour of the crowd, which they felt had vindicated their own approach to the demonstration.

An explanation for the relatively few arrests was offered by one of the organizers on local radio.

> One or two policemen . . . and one or two of the crowd . . . have acted out of the spirit of how the whole thing has gone. I've been speaking to senior police officers. They're very pleased with the whole tone and spirit of the demonstration. I'm more than satisfied with how the vast majority of police have handled themselves. I regret that some people, on both sides, did allow it to get into a situation where there have been some people carted off.   (Radio Sheffield 29 April)

The police view, expressed to us by the Deputy Chief Constable in interview, was that only a few of the demonstrators 'allowed the situation to go to their heads a bit'.

It is worth considering these factors in more detail to see whether they constitute a sufficient explanation for the absence of disorder and to draw some general propositions from this particular case.

Police policy towards the demonstration sought to balance the physical safety of the Prime Minister against the right of the local community to make an orderly protest. Their preparations for the visit began as soon as the invitation was accepted. The local industrial relations climate was monitored, since a major dispute involving the miners or steelworkers would add a new dimension to the demonstration. Previous instances of visits to the area by Prime Ministers were examined but found to have limited use, since none included a situation where local authorities were in direct and daily conflict with central government.

The police were therefore aware of a potential for violence but saw it as their role to pre-empt it in the first instance, while being in a position to respond quickly to any that might occur. Thus from the outset the police were anxious to negotiate with the organizers to achieve a form of protest which would minimize the possibility of disorder. This police concern to negotiate complemented the organizers' wish to avoid anything likely to detract from an image of responsible protest. Both sides thus had quite specific reasons to ensure that liaison was established, maintained, and effective. One specific agreement was that the demonstration should be confined to a specific location, the forecourt of the city cathedral, directly opposite the Cutlers' Hall. For their part, the police raised no objection to the erection of a platform for speakers.

The organizers made a concerted attempt to define the demonstration as an orderly protest, disavowing any intention to create disorder. In local media interviews, they consistently warned against giving Mrs Thatcher the opportunity to dismiss the demonstrators as a mob and stressed that the protest was not aimed at her personally but at the policies of her government. One of the Unwelcoming Committee's leaflets distributed on the day of the demonstration appealed to demonstrators to 'remain peaceful and disciplined, for it has never been the aim of the organisers to try and physically prevent the Prime Minister from attending our local dignitaries' "Beanfeast" '. Such statements could not alone guarantee an orderly outcome but helped set the tone of the demonstration.

The demonstrators were not in any case predisposed to violence. In replies to one of our survey questions about who would welcome disorder at the demonstration, 'Mrs Thatcher', 'the media', and 'the police' were most often nominated. The 'small minority' of the crowd seen by some to share this vested interest in disorder did not include any of the respondents themselves.

Other characteristics of the crowd were relevant. That most came from Sheffield was seen to be important by the police, who in interview referred with some parochial pride to 'a stable, solid community' who were 'highly responsive to authority'. Class composition and regional culture both reinforced the value placed on order as a political tradition. Most of the crowd were seasoned demonstrators (77 per cent had demonstrated before, 69 per cent in the last sixteen months) who recognized the rules of the political game. Those who brought their children along indicated both the intention and the expectation that the demonstration would remain orderly.

There were also conscious attempts to channel the attention of the crowd. A festive atmosphere was induced by the provision of entertainment, from balloons to music. Political speeches provided an orderly rallying point for the crowd. The decision of the Provost of Sheffield Cathedral to permit the erection of the platform was regarded as crucial by both police and organizers. As one of the latter explained in a radio interview, 'the decision was absolutely key in making sure that the demonstration was orderly' (Radio Sheffield 29 April 1983). The one minute's silence also served to focus and express the crowd's feelings, while the Alternative Feast of Fun provided a specific incentive to disperse.

Specific police tactics were clearly designed to prevent disorder. It was decided at the outset primarily to use local officers. Reinforcements were brought in from outside, but only as a precautionary measure, as the Deputy Chief Constable explained to us at the time:

> We're bringing in policemen from West Yorkshire. Whether we use them depends, of course, on how the demonstration goes. But I do stress that it has been the organizers' intention, and we've had an awful lot of co-operation from them, that it will be a powerful and dignified demonstration. I would hope not to use very many policemen. But, of course, you've got to cater for those people who come down there purely to cause trouble.

He felt that the respect for authority in the local community, combined with the insignificance of left-wing sects and anarchist groups, made his task easier than it would have been in some other cities. Hence he felt able to accord some trust to the crowd and its organizers.

There were nevertheless special measures taken to minimize the possibility of confrontations, especially between demonstrators and guests. The police insisted that the guests be transported to the Cutlers' Hall by coach. This prevented both guests and demonstrators from provoking each other, while allowing some ritual insults to be exchanged in a relatively harmless form.

Before and during the demonstration, the police discouraged anything which might provoke the crowd, opposing a mooted counter-demonstration by Conservative trade unionists. Inside the hall on the day one of the guests, a local Conservative politician, was threatened with arrest if he persisted in making gestures and waving a blue handkerchief at the crowd.

Compliance with the police request to hold the demonstration in the confined space of the cathedral forecourt enabled the erection of crash barriers early in the day. As the crowd built up slowly behind them, the numbers of police increased gradually. The Deputy Chief Constable validated this strategy in interview:

> The essential thing is to get there before the crowd. If the crowd are there before you, you've got to use force, normally, to get them back, so immediately you're on the wrong footing. The crowd, by and large, will fall in behind whatever you erect.

The crowd made no attempt to cross the barriers and the police rarely crossed the other way. Only a few officers, mainly in pairs, were stationed in the crowd, which was largely stewarded by volunteers from the Amalgamated Union of Engineering Workers (AUEW). The fixed location of the crowd further enabled police carrying radios to patrol the surrounding rooftops and pinpoint any potential sources of trouble. Action by the police was directed against identified individuals for specific offences, not indiscriminately against the crowd as a whole. Occasionally, the crowd actually assisted police officers in making an arrest, an indication of both the legitimacy accorded to police tactics on the day and an identification with the official version of the purpose of the demonstration. The police had helped to cultivate such a relationship, those officers stationed directly in front of the crowd having taken every opportunity to chat and indulge in good-natured banter. This was a deliberate ploy; in the initial briefing they had been exhorted to 'jolly the protestors along'.

Summary

Despite the disorders which had taken place during recent visits of Mrs Thatcher to other parts of the country, her visit to Sheffield passed off peacefully. This seemed attributable to four factors. Firstly the organizers adopted the view that disorder would not be in their political interests and set out to define the objectives of the demonstration in these terms. They also showed the ability to discipline and channel the behaviour of the crowd. They liaised closely with the police, whose policy of low-key policing throughout the event was the second important factor. The police succeeded in determining that the third factor, the venue, would maximize their ability to control and survey the crowd. Finally the crowd itself showed no inclination to challenge the authority of either the organizers or the police, a view consistent with its composition and political outlook.

None of these positive influences were present at our second case study, the two NUM rallies held in Sheffield during April 1984.

2
NUM rallies in Sheffield, April 1984

Background to the first rally

The two rallies discussed here took place in April 1984 outside the NUM headquarters in Sheffield city centre. The miners' strike had been in progress for five weeks when the first rally took place. The strike had begun as a result of a decision to shut Cortonwood Colliery in Yorkshire, an area where support for the strike was strong. Elsewhere resistance to the strike among miners had been growing, especially in Derbyshire and Nottinghamshire. Opposition had crystallized around the demand for a national ballot of the membership. The NUM executive, which had so far supported the strike, arranged a meeting for 12 April at NUM headquarters to discuss a motion calling for a national ballot proposed by the Leicestershire area. The first rally was a lobby of executive members attending that meeting. Subsequently, the matter was referred to a Special Delegates' Conference, which was the occasion of a second mass rally at the different venue of Sheffield City Hall on 19 April.

Heavy picketing of working mines had already provoked confrontations with the police. A miner had been killed at Ollerton in Nottinghamshire. The existence of the police National Recording Centre had been revealed and the police had begun to prevent the movement of pickets. Some were stopped and escorted on their way to Sheffield (East and Thomas 1985, 139).

At the time, probably a majority of all miners did support the strike, but not the 55 per cent required for endorsement by ballot. The issue before the NUM executive and subsequently the Delegates' Conference was thus vital. For the striking miners, concession of a national ballot would take much of the impetus out of the strike. For non-striking areas, the failure to hold a ballot would be undemocratic and validate their refusal to join the strike. At both rallies, those demonstrating were striking miners, opposed to a ballot and its advocates.

The rallies occurred early in the strike, two months before the mass picket of Orgreave and the first of our community disorders in Maltby. Both rallies had the immediate political objective of persuading the union's leadership to continue to endorse the strike.

Overview of the first rally

The first rally took place on 12 April outside the NUM's national headquarters in St James's Square, Sheffield. A subsequent police report emphasized that the headquarters was in 'a multi-occupancy office block in the centre of Sheffield, with very little room to accommodate large numbers of demonstrators outside' (South Yorkshire Police 1985, 4). Large numbers there turned out to be. The same report estimated that 7,000 miners from throughout the United Kingdom were present, with 2,000 police officers drawn from six separate forces.

The arrival of representatives of pro-ballot areas, such as Ray Chadburn and Henry Richardson from Nottinghamshire, was greeted by extensive pushing and shoving as the demonstrators surged forwards, jeering derisively. Surges of support signalled the arrival of executive members opposed to the ballot, such as Peter Heathfield and Mick McGahey. In both cases the police prevented the demonstrators from reaching their targets.

Our researcher present noted that on numerous occasions the demonstrators linked arms and surged violently into the police ranks. Punching, kicking, and hair-pulling took place as miners and police clashed. A wall of police officers standing ten deep held off a succession of charges and kept the miners thirty yards clear of the NUM building. Then, by setting up a chant of 'one, two! one, two!' the police would succeed in pushing the demonstrators back to the rear of the courtyard. Missiles were thrown in retaliation, particularly by those miners suffering the worst effects of the crush.

Shortly before the meeting of the executive, NUM President Arthur Scargill appeared at an upper-floor window of the multi-storey building to impress upon his members that:

> This is yet another example of a police state. We will do everything in our power to stop the closure of our pits, the butchery of our industry and the sacking of our members.
>
> (*Yorkshire Post* 13 April)

The response was a further surge in the crowd.

At the end of the executive meeting, Mr Scargill emerged from the NUM offices to inform his members of two decisions. Firstly, the motion calling for a national strike ballot had been ruled out of order and would be referred to a Special Delegates' Conference on 19 April. Most knew it was likely to be rejected then. Secondly, the Delegates' Conference would also consider amending the union rules so that a simple majority of ballot votes, rather than the 55 per cent stipulated by present rules, would be a sufficient to authorize a national strike.

Plainly euphoric at this outcome, the demonstrators engaged in their final and most concerted push against the police line. It seemed to our observer that this was intended as a departing gesture of defiance and show of solidarity.

After the first rally

After the rally, a small number of demonstrators remained behind to await the emergence of the Nottinghamshire delegates, Ray Chadburn and Henry Richardson, who were set upon and jostled by miners as they tried to reach the car park. Asked later by television reporters what they thought of their reception, the two men declined to condemn their assailants, preferring to criticize in public their own Nottinghamshire members whom they urged to 'get up off their knees' and stop being 'scabs' (both BBC and ITN Main News 12 April).

Later in the day, police officers were summoned to several public houses in response to complaints about miners' behaviour. During one such incident, two miners were ejected by the landlord of the New Inn opposite the Trades and Labour Club in Duke Street. This was to have repercussions a week later.

Directly after the first rally, a long line of miners marched five-abreast through Sheffield City Centre towards a main road out of the city, the Wicker, where many of their coaches were parked. At first the accompanying police tolerated the situation but, as the miners' procession meandered unpredictably through the streets, bringing traffic to a standstill, the officers became visibly more frustrated by their inability to control the situation.

The marchers eventually reached Lady Bridge leading to the Wicker. At this point a senior officer arrived on the scene, accompanied by a unit of reinforcements. He gave orders to clear the road. Almost at once, in the words of one witness,

> the hitherto tolerant behaviour of the police escort suddenly
> changed to one not only of complete intolerance, but to one of

positive aggression. Police began to push and thump the miners in their backs. The unfortunate individuals then proceeded to turn around . . . they were grabbed by one lot of policemen and thumped in the abdomen by others. . . . Other miners were being pinned to the ground and assaulted. At no time did I see a single blow struck by a miner at the police.

(Sheffield Policewatch report no. 1)

Field notes made at the time corroborate this account. Some miners were pushed on to the kerb, others were kicked on the body and legs by police officers herding them towards their coaches. Anyone who protested was unconditionally arrested – sometimes by six officers at a time.

Analysis of the first rally and its aftermath

Such incidents contributed to an image of the rally as essentially disorderly. By the end of the day, fifty-five people had been arrested and forty-two officers were injured, six requiring hospital treatment. Most accounts took their lead from opinions expressed at the time by the Deputy Chief Constable of South Yorkshire, who blamed Scargill's intervention for inciting disorder (*Yorkshire Post* 13 April).

This was only partially accurate. Though Scargill's intervention did nothing to calm the situation, it was already inflamed before he appeared. A more considered view in retrospect was expressed to us later by the Deputy Chief Constable. His account is worth considering in full:

What you got at that meeting was a large number of people who did not like certain members of the NUM Executive. To quote a few names, there was Bell from the white-collar section, and Chadburn and Richardson from Notts. Now, the attitude of the Nottinghamshire miners was that they should continue to work and the vast majority there believed that those lads who were on the moderate wing of the Executive would be voting against their wishes. So, one of our principal objectives was to ensure that everyone – whether a Scargillite, a McGaheyite, a Bellite, or whoever he might be – who had business in that NUM building was able to get in and get out without being physically assaulted. Now, in one respect we failed because the leader of the Nottinghamshire miners was assaulted, as was a leading reporter from one of the television networks. I think with hindsight the police were not as sure, as professional, as we were when the strike developed. This was the first occasion that so many policemen had been involved. New tactics were involved and new disciplines were being implanted. And the ground was taken in the middle by miners, I think from South Wales, who took over a kiosk type of place from midnight onwards. You have to ask why they had taken it over from midnight for something which wasn't going to start until eleven o'clock in the morning.

So there was potential for disorder, particularly as a number of people had drunk quite a lot and travelled quite a long way. It was a bit like caging up a load of football supporters who had travelled a long way, only to be kept hanging around for up to twelve hours to see their heroes. The potential was all the more obvious, given that most picket-line confrontations do not take place in the middle of a major city. All those people had moved into a confined space in the midst of some of the most expensive business properties in the middle of a major city that did not particularly want them there. They were within a hundred yards of the prestigious Cutlers' Hall and very close to the offices that run down the High Street. There were six or seven thousand people, all from out of town, all wondering around aimlessly, trying to eat, drink, urinate. You had all the ingredients.

As the last metaphor reveals, the police view was that this first rally was a recipe for disorder. Almost everything was wrong. The rally was in a confined space with no room for police manoeuvre. There was a mis-match between the established police tactics for handling a picket and the physical location in a city centre. Strategic places within the setting had been commandeered by miners, who had arrived before the police. The crowd were none too sober, restless, and on edge. They did not know the city and so could behave with the recklessness of strangers. They expected and were given the opportunity to direct their anger against political opponents.

The time and place of the rally, the composition and mood of the crowd, the presence of symbolic enemies, and the absence of effective leadership were in our view important characteristics which did predispose the rally to disorder. What happened on the way back to the coaches was that the police seized the opportunity to do what they had been incapable of doing in St James's Square, and remove the miners by force. The situation could easily have been avoided had the officer arriving on the scene decided otherwise, but experience of the preceding rally was hardly likely to make any officer take a tolerant view. Police-initiated disorder appeared to counter-balance that initiated by the pickets. This pattern was to re-assert itself after the second rally, despite concerted attempts made to change the dynamics of the rally itself.

Background to the second rally

The issues which concerned those miners at the second rally and the political context in which they were mobilized had not changed in a week, nor had relationships with the police improved. But the background to the second rally had changed in one significant respect: it had the first rally as its immediate context. In different ways, neither police nor pickets felt they had come well out of the publicity given to the previous rally. Local City Council leaders, including those who had been directly involved in the organization of the Thatcher demonstration, offered themselves as intermediaries. Members of the Police Authority were also active, as the Deputy Chief Constable explained in a subsequent interview:

> There was direct liaison between ourselves and the leader of Sheffield City Council – that, and the direct involvement of the South Yorkshire Police Committee. It was our intention to obtain the co-operation of the NUM, which we hadn't had, to provide a carnival type atmosphere. There was very bad publicity for the NUM for what happened at the first week . . . the hopeful intention was that they would be able to police themselves, so that any suggestion of police provocation could be debunked.

The police were therefore seeking to 'normalize' the rally into an ordinary demonstration. They were anxious not to appear to be dramatizing the situation, the Chief Constable being advised against a premature return from holiday. The NUM consulted Sheffield Trades Council about crowd management strategies The results were very clear on 19 April.

Overview of the second rally

The Delegates' Conference held on 19 April required a larger venue than the NUM's own premises could provide, so it was held at Sheffield City Hall. This is a large rectangular building surrounded on all sides by slip roads with a large paved forecourt, as noted in the police report. 'The space has its own boundaries, therefore making it unnecessary to cordon areas off with police officers' (South Yorkshire Police, 1985, 5). All this was a different setting from the claustrophobia of St James's Square. The same number of miners were present as at the first rally, but there was a gradual build-up of their presence and none attempted to arrive the previous night.

Other aspects of the rally had been negotiated with the NUM through intermediaries. The police were happy for NUM marshals to be the main controllers of the crowd in the first instance. This real difference in the police approach was noticeable to outsiders, such as Vincent Hanna of BBC's Newsnight programme:

> 7.45, and a police decision is made to have breakfast. There are two hundred officers on duty with four hundred more on standby. A week ago in Sheffield there was violence after the Miners' Executive meeting and today police appear to want to restore some strained relationships with the union. So they walk in twos instead of groups and, it is rumoured, even offered the police band to entertain the crowd. It was declined. Today, the operation is deliberately low-key.
>
> (BBC Newsnight 19 April)

The NUM heeded the advice of the Trades Council to take several measures designed to minimize the possibility of disorder. A platform was erected opposite the City Hall. The 7,000 demonstrators were kept occupied listening to a succession of speakers and entertainers. Malcolm Pitt, President of the Kent Area NUM, repeatedly urged the miners to refrain from violence which would be exploited by the media. The NUM's marshals sought to minimize contact between the police and their members. The police reciprocated:

> It's 9.30, with seven thousand miners now in the square, and the delegates begin to arrive, pushing through a noisy, if good-tempered, line of NUM marshals. The police are spotted approaching and there is instant chanting. An inspector rushes in to send them away. It's still a low-key day.
>
> (BBC Newsnight 19 April)

The Nottinghamshire delegates whose arrival the previous week attracted violent attention had in the interim publicly dissociated themselves from the views of working miners. They were thus no longer the identifiable enemy, a status confirmed by Arthur Scargill's decision to accompany them personally into the hall.

The rally was entirely peaceful. No arrests were made during it. In mid-afternoon, Arthur Scargill appeared on the platform outside the hall. He informed those present that the Delegates' Conference had rejected the call for a national ballot but had passed the motion reducing the majority required in such a ballot from 55 per cent to a simple majority of votes cast. This news set up chants of 'Here we go! Here we go!'. Malcolm Pitt then called for an orderly return to the coaches and the crowd began to disperse peaceably. The *Sheffield Star* of 19 April was headed 'Miners make it a gala' and referred to the low-key police presence and to singing and dancing, which established a mood 'just like Blackpool on a Bank Holiday'. But on two separate occasions, disorder did break out.

The first, of which we only have police accounts, occurred during the afternoon. A caterers' van arrived with supplies for an evening function and was raided by hungry miners. The police intervened and were attacked:

> The attacks upon the police officers were so violent that the officers were required to draw their truncheons to protect themselves. Several police officers were surrounded by drunken, violent demonstrators and beaten severely, their colleagues being forced to mount rescues, and having to use their truncheons in order to do so. More police officers attended the scene, and riot shields were despatched, but in the event not deployed even though police officers came under a barrage of missiles comprising house bricks and bottles. The situation eventually calmed, with demonstrators being coaxed onto their waiting coaches and escorted out of the city.
>
> (South Yorkshire Police 1985, 5)

It is perhaps as well that this incident did not happen earlier in the day, when it might have become just the sort of flashpoint to destroy the tenuous truce between police and demonstrators. The police had no option but to intervene. Their agreement with the NUM did not extend to permitting theft. Disorder followed police action which was clearly, from the evidence we have, valid and appropriate. The second incident was rather different.

After the second rally

The origins of the second incident lay in a complaint later that afternoon from the licensee of the New Inn public house opposite the Trades and Labour Club, about a mile away from the City Hall. Miners were alleged to be kicking on the door, demanding to be let in. The establishment had been deliberately closed at lunchtime because of the incident there after the previous week's rally when two miners had been ejected. Responding to the complaint, a group of police officers approached a larger group of miners.

According to Assistant Chief Constable, Tony Clement, of South Yorkshire Police:

> Initially the police were heavily outnumbered and two officers who were trapped in a doorway drew their truncheons to protect themselves. According to the licensee of the public house, the miners had come from the Trades and Labour Club after a long drinking session and many were drunk.
>
> (Quoted in the *Yorkshire Post* 21 April)

Subsequent police accounts emphasized that when vanloads of reinforcements came to the assistance of their colleagues, they were immediately confronted by a 'drunken mob' emerging from the club. This was the version proposed by a police constable later in court. 'They were staggering about and shouting, from which I could only draw the conclusion that most, if not all, were under the influence of alcohol' (*Sheffield Morning Telegraph* 17 October). Police also claimed that a group of miners charged at them, chanting 'Here we go! Here we go! Here we go!'

A rather different version of the event was presented by several eye-witnesses, including two local Labour MPs, Richard Caborn, the Member of Parliament for Sheffield Central, and Bill Michie, the Member for Sheffield Heeley. In his voluntary statement subsequently given to the police, Richard Caborn decribed how at around three o'clock he was outside the club giving directions to some Durham miners on how to get back to their coaches. It was his view that the miners were leaving the club in an orderly fashion when the police arrived. His statement went on:

> Two police vans arrived and parked at the traffic lights in Duke Street . . . on the city centre side of the lights. The vans unloaded and I think about twenty police constables got out, and started to walk diagonally across the road towards the club. I walked towards the police constables in front of the miners looking for the person in charge, an inspector or sergeant. I could see only police constables. I put my arms up and addressed the police generally, saying, 'There is no trouble in this club. I am a trustee of the club and a Member of Parliament for this area.' I said this as I was walking towards the police constables and they were walking towards me. I heard a police constable say to me, 'Fuck off'.

A confrontation ensued and police began to arrest miners indiscriminately. Two police officers chased a miner into the crowded club entrance and drew their truncheons. As Caborn appealed to the officers, he was knocked to the ground. Rising to his feet, he saw a police officer hitting the club sign with his truncheon and shouting at the miners, 'Get back, you bastards!'. Richard Caborn later gave evidence in court that the police constables involved seemed very young and leaderless: 'I looked for either an Inspector or a Sergeant, but could find neither . . . there seemed to be absolutely no one in charge' (*Sheffield Morning Telegraph* 18 October). Caborn did eventually locate a police inspector, who was unable to specify who was in charge.

Media accounts emphasize that police reinforcements were constantly arriving on the scene. A procession of police vans, said to have contained mostly West Yorkshire police officers, was observed stretching back for a quarter of a mile (*Sheffield Morning Telegraph* 24 April). Several eye-witnesses described the aggression as largely one-sided:

> I was really shocked to see it in Sheffield. The police were very forceful. We saw them grabbing miners and pulling them about. One policeman pushed a miner down the grass bank and another knelt on top of him. I found it quite upsetting. The miners did not seem to be doing anything.
>
> (Female witness in court, quoted in the *Sheffield Morning Telegraph* 19 October)

Meanwhile the second MP present, Bill Michie, was trying to calm the situation but was arrested by two police constables. When Caborn tried to explain that Michie was an MP, one of the officers responded 'What's an MP?' Michie was nevertheless released.

The two MPs asked for the miners' coaches to be sent. According to Michie, the attempts by NUM stewards to move their members away were hampered by the growing police presence and by the build-up of angry miners refusing to leave the area until they were told where their arrested colleagues had been taken. Some miners staged a sit-down protest in the centre of the road, but NUM officials persuaded them to abandon it.

At this point, the Durham Area representative on the Executive arrived. According to his signed statement, the police prevented him from defusing the situation. No one would negotiate with him. His attempts to use a loud-hailer to get the miners to disperse were undermined when a policeman snatched it from his hand, a gesture which infuriated the miners. The police ordered everyone immediately to board the buses which had arrived. This only produced the response that those already on board got off again. In the ensuing mêlée, the executive member was knocked out and had two of his ribs broken. He was taken to hospital, where he spent two days.

The *North Eastern Journal* claimed that the Durham official was one of eighty-two miners and ten police officers who had received injuries during the course of the incident. No less than sixty-eight people were arrested before order was restored.

Even media and legal accounts of the incident tended to be critical of police behaviour. The *Sheffield Morning Telegraph*, a Conservative newspaper generally supportive of the police during the strike, pointed out in an editorial on 21 April that:

> The police authorities have been unable or unwilling to answer Richard Caborn's claims that a force of young constables – without even a police sergeant to control them – launched into a public, and by all accounts, ugly brawl in a Sheffield street. These were not police officers aware of this city's tolerance of peaceful demonstrations, but officers from an outside force, presumably with no knowledge of the average miner other than a fear that any miner is a bobby-basher.

At the subsequent trial of eight Durham miners accused of various public order offences during the incident, the defence counsel referred to the way 'the normal constraints of police behaviour got thrown overboard'. He accused the police of behaving indiscriminately and said that the situation could easily have been defused had they shown greater co-operation. The presiding magistrate dismissed the charges against four of the defendants, though found the others guilty as charged. He nevertheless criticized the police evidence as 'unconvincing and unsatisfactory', adding 'I am not satisfied that the police were as tactful as they might have been' (*Sheffield Morning Telegraph* court report 20 October).

Analysis of the second rally and its aftermath

The second rally on 19 April and the incident which followed it showed both how order can be maintained in the most adverse circumstances and how easily it can break down when its main supports are removed. Those supports had to be built up after the first rally, when their absence had allowed disorder to prevail.

The successful implementation of measures to ensure order at the second rally crucially depended on the establishment of communication between the organizers and police. This was achieved through the involvement of members of the local council, the County Police Committee and Sheffield Trades Council. These were bodies with an institutional legitimacy both sides could acknowledge. An implicit bargain was struck between police and union, neither of whom wished to see a repetition of the previous week's events. The police strategy was expressly designed to reflect the spirit of this agreement. The numbers of police deployed were small given the numbers of demonstrators and most were held in reserve. They sought to avoid provoking demonstrators by their actions or too obvious a presence. Immediate control of the demonstrators was conceded to the union's own marshals.

The NUM as organizers took seriously their responsibility to control the behaviour of the crowd. The activity of marshals, the erection of a platform for speakers and entertainment, the appeals to avoid violence made by prominent and respected leaders, all acted to channel and discipline the responses of the crowd.

Other factors not necessarily in the immediate control of police or organizers helped. Unlike that for the first rally, the venue for the second allowed space for the demonstrators to move about and the police to keep their distance. It was also away from busy shopping or business areas, where the police would have felt obliged to secure the safety of nearby buildings and passers-by.

The demonstrators' principal targets had also been removed. The Nottinghamshire delegates' clarification of their position made them allies rather than enemies. Arthur Scargill's decision to accompany Chadburn and Richardson reinforced the point.

In these ways a different definition of the situation had been achieved. The police showed no interest in confrontation and did not wish to intervene unless absolutely necessary. The NUM was officially and openly committed to avoiding violence. In modifying their own behaviour to achieve these goals, police and organizers also modified the behaviour of the crowd. It remained volatile, occasionally prone to take advantage, as the incident with the caterers' van showed. But they were not presented with visible enemies in the form of police lines or representatives of working miners, and generally appeared ready to take a lead from the official union position.

Such controls on the definition of the situation and the resulting appropriate behaviour were absent from the incident outside the Trades and Labour Club. This happened some distance from the main demonstration, physically removed from the arena where a negotiated compromise prevailed. The police officers involved were young, from West Yorkshire, and without the leadership of a senior officer. The original agreement had been negotiated and maintained by older and very senior officers from South Yorkshire. As long as they were in charge, they could ensure that all police officers acted within the letter and the spirit of their instructions. Without these guidelines, the complaint from the licensee was interpreted less as an incident to investigate than as a signal for immediate and decisive action. The number of police officers who responded, their demeanour and willingness to draw truncheons, their vilification of anyone who tried to mediate, all indicate a lack of discipline and control. There seems to be little doubt that in this instance disorder was wilfully cultivated by members of the police force. Theirs was the responsibility for breaking the agreement which had otherwise kept the second rally free from disorder.

Summary of both rallies

Two miners' rallies were held in Sheffield city centre in April 1984 during the miners' strike. The first, to lobby members of the executive discussing a formal proposal for a national pit-head ballot, involved violent clashes between police and demonstrators. The venue outside NUM headquarters was an enclosed square, the most strategic points of which had been commandeered by demonstrators the night before. Miners periodically surged towards the entrance to the NUM building in attempts to express derision or support for the views of individual members of the union executive. The police endeavoured to hold and force them back. A speech from Arthur Scargill did nothing to calm the situation. As they left, two Nottinghamshire delegates were attacked. As a procession of miners subsequently returned along a main street towards their coaches, a police decision to move them off the road resulted in arbitrary and violent arrests.

The absence of liaison between police and organizers before the first rally was rectified by the time of the second a week later, owing to the intercession of local council and trade union leaders. The rally was to lobby a Delegates' Conference, held at the City Hall, surrounded by more open and manageable space. The police decreased their numbers, deployed police officers selectively, and avoided acts which could be seen as provocative. The union undertook to police its own demonstration through marshals, provided speeches and entertainments to keep the crowd occupied, and explicitly disowned violence. Neither police nor union representatives were presented to the demonstrators as obvious targets. There were no incidents and no arrests during the rally. At the very end of the rally, there was a brief confrontation following the theft of food from a caterers' van. A more serious incident occurred when police response to a complaint from a public house licensee took the form of violent assault on miners outside a Trades and Labour club.

As in the case of the earlier 'Thatcher Unwelcoming' demonstration, the key factors were the organizers, the police, the venue, and the crowd. Each of these were out of control during the first rally and had to be brought under control for the second. Enabling this to happen was a dramatic improvement in the extent and nature of liaison between the police and the organizers of the demonstration. The mechanisms by which order might be maintained were negotiated between these parties.

The fragility of this agreement was evident in the way the incident after the second rally duplicated events after the first, despite the very great differences in the rallies themselves. Left to their own devices, junior officers forsook any attempt at negotiation and attempted to impose their will by force.

Both rallies had as their background the early stages of the miners' strike, a context of developing conflict within the union and between pickets and the police. In the first rally the latent antagonism arising from such conflicts was allowed full expression. In the second, it was deliberately and successfully controlled. But on the margins of both rallies any existing controls broke down, on both occasions as a result of sudden and arbitrary police action.

3
Understanding demonstrations

Comparison of case studies

The 'Thatcher Unwelcoming' demonstration of 1983 and the two NUM rallies of 1984 were separated by exactly one year, during which the miners' strike had introduced new levels of conflict and controversy into the national political arena. The splits within the union, the extraordinary powers assumed by the police, and the daily nature of picket line interaction had together begun to ensure that any event associated with the miners' strike was potentially disorderly. In April 1984 the full potential for disorder had yet to be realized but its dimensions were becoming apparent.

Thus the political backgrounds of the demonstrations constitute one high-level explanation for the propensity to disorder. Yet attention needs also to be focused on lower levels of explanation, such as the physical location of the demonstrations. The Thatcher demonstration and the second NUM rally were held in relatively open spaces, where the possibility of damage to adjacent buildings or interference with passers-by was slight. By contrast, the first rally was in an enclosed space in the centre of a busy business district, affecting the room police had for both physical and legal manoeuvre. Physically, it was impossible to erect barriers to divide the crowd from the police or to agree on any neutral territory. Thus there was a continous contest over space. Legally, there was the need to protect members of the executive and the public in the vicinity from assault. Neither the police response nor their interpretation of the law could be flexible.

On the other two occasions, the Thatcher demonstration and the second NUM rally, the police were able to determine the location of the demonstrators beforehand. They defined the boundaries of crowd activity and monitored it closely. Necessary police action was directed against isolated and specifiable individuals rather than the crowd as a whole. Most officers were kept behind the established boundary, and reinforcements kept out of sight. Officers could be deployed in the crowd in pairs rather than having to foray in groups. Such strategic advantages were supplemented by complementary tactical decisions, to use mainly local police officers and establish a rapport between police officers and demonstrators.

The ability of the police to confine, observe, and patrol the crowd required the co-operation of the organizers. In all three instances studied, the police declared their willingness to negotiate without conditions, enhanced by the idea that there was a 'Sheffield tradition' of peaceful demonstration and firm but tactful policing.

Moreover, the organizers of the Thatcher demonstration and the intermediaries who emerged between the two rallies were not an *ad hoc* grouping. They were members of the local political establishment, in Sheffield coterminous with the Labour Party and trade union movement. As elected representatives and controllers of the City and County Councils, they had constitutional legitimacy and also comprised the majority on the County Police Authority. Additionally, and this is crucial, the police had reason to believe that they would in practice be able to control the crowd. In the case of the Thatcher demonstration, the 'labourism' they represented was far stronger than any alternative groups of the left. In the second rally, the police took the calculated risk that the NUM could not afford to lose control of the crowd, despite what the police had seen as their deliberate refusal to control the first rally.

It was not just the existence of an organizing group or even its willingness to negotiate which were crucial, so much as police perception of the leadership as responsible, legitimate, and effective: actually and not just nominally in control of the situation. Had there been doubts about this, police participation in any agreements would have been provisional and conditional. Only if the leadership was seen to want to avoid disorder and to have the power to control the crowd, could any bargains be struck.

In this, as in much else, the role of the organizers was central. The strategies they adopted at the Thatcher demonstration and the second NUM rally were identical, and not just because some of the same people were involved in the organization. At both, the organizers publicly disavowed violence, offering to demonstrators the pragmatic argument that it played into the hands of political enemies. The use of stewards signalled to the police a real desire to control the crowd, and to the demonstrators that control was being exerted on their behalf by their own members. For all concerned, this represented effective self-policing. The erection of platforms enabled entertainers and speakers to affirm the sentiments of the crowd within the tone established by the organizers. All these were ways in which the organizers could seek to control the crowd but they still required a good deal of co-operation from the crowd itself.

The crowd at the Thatcher demonstration was visibly different from that at the two NUM rallies. A largely middle-class crowd, half of whom were women and children, was likely to respond differently from a crowd of working-class men. The Thatcher demonstration was also a largely symbolic gesture of dissent. There was never any serious intention to prevent either the guests or Mrs Thatcher from entering the Cutlers' Hall. By contrast, at the first rally at least, the miners felt they could influence the actual course of events, in this case the decision to be taken by the miners' executive. They were also presented with individuals they could identify as targets for their agitation, notably the two Nottinghamshire delegates and the police themselves. During the four weeks of the strike they had come to see the police not as neutral arbiters of the law, but as part of the armoury of the state ranged against them. The crowd at the Thatcher demonstration had a less personal and intense view of the police. The only other targets for their activities were coaches full of guests whom they treated with mockery and derision rather than hatred. Mrs Thatcher was a target for their abuse but not, as many speakers emphasized, for any other activity. She was in any case never visible to most of the demonstrators.

Thus, at the Thatcher demonstation, we had a largely middle-class crowd of all ages and both sexes making a moral protest against a Conservative government. At both rallies, the crowd consisted exclusively of working-class male trade unionists engaged in what they saw as a struggle to defend their jobs and communities. It does not need a social scientist to predict that the first crowd is more likely to be orderly than the second.

However, the potential for any crowd to be involved in disorder is not fixed by its composition or political objectives. Collective trade union activities can be orderly even in the middle of long-running disputes, as is shown by our later example of picketing during the 1980 steel strike as well as by the second NUM rally. As incidents at universities occasionally show, it is not always the case that middle-class, sexually-mixed crowds are necessarily orderly. Even the presence of mothers with their children may not pre-empt disorder, as was frequently the case at Greenham Common. Any crowd can be provoked or provocative.

Disorder is not given in the composition, outlook or predisposition of any crowd. Much depends on the crowd's definition of the situation, since this delimits the situationally-appropriate behaviour. Such a definition may be drawn in part from the wider political context, as happened throughout the miners' strike. It may also be developed by the activities of organizers and police. They have some control over the immediate circumstances and environment. The 'tone' of the event may be as important in explaining order and disorder as the composition and attitudes of the crowd.

We can now list the factors we have discovered to affect the degree of order at a demonstration. The following are the optimum conditions for the maintenance of order at a demonstration:

1 A routinized political context
2 A flexible interpretation of the law
3 An isolated and open setting
4 A preparedness amongst organizers and police to undertake serious negotiations
5 A police ability to limit the crowd's movements and survey its activities
6 Police strategies involving local officers, partly deployed in small groups, with reinforcements out of sight
7 A police perception of the organizers as united, responsible, and effective
8 A disavowal by the organizers of any form of violence
9 A use of stewards, speakers, and other devices to channel and control crowd behaviour
10 A rationale for the crowd to dissociate itself from violence
11 A respect for organizers and police amongst the crowd
12 A crowd of mixed ages and sexes
13 A commitment by the crowd to exclusively symbolic goals even where the possibility exists for more direct action.

These are not as yet grouped into categories, given any sort of priority, or systematically interrelated. Even in this crude form, they do appear to work for the examples we have studied. For instance, they can specify exactly how the second NUM rally was made to be more like the Thatcher demonstration than the first rally. The role of the negotiation is revealed. Most of the factors predisposing a demonstration to greater or lesser disorder stem initially from the interaction between police and demonstrators beforehand, which can 'define the situation' for the crowd.

These propositions are, however, still only derived from three instances occurring in a short time-span within one city. These were also static, not moving demonstrations, with crowds no more than two or three thousand strong. It remains to be seen whether what we have discovered can be generalized to larger and more mobile demonstrations at other times and in other places.

Vietnam war demonstrations, 1968

In an excellent study of one of the 1968 anti-Vietnam war demonstrations, Halloran *et al.* (1970) suggest that a turning point in the post-war history of political demonstrations occurred in 1961. On this occasion 1,314 people were arrested during a demonstration in Trafalgar Square organized by the Committee of One Hundred, a splinter group from CND committed to civil disobedience. Halloran *et al.* (1970, 57) hold this incident to have marked 'a new phase in the relationship between police and demonstrator' with the police adopting tougher attitudes and encountering more active resistance from demonstrators.

The international student movement which grew in the 1960s used the mass political demonstration as one of its main strategies, especially to voice opposition to United States involvement in the Vietnam war. In October 1967, the Vietnam Solidarity Campaign (VSC) held its first mass demonstration. Five thousand attended a rally in Trafalgar Square, after which many marched to the United States Embassy in Grosvenor Square. Attempts were made to breach a police cordon and objects were thrown from the crowd. The rejection of non-violent tactics, which had developed into resistance to arrest, now occasionally took the form of unprovoked attacks on the police.

In March 1968, the VSC organized a further demonstration in which 25,000 people assembled in Trafalgar Square and marched to the United States Embassy to hand in letters protesting about the war. Demonstrators broke through a police cordon and grouped in front of the embassy, where additional police were stationed. Missiles were thrown and eventually mounted police were used to clear the square. During the ensuing mêlée 280 people were arrested.

Halloran *et al.* suggest that from this point on, demonstrators and police both had 'two possible approaches to future demonstrations. They must either seek to avoid possible situations of confrontation or accept the possibility that future demonstrations might become increasingly violent' (1970, 73).

A further demonstration on 27 October 1968 was better organized by both sides. The organizers chose a route from Charing Cross to Hyde Park, where a rally was to be held. In all their publicity, violence was disowned and demonstrators were asked not to go to Grosvenor Square. Declining to appoint marshals, the organizers nevertheless made every effort to channel the sentiments of the crowd. Much stress was placed on symbolic gestures, such as the handing in of a letter of protest at 10 Downing Street, and a ceremony commemorating the Vietnamese dead at the Cenotaph.

The police raised no objections to the route and made no attempt to confine or divide up the march. Traffic was diverted or halted. Police walked alongside the marchers and though reinforcements included mounted police, they were kept out of sight. For the most part the crowd followed the lead of the organizers, confronting neither the police nor groups of taunting bystanders.

> The main march was thus characterized by non-violence and cordial relations between police and marchers, as both groups sought to minimize the possibility of violence by avoiding those tactics and situations which had elicited antagonism on previous occasions. (Halloran *et al.* 1970, 76)

Despite a general tension evident early in the day, most of the 60,000 demonstrators marched in reasonable order to Hyde Park. Two small and separate groups broke away from the main march and descended upon the United States Embassy. A police cordon successfully held them back, refraining from deploying truncheons or police horses as they had done a year earlier.

These demonstrations are important because they represented turning-points in the willingness of minorities of demonstrators to direct violence at the police, and because, despite the apparent success of the tactics employed at the second demonstration, police perception was that they could no longer rely on traditional methods of crowd control. Police tactics such as the wedge, snatch squads, and the Special Patrol Group (SPG) came after these demonstrations, as riot shields and dispersal tactics would follow the inner-city riots.

Despite the lapse of twenty years since these demonstrations, similar factors to those identified in our Sheffield case studies emerge as differentiating the orderly from the disorderly demonstration. The corrective measures taken after the March 1968 demonstration parallel quite closely those taken between the NUM rallies: the instigation of negotiations between the police and the organizers and their consequent agreement about aspects of the demonstration, especially the route and the style of policing; the overt commitment of the organizers to peaceful protest and their concerted attempts to control the crowd; the preparedness of the police to divert and stop traffic, supervise the march lightly, and keep reinforcements out of sight.

However, these were large, moving demonstrations held in the very different political climate of the 1960s. To find more precise correspondence with our Sheffield examples we need demonstrations which are local, static, relatively small-scale, and comparatively recent. Ideally we should also like examples of orderly demonstrations. These do not unfortunately result in committees of inquiry or attract the attention of academics. For instance, the order maintained at the massive CND demonstrations in London in the early 1980s has been taken for granted as not requiring explanation. So some of the biggest political demonstrations ever held in this country have hardly been analysed at all.

Consequently, we have settled for two examples which appear similar to our own case studies. These are the planned demonstration against a National Front election meeting in Southall in 1979 and a student protest against the visit by Leon Brittan, the Home Secretary, to Manchester University in 1985.

Southall, 1979

Various accounts exist of this demonstration (Warpole 1979, Rollo 1980, Southall Rights 1980, Harman 1982, Jefferson and Grimshaw 1984). Here we shall rely mainly on the most detailed account of matters of fact, to be found in the Report of the NCCL Unofficial Committee of Enquiry (1980). We shall also use some of its interpretations, supplemented by Jefferson and Grimshaw's construction of the police perspective.

During the General Election campaign of 1979, the National Front declared its intention to hold a meeting in Southall, an area of West London with a large Asian population within a parliamentary constituency where the Front were fielding a candidate. Ealing Council, having been advised it would be illegal for them to ban the meeting or dictate where it should be held, granted the National Front the use of Southall Town Hall for the meeting on 23 April 1979.

At a meeting of the local Asian community, it was decided to hand in a petition to Ealing Town Hall the day before the meeting. On the day itself, all shops would close at 1 p.m. and a peaceful sit-down protest would be held outside Southall Town Hall at 5 p.m. The Southall Youth Movement was absent from the meeting and planned a picket for midday. The Anti-Nazi League and other left-wing groups advocated a more confrontational style of protest than that favoured by local leaders. These differences of objectives and emphases were to have serious repercussions.

Representatives of the demonstration co-ordinating committee met local police officers and an officer from Scotland Yard on 17 April. No objection was made by the police to the plans for a peaceful sit-down protest, though it was mentioned in passing that the local force would not be in charge on the day.

On 22 April, a march of between 3,000 and 5,000 people was held to hand the petition in to the local council. Though the petition was eventually handed in, the march was poorly stewarded and heavily policed by officers from Scotland Yard's A8 Public Order Division. Several arrests were made, some involving mounted police. The march was, in retrospect, a sign of what was to happen the next day.

On 23 April, members of the Southall Youth Movement who began to congregate at midday were immediately dispersed by the police, with forty or so being arrested. Meanwhile, the main co-ordinating committee had met to discuss arrangements and appoint stewards. The situation outside the Town Hall deteriorated as the police cleared everyone from the immediate vicinity and cordoned it off. 'Thereafter, for the rest of the day, there was no possibility of a single demonstration nor of any effective unified leadership of the demonstrators' (NCCL 1980, 34).

All four roads leading to the Town Hall were cordoned off. Demonstrators who responded by pushing against the cordon were charged by the police. Second cordons were formed behind the demonstrators, effectively trapping them. At around 5.15 p.m. police allowed a sit-down protest to take place between the two cordons, before forcibly dispersing the crowd and arresting those who resisted. An attempt to break through the police cordon on the eastern side was rebuffed by the Special Patrol Group, until then held in reserve. Arrests and violence followed, culminating in the full-scale police attack on 6 Park View Road, an impromptu legal and medical aid centre.

As the National Front meeting began at 7 p.m., the second cordon was removed from the western side but when stones were thrown and windows broken, snatch squads and baton-charges were used to arrest and disperse demonstrators. During this period a demonstrator, Blair Peach, was killed. At 9.30 p.m. the meeting ended. Demonstrators dispersed, the cordons were removed, and by 10 p.m. traffic was being allowed back into the area. Altogether 345 people were arrested.

The following day, the police blamed the violence on outside agitators while politicians blamed right- or left-wing 'extremists'. Asian community leaders called for an investigation into the death of Blair Peach and into the whole question of police behaviour, especially that of the Special Patrol Group. In a report to the Home Secretary, the Metropolitan Commissioner claimed that the decision to cordon off the Town Hall was taken only as a response to the disorder caused by the Southall Youth Movement's attempt to stage a picket; that at all stages the police were reacting to crowd violence; and that most of the problem lay in outside agitators who had come just to cause trouble.

The NCCL inquiry team argued the opposite. Most if not all of the crowd violence occurred during and after police action against it. There was no evidence that outsiders were significant in numbers or influence. Disorder was seen as arising from police activity. 'The policing of the demonstration was a vital and active, not merely reactive, factor in the events of the day' (NCCL 1980, 150).

The inquiry criticized the decisions made by the police and their manner of execution. Cordoning off the area planned for picket and sit-down protest effectively removed the right to demonstrate. Local arrangements made between police and community representatives were ignored and self-stewarding rendered impossible. The police were shown to have acted with extreme violence to all demonstrators.

Many of these and related charges remained and remain unanswered. Jefferson and Grimshaw (1984) have reconstructed the logic of police actions. They argue that the police had been sensitized by a recent series of confrontations between the Anti-Nazi League and the National Front to expect trouble. The ruling that the meeting was a legal part of the electoral process further endorsed a hard line. The location of the Town Hall at a cross-roads prevented identification of one focal point for police containment of the crowd. The number of, and differences between, the protesting groups gave no indication that any leaders would or could control the crowd. Hence the police chose to prevent any demonstration and to forcibly disperse the crowd, whose resistance resulted in disorder.

On the basis of this and our previous examples, a consistent set of factors are emerging as more or less conducive to order and disorder. Before outlining these in more detail, we want to test them against one final example.

Manchester University, March 1985

For an account of what happened at a demonstration at Manchester University in March 1985, our source is yet another unofficial inquiry, this time convened by the local authority (Report of the Independent Enquiry Panel, Manchester City Council 1985). The police again declined to give evidence, since the Police Complaints Authority had launched their own investigation, subsequently published in a heavily censored version. If what follows is therefore a partial view, we can only stress that this is the only publicly available account, one which is commendable in its thoroughness but inevitably incomplete.

At the end of 1984, the Manchester University Conservative Society invited the Home Secretary, Leon Brittan, to speak. The meeting was arranged for 1 March 1985, in the final month of the miners' strike. The previous year Michael Heseltine, then Defence Secretary, had been covered in paint when arriving to speak at the university.

The Students' Union agreed that the Home Secretary had every right to speak and took steps to ensure that he would be able to. The number of security staff was increased. Entry to the meeting would be by ticket only and on production of a student identity card. Though student facilities in the building would be open as normal, only two entrance doors would be open, one at the front and one at the back. In the week before the visit, there was formal discussion of these arrangements with the local police, including visits by them to the Students' Union building. From quite early on, the Union Executive and the manager of the building expressed the view to the police that the Home Secretary should enter through the back door.

Several student groups declared their intention to demonstrate against the Home Secretary. One 'Stop Brittan' leaflet, proclaiming an intention to prevent the Home Secretary from entering the Union and claiming the support of the Labour party and CND, was circulated amongst students, despite being disowned by these organizations and the Students' Union.

The Home Secretary was due to arrive at 7.40 p.m. By 7.10 p.m., between four and five hundred demonstrators had assembled on the steps in front of the Union and on the surrounding pavements. A group of thirty or so police officers marched along the road to the steps, formed a wedge and without warning proceeded to clear the steps. When students resisted, police reinforcements were summoned and the students removed by force. Witnesses at the inquiry alleged racist and sexist abuse by the police and instances of violent assault. It was not denied that students answered and pushed back. By 7.20 p.m., the police had established control of the steps. Some officers entered the building and began to dictate who could leave and enter it.

The Home Secretary arrived and was rushed into the building, surrounded by Special Branch and uniformed officers. An egg was thrown from the crowd and one demonstrator made an unsuccessful attempt to strike the Home Secretary, who was otherwise unharmed as he entered. He spoke to an angry and noisy audience, leaving at 8.20. When he had gone, police used considerable force to disperse the crowd, including those coming out of the meeting. Forty demonstrators and ten police officers were injured. Forty demonstrators were arrested, of whom thirty-three were charged.

Again we must ask about the logic behind police strategy. A photograph of a police briefing diagram, fortuitously made available to the inquiry, showed that the police had meticulously planned their operation. Thus their supposed negotiations with the Students' Union had in fact been bogus, since they were committed to a quite different form of policing the demonstration from that which had been expected.

This strategy was clearly influenced by high level government views, especially the Home Secretary's insistence that he would enter by the front door. Presumably, the spectacle of a Conservative Home Secretary 'ducking in by the back door' was incompatible with the image projected by the government during the miners' strike.

The police decision to take the demonstrators by surprise avoided awkward questions about their legal jurisdiction over the Students' Union which might otherwise have arisen. Some of the advance publicity for the demonstration may have confirmed police suspicions that some elements intended to prevent the Home Secretary entering the building.

There is a kind of logic here which cannot be extended to the decision, after the Home Secretary had left, to disperse the crowd forcibly rather allowing it to disperse naturally. Unlike much of their previous conduct, this cannot be justified by their need to protect the Home Secretary. It seemed simply gratuitous, indicating a general view that the crowd were to be forcibly denied the right to be there at all.

The report of the Police Complaints Authority was published in March 1987. Press accounts suggested that the Director of Public Prosecutions insisted that some passages be removed, since they would prejudice the trials of three police officers and one student who had been charged with offences arising from the demonstration. Even so, the report admitted that there had been clear cases of assault by unidentifiable police officers on demonstrators. It was further suggested that passages omitted from the published report were highly critical of those senior officers responsible for police conduct and absolved the Students' Union of all blame (*Observer* 1 March 1987). As one newspaper editorial put it, 'The result is a PCA report which acknowledges that a lot of serious things occurred but which fails to come up with a detailed explanation for them' (*Guardian* 2 March 1987).

Such an explanation, we suggest, lies in the way the police accepted a brief from political sources to discharge their duties in a manner which showed scant regard for the rights of demonstrators and even for the law itself. Disorder was anticipated and instigated by those with the responsibility of preventing it.

Towards a model of disorder and order at demonstrations

The demonstrations in Southall and Manchester closely parallel the incidents we observed in 'Sheffield. Both were static demonstrations on 'home' territory. The Manchester demonstration corresponds to the 'Thatcher Unwelcoming' as a protest against a leading member of government. The Southall demonstration was, like the NUM rallies, directed at the occurrence of a political meeting. Both the 'Thatcher Unwelcoming' and the Southall demonstrations bore the imprint of the communities where they occurred, whilst the NUM and university demonstrations involved homogeneous interest groups.

There are also real differences in the location, contexts, membership, objectives, and dynamics of each demonstration. Still, there are sufficient broad similarities for us to make direct comparisons. We can take the factors earlier identified as crucial in determining order and disorder at the first two case studies and extend them to Southall and Manchester. The results can be seen in table 3.1. By reading across the table, it is possible to identify those characteristics which most consistently distinguish the disorderly demonstration from the orderly one.

Table 3.1 Factors predisposing static demonstrations to disorder

Factor	Mrs Thatcher (1983)	First NUM rally (1984)	Second NUM rally (1984)	Southall (1979)	Manchester (1985)
Political and legal context					
Absence of intergroup conflict	yes	no	no	no	no
Flexible legal obligations	yes	no	yes	no	no
Physical venue					
Relatively open space	yes	no	yes	yes	no
Other buildings and persons unaffected	yes	no	yes	no	yes
Organizers					
Prepared to liaise with police	yes	no	yes	yes	yes
Open disavowal of violence	yes	no	yes	mainly	yes
Use of self-stewarding	yes	no	yes	yes	no
Organized speakers and entertainments	yes	no	yes	no	no
Ability to control crowd	yes	no	yes	unknown	no
Police					
Prepared to liaise with organizers	yes	yes	yes	nominally	nominally
Perceive organizers as effective	yes	no	yes	no	no
Present before crowd	yes	no	yes	yes	no
Able to dictate layout	yes	no	yes	yes	no
Easy surveillance of crowd	yes	no	yes	no	no
Largely scattered deployment	yes	no	yes	no	no
Use of mainly local officers	yes	no	yes	no	yes
Reinforcements hidden	yes	no	yes	no	no
Crowd					
Disavowal of violence	yes	no	mostly	unknown	unknown
Accepting organizers' leadership	yes	yes	mostly	unknown	unknown
Accepting police tactics	yes	no	mostly	no	no
Mixture of ages and sexes	yes	no	no	yes	mixed sexes
Making symbolic gesture	yes	no	yes	unknown	yes
Visible targets absent	no	no	yes	no	no

We do not intend to work through the details of each demonstration again. Examples can be extracted from the table and the accounts given earlier in the chapter. Our final comments are aimed to construct some general propositions about order and disorder at static demonstrations. We must emphasize again that we are insisting that order, no less than disorder, has to be explained.

We start with the *political* and *legal contexts* which have quite specific effects on the nature of a demonstration, largely independent of events and behaviour on the day. Especially important for the political context is the nature of existing conflict between those demonstrating and those they are demonstrating against. Conditions for disorder might be least where the political context is a diffuse conflict between a Conservative government and broad alliance of radical groups. It might vary in its intensity but such a demonstration is mainly an extension of the normal expression of dissent within democratic processes. Less normal and institutionalized are occasions when a group of trade unionists is engaged in a national struggle in defence of its livelihood or when an immigrant community and its allies are seeking to object to an alien presence of racists in its midst. These are uninstitutionalized conflicts whose boundaries are undefined.

The legal context may similarly affect conduct and attitudes, especially those of the police. Where they have themselves formulated, or had formulated for them, a particularly rigid interpretation of their legal obligations, their response will be less flexible, they will be more prepared to attain their objectives with maximum force. There is always an overriding objective to protect the targets of a demonstration from physical harm, but exactly how this is achieved and the extent to which different ways of achieving it can be considered, depend upon how and by whom the legal context has been defined. This affects specific police decisions about where demonstrators can stand, how far traffic and the public can be inconvenienced: the terms on which the police will tolerate any demonstration at all.

The rigidity of such a definition of the law will affect how far it is seen as just by the demonstrators. If they perceive the application of the law to infringe on their rights then they may withdraw their respect for the law and those who administer it, the police. At Southall, for example, the demonstrators did not respect a law which defended the right of the National Front to hold a meeting but failed either to defend the immigrant community from racist abuses or uphold its right to demonstrate.

At the 'Thatcher Unwelcoming', by contrast, the rights of Mrs Thatcher and other guests to attend the feast, and of the police to defend that right, were accepted by the demonstrators, as was their right to demonstrate by the police.

The political and legal contexts will shape police and demonstrators' perceptions of the *venue* for the demonstration and its potential for permitting disorder. The more control the police feel they can establish over the space to be occupied by the crowd, the more they will feel able to control the crowd itself. Factors militating against this felt sense of control appear to include the proximity of public thoroughfares or shops and offices, the existence of several routes to and from the venue, and restricted room to move both officers and the crowd about. If the only effective barrier to be used is that of a police cordon, then confrontation with the demonstrators is almost inevitable. The site of the crowd affects where officers can initially be deployed, how far the local police can manage the crowd unaided, and how quickly reinforcements would have to be mobilized. The characteristics of the venue contribute to the police sense of how far they can contain the crowd and any disorder which may break out, as does their perception of the crowd and its organizers.

Perception of the organizers will obviously be influenced by police knowledge of their status and experience. The *police* are generally willing to negotiate in principle, since this potentially makes their job easier. In some situations, though not any we have studied, such negotiation might be a simple statement of the conditions under which the police will tolerate the demonstration, in effect the procedure anticipated in the 1986 Public Order Act. Where organizers are seen as authoritative, or at least having good reasons for avoiding disorder, they may be given the opportunity to achieve that objective, through self-stewarding and other means of crowd control. However, where organizers are perceived as disunited or ineffectual, then they will be in practice ignored and not given any opportunity to demonstrate their crowd control abilities.

The *organizers* have, then, to use the negotiation process to establish their own credibility in the eyes of the police. Should they fail in this, then any agreements reached will not be implemented. Refusal to negotiate with the police thus guarantees the police a 'free hand'. Willingness to negotiate is not enough, for the organizers must also know how to control the crowd. The differences between orderly and disorderly demonstrations do stem in part from the ability of the organizers to establish themselves as recognized leaders who can in practice focus the attention of the crowd and provide symbolic mechanisms to express its feelings. But of course, the ability of organizers to control the crowd depends on how far the crowd is willing to be controlled.

We come finally, and by design, to the *crowd*. A police account would no doubt begin with the crowd, on the assumption that they will be the main potential source of disorder. They may read off the likelihood of this from their observations and anticipations of the crowd: its size, composition, intentions, mood, and, often, sobriety. The police look particularly for the organized presence of 'political extremists' whom they see as prepared to use a particular issue as cover for an attack on authority in general. Other factors taken as signs of trouble include any indications of drunkenness among the crowd.

Influential though fringe political groups and drunkenness may sometimes be, they seem too simplistic to explain the attitudes of the crowds we have studied. Our survey of the 'Thatcher Unwelcoming' crowd showed a clear consensus that both moral and political reasons existed for them to avoid violence. The NUM rallies both showed a quite definite preparedness to use violence to achieve political objectives. The inquiry team at Manchester formed the view that the students did not appear to be contemplating violence. Of the intentions of the crowd at Southall we have no evidence at all, since it was never allowed to congregate and establish an identity.

We can thus offer only the most tentative outline of the influences which seem to structure any crowd's propensity to disorder, which include its composition, motives, and sense of justice.

Variations in the sex, age, and class composition of demonstrating crowds do not always have consistent effects. The presence of women and certainly of children does tend to minimize the possibility of violence, if only because their very presence is itself a statement that violence is not expected. But, as Southall and Manchester showed, the gender of the demonstrators is not important in determining police action. Youthful crowds seem more likely to accept violence as legitimate, though not all the rallying miners were young. The middle-class ethos of the Thatcher crowd militated against violence, though students, largely drawn from the same class, may not accept such a definition of responsible behaviour. In short, any generalization about the composition of crowds can immediately be qualified by contrary examples from our case studies. The issue is further complicated by the fact that in many instances the crowd were as much victims of disorder as instigators of it. The most volatile crowd at a demonstration will be one composed principally of young men, not least because they share a predisposition to violence with the police.

But even when young and male, political demonstrators are not football hooligans, whatever police and press may think. They have a political reason for what they are doing. They will have a sense of what they are trying to achieve and of the most effective means of achieving it. The conventional sociological distinction between 'symbolic' and 'instrumental' action may be useful here. Demonstrators who see themselves as making a gesture of moral or political dissent may recognize limits to its expression. They may be satisfied if their sentiments find suitable symbolic embodiment. This may be insufficient if the original motive for a significant number of demonstrators is to prevent, or alter the course of an event, or to seek revenge on an individual or group. At the first NUM rally, and possibly for a few of the Southall crowd, there was a real desire to physically attack opponents. This was thought by the police, though never proven, to have been the case at Manchester. It was certainly absent from the 'Thatcher Unwelcoming'.

It seems rare for a crowd at a demonstration to be united in holding an instrumental objective, one factor which differentiates demonstrators from pickets. Such a purpose involves the redefinition of a demonstration away from its function as a means of expressing an opinion, towards its use as a pretext for physical attack upon political opponents. It may be that this is a trend which is becoming established in the context of increasing political polarization in British society as a whole. This definition of the situation was not, however, held by any but a small minority of those in attendance at the demonstrations we have studied.

These aspects of the political and legal context, the venue, the police, the organizers, and the crowd, are those we take to be crucial in determining the degree of orderliness at a demonstration. The construction of table 3.1 (page 64), as a series of presences and absences, rather simplifies a complex reality. We cannot in practice calculate the 'disorderliness potential' of a given demonstration. Nor can some factors necessarily be given more weight than others. However, we do wish to stress the importance of the police role. With the exception of the 1968 demonstrations and the first NUM rally, where some members of the crowd were bent on violence, most of the disorder in the cases we have reviewed resulted from police action. Different kinds of action, based on real negotiation and a balance between the law and the right to demonstrate, might have averted disorder. This was the case at both the 'Thatcher Unwelcoming' demonstration and the NUM rally, and is presumably so for the vast majority of demonstrations which remain peaceful.

What informs police strategy is often the political definition of the situation, especially as formulated by members of government. The policing of demonstrations is invariably a political matter, involving as it does the right to protest against authority. When the police become partisan in deed or word, disorder will result. As we shall see in part two, this proposition also applies to mass picketing.

Part two

Picketing and disorder

Introduction

This section comprises a comparison of two well known examples of industrial mass picketing occurring in the Sheffield area. One is the mass picket of Hadfields, a private steel firm, during February and March of the 1980 steel strike. The other is the mass picket of the British Steel coke depot at Orgreave on the outskirts of Sheffield during the miners' strike in May and June 1984. The first was characterized by occasionally violent skirmishes between the pickets and the police, the second by a series of pitched battles over a period of three weeks. Central to our analysis is consideration of why the two events should have turned out so differently.

The Hadfields case study is based on retrospective interviews with twenty officials and rank-and-file members of the Iron and Steel Trades Confederation and twelve members of the South Yorkshire Police Force, varying in rank from constable to inspector. We also used a very detailed account of their operations given by the South Yorkshire Police in a report to the Home Office. This was supplemented by coverage in the local Sheffield and Yorkshire press at the time. Other accounts of the strike, notably those by Docherty (1983), Hartley *et al.* (1983), and Geary (1985) have been used for background information and evidence on the Hadfields picket.

The events of some of the most dramatic days at Orgreave were witnessed in person by our field researcher. National and local press, television and radio were carefully monitored for journalists' own accounts and their interviews with others present. Forty-two members of the Yorkshire and North Derbyshire areas of the National Union of Mineworkers were interviewed. The Chief Constable of South Yorkshire, his Deputy Chief Constable, and the Superintendent in charge of operations also gave us lengthy interviews but were unable to comply with our request to interview junior officers from Police Support Units. The daily reports of the civil liberties' organization Policewatch provided detailed accounts of events. The voluminous literature on the miners' strike was culled for information on Orgreave, the most useful being Beynon (ed.) (1985), Callinicos and Simons (1985), Coulter *et al.* (1984), Fine and Millar (eds) (1985), Sunday Times Insight Team (1985), and McCabe and Wallington (1988).

Chapter four deals with Hadfields, and chapter five with Orgreave. In chapter six we set a comparison of the two events in the context of instances of mass picketing which preceded and followed our two case studies, to ascertain contemporary trends in the level of disorder on such occasions. Our discussion here contains reference to the work of Clutterbuck (1977), Kahn *et al.* (1983), and especially Geary (1985).

4

The Hadfields mass picket, February 1980

Background

The picketing of the Hadfields private steel works on Vulcan Road in the Sheffield district of Attercliffe was a development of the 1980 national steel strike. The background to the actual dispute is well documented elsewhere (Bryer *et al.* 1982, Docherty 1983, Hartley *et al.* 1983) and a brief recapitulation is adequate for our purposes.

The origins of the dispute lay in the rapid decline of the British steel industry during the mid-1970s. Partly the result of the world recession, this was also a consequence of successive British governments artificially depressing steel prices in order to provide cheap raw materials for manufacturing industry. The side-effect was to restrict profitability and hamper new investment in the industry.

The British Steel Corporation (BSC) reacted to declining demand by restructuring the public sector into five main areas of steel production, one of which was Sheffield. A major redundancy programme was instigated, largely with the acquiescence of the main steel union, the Iron and Steel Trades Confederation (ISTC). With the accession to power in 1979 of a Conservative government committed to a hard-line monetarist policy, even more stringent policies were required.

In July 1979 the Industry Minister, Sir Keith Joseph, announced that from March 1980 BSC would receive no further money to cover its losses. In the following autumn the ISTC were presented with a wage offer of 2 per cent plus local productivity bonuses, at a time when inflation was running at 17 per cent.

On 7 December the ISTC gave notice of its intention to call a national strike for 1 January 1980 unless the offer was improved. Four days later the BSC Chairman announced that the 2 per cent wage deal was now conditional upon a 30 per cent reduction of the entire workforce. A strike seemed inevitable.

There can now be little doubt about the government's willingness to confront the steelworkers. Ministers were already committed to the closure of unprofitable public sector capacity and the related objective of trade union reform. The 1978 Ridley Report had previously nominated the steel industry as a favourable battleground (*The Economist* 27 May 1978). By contrast, the ISTC's right-wing leadership went into the strike reluctantly, searching for a compromise to the last (Kelly 1981).

Such uncertain leadership produced little co-ordination of the rank and file. The responsibility for organizing the membership was left to regional strike committees. Organization within the relatively militant South Yorkshire area had already been given some impetus by an existing dispute at the Stocksbridge works over the sacking of a militant shop steward. As ISTC's General Secretary, Bill Sirs, was approaching the BSC management in the first week of the strike with a compromise productivity deal, the South Yorkshire workers were re-formulating their demands for '20 per cent and no strings attached' (Hartley *et al.* 1983, 33).

Sirs had initially called for a 'short, sharp strike' (Docherty 1983, 163), but the BSC's own stocks were very high and there was sufficient capacity in the private sector to meet any immediate shortfall in supply. It was their understanding of the strategic role of the private sector which led South Yorkshire pickets to ignore the union's national policy of confining action to the public sector. Instead they chose to selectively picket the eastern seaports and local private companies. It was within this context that the picketing of Hadfields developed into a major symbolic struggle.

Initially, the decision to picket Hadfields was taken because its products were, more so than any other local private steel company, in direct competition with those of BSC. There was also an allegation that the firm was profiteering from the strike. Other reasons made it seem imperative to local ISTC members that Hadfields should be put out of action. Amongst these was the need to restore some credibility to the strike in the eyes of Transport and General Workers' Union (TGWU) lorry drivers who argued that they were entitled to cross picket lines, since the ISTC couldn't even get all their own members out on strike. It was also felt that the closure of Hadfields would serve as an example for other private steel workers in the locality to follow. Many strikers were further provoked by the public pronouncements of the outspoken Hadfields Chairman and the refusal of the local ISTC convener to condone the picket.

The majority of the Hadfields workforce were members of the

ISTC, with most of the rest in the Amalgamated Union of Engineering Workers (AUEW). There was latent hostility amongst ISTC members in the private sector to local action by public sector workers. Differences of interest between the two groups which had been developing since the partial nationalization of 1967 were exacerbated by the fact that the BSC's proposals did not directly affect the private sector. As the picketing activity increased, Hadfields' workers also came to resent what they saw as attempts to intimidate them into strike action.

Overview of events

Picketing of Hadfields began in January 1980. During its earliest phases, the number of pickets was relatively small. The pattern quickly settled into a routine: workers and lorry drivers would be stopped by pickets but allowed to go on their way if not persuaded by argument. The police supervised the proceedings but intervened only occasionally and with tact.

Some arrests were made in the early stages of picketing, generally when someone broke the ground rules which had been established. One such example occurred on 8 January. Pickets trying to persuade a lorry driver not to cross the line were asked to move by a police inspector before they felt they had been given a sufficient opportunity to present their case. The pickets reacted by blocking the works entrance; the police formed a wedge and drove in to disperse them. Six pickets were arrested. Such breakdowns of accommodation between police and pickets remained sporadic until the mass picketing of the following month.

On 1 February the House of Lords overturned the decision by Lord Denning to grant an injunction restraining the ISTC from calling out the private sector. On 4 February the Hadfields workers reluctantly joined the strike, only to vote to return six days later. The public sector strikers' response was to stage the first major mass picket of Hadfields.

According to Hartley *et al.* (1983, 67), mass pickets of this type

can be taken as evidence of a high motivation to win on the part of the strikers . . . (and) may also be seen as a tactic deployed by the strikers to assert their concept of order on the picket lines against that of the police in a situation where no accommodation seemed possible.

The introduction of mass picketing signalled an intensification of action, simultaneously reflected in the picket leaders' decision to abandon their previous policy of communicating their intentions to the police (South Yorkshire Police 1980, 4). As a result, the police were considerably under strength when several hundred pickets arrived at Vulcan Road on 12 February and broke through a hurriedly assembled police cordon. Police reinforcements quickly arrived and the bulk of the day's arrests were made as they successfully regained control of the situation. Both police and pickets approached the next mass picket with greater organization and resolve.

Arthur Scargill and 300 Yorkshire miners joined the mass picket of 14 February. Their presence may have been a source of concern to the police since 'outsiders', in their view, tend to politicize the mass picket and thus raise the police's expectations of violence (Kahn *et al.* 1983, 88–9). Thus the police policy of sensitive handling was under pressure from such new elements in the situation. Another was the presence of a sizeable number of strikers whose unique experience of the dispute had equipped them with a more aggressive approach to picketing than had become routine at Hadfields. One local picket described to us the first time he encountered the 'Warrington Brick Brigade', a group of Cheshire steel workers who had been given their name by the Chief Constable of Merseyside.

> They said 'All the tall lads go to the front, we're going to throw bricks as the lorries come out'. I thought 'Well, they're kidding! They can't do that!' . . . Any road, the gate opened up and a lorry driver started revving and shot forward. And – I'm not lying – there were bobbies all over the place, and they were physically pulling the bobbies away. And then the bricks came over! It was a real eye-opener and I thought 'Well, this is what it's all about'.   (South Yorkshire picket, in interview)

Such groups remained a minority influence, since few other pickets followed their lead. As a consequence, they were more easily singled out for police attention (Docherty 1983, 7; *Sheffield Star* 19 March 1980).

Two main flashpoints occurred on that day: the first one when a bus accidentally set down a group of Hadfields workers too early and the police cordon was too weak to contain the pickets at that point; and the second when a group of pickets tried to block the main entrance. The police reacted decisively each time, but there is no evidence of any over-reaction on their part. The lack of widespread opposition from the pickets to the twenty-two arrests made on the day owed much to the relationship built up with the pickets during the preceding eleven weeks of the dispute.

In the month afterwards, there was no significant picketing activity at Hadfields, even though the workers had decided to go back to work. The next confrontation was on 14 March. This mass picket occurred in the aftermath of a mass picket of the Sheerness Steel Works on the Isle of Sheppey in Kent on 22 February. In the week prior to the picket of Sheerness, newspapers orchestrated a campaign against the impending picket, one carrying the headline 'Isle of Fear' (Docherty 1983, 198). Handbills depicting Lord Kitchener saying 'Your Island Needs You' were distributed and signs appeared in local shops saying 'No Pickets Served'. On the day of the picket, coachloads of South Yorkshire steel workers were intercepted and searched by the police. On the picket line itself, the tactics of the Metropolitan Police prompted accusations of brutality (Docherty 1983, 199).

This experience left a deep scar on many of those involved.

There were a particular time when we had been marching round Sheerness. Police had thrown a cordon across the road and we went to go through. One of them grabbed me. There were a large wall, I can't remember the name of the streets, a high wall, they got me up against that, about five of them, and kicked bloody hell out of me.

(ISTC official quoted in Geary 1985, 111)

The president of the Kent area of the NUM led a contingent of 300 miners to Sheerness and felt the police behaviour on that day was a revelation to many present.

They would not accept that the police could act in this way. They'd seen the friendly neighbourhood bobby and that wasn't what we were putting forward. But after Sheerness, there was a unified chorus of 'Maggie's Boot Boys!' I think the lesson was well learned.

(Malcolm Pitt interview, ATV: A Question of Leadership 14 August 1981)

The 12 March picket of Hadfields also occurred at a time when national support for the strike was waning amidst growing criticism of the role of central union leadership. The picket was specifically designed to demonstrate the high level of morale that still existed in the South Yorkshire area. After Sheerness, the pickets marched on Hadfields, harbouring a new attitude towards the police:

> There was no way I was going to be knocked about again. I was just fed up. I mean, Sheerness will never go out of my mind. It was a debacle. From then on, if someone was going to kick me, I was going to belt 'em back. And I think there were a lot of people felt like that.
>
> (South Yorkshire picket, in interview)

Made aware of the pickets' intentions, the local police had called for reinforcements. Police expectations of violence were high:

> Most of the police had been on duty for more than six hours by the time the pickets arrived at Vulcan Road yesterday. Eight coachloads of Manchester police had been sitting outside Attercliffe police station since dawn. By lunchtime they were probably desperate for anything to happen. As one officer had put it in the morning, 'I hope something happens today after we've called in all those reserves, or we'll be looking a bit silly'. (*Sheffield Star* 13 March 1980)

Even so, the precise nature of the pickets' arrival – two separate contingents from Rotherham and Stocksbridge, marching briskly towards Hadfields down different access roads – momentarily surprised the police, who quickly fanned out across the streets to impede their progess. At this, the pickets charged the police, fighting first with those in the line then with reinforcements brought up. Seventy-five arrests were made before the remaining pickets withdrew. Clearly, there had been a total break-down of the norms governing non-violent picketing.

Analysis

Hadfields might well have been the setting for a far greater confrontation had the ideological climate been different. The dispute was widely defined as a 'routine' industrial strike, with none of the political rhetoric which was to be invoked during the course of the coal dispute. As Kahn *et al.* (1983) have pointed out, the police are apt to respond more vigorously when they see a mass picket as politically motivated.

Further, the policing of the strike was organized and controlled at local level, in accordance with the 'Hearts and Minds' philosophy practised by South Yorkshire Police:

> Bearing in mind that almost every family in Sheffield is

connected in one way or another with the steel industry, my task during the early part of this year was clear – the South Yorkshire Police had to maintain order but at the same time be fully conscious of the overriding importance of performing its task with tact and diplomacy.

(South Yorkshire Police 1980, Appendix F, 2)

Our conversations with steel workers tended to corroborate the view that the police regularly 'went out of their way' to appear sympathetic. For example, one picket told us, 'One day, twelve officers arrived at a picket with "We support the steel strikers" badges on. They would talk about football, relatives in the industry, anything to keep on friendly terms.' This day-to-day relationship was considered crucial in helping the police to understand the precise 'mood' of the pickets.

We were looking at the mood for eleven weeks. If we had not looked at the mood of the pickets for eleven weeks and had 1500 people in Vulcan Road on Valentine's Day and they had all been of one mind, which they were not, we would have had a riotous situation.   (South Yorkshire Police 1980, 42)

On St Valentine's Day itself, police officers from four other forces were drafted in but mainly waited on standby. Local policemen were used instead and, significantly, allowed sufficient time to acclimatize to the mass picket. This police strategy even survived moments when the police felt defensive.

We pulled down the road, we formed up in a unit and we marched down not really knowing what to expect and, I think, rather tense with the adrenalin flowing. And the pickets are singing 'Hokey Cokey' and you think 'What's going on?' Then they shout 'Halt!' before the commanding officer shouts halt, so half the team halts and the other half doesn't, and it's very funny. They all jeer and laugh which, to begin with, makes you very angry because we're proud and we're trained to march. Then they – the commanding officers – say: 'Right! That section: down there!' . . . And we all stood there feeling quite tense and then, gradually, one or two snippets of conversation started up and everybody relaxed a bit and the tension began to subside.   (Police Sergeant, in interview)

An ISTC official interviewed by Geary appreciated that he had been let off leniently:

I was arrested at Hadfields. I knocked this fucking copper down and the only thing they did to me were to keep me handcuffed longer than the rest. I were expecting getting bloody cracked when I got in cells at police station, but other than keeping me longer than anybody else there were nobody came near me whatever. If I'd been out of the area I reckon I'd have got bloody hammered.   (Geary 1985, 112)

An even more striking example of the enduring commitment of senior South Yorkshire Police officers to maintaining friendly relations concerned an incident on St Valentine's Day when the commanding officers decided not to attempt to disperse a spontaneous sit-down protest:

> As they were passive and the workforce had entered the premises, a decision was taken not to try and move them. This, in my view, was sensible police strategy and permitted the breach of a relatively minor law in preference to creating violent scenes.   (South Yorkshire Police 1980, Appendix B, 3)

However, many junior ranking officers took a dim view of this tactic. For, whilst the pickets may have considered the protest perfectly justifiable in terms of culturally derived appeals to 'solidarity', such action came into conflict with the police's own occupationally inculcated emphasis on respect for legal authority (Holdaway 1983, Manning 1977). Junior officers recalled the incident with some resentment.

> I think, to be honest, some of us who were at the bottom end – the sharp end – felt that politics took over on occasions and that we had to 'be careful' when, had it been a 'football hooligan' situation or a 'Saturday night' situation, the people who were causing trouble may well have been arrested, shall we say, 'somewhat more quickly'. We often felt that people should have been dealt with because they were breaking the law.   (Police Sergeant, in interview)

Left to their own devices, such junior officers would have forcibly removed the pickets. That they did not is almost entirely due to the amount of discretion exercised by senior officers. This discretion was framed by a general desire to maintain positive relationships with the local community, helped by a definition of the dispute as fundamentally apolitical.

This basic police policy evoked a positive response from the pickets. Police officers were regarded for the most part as 'only doing their jobs' and seldom was it suggested that they were playing a 'political' part in the dispute. The resulting goodwill on both sides encouraged a routinized form of normal picketing behaviour in which the police and pickets tried to accommodate each others' goals and objectives. Thus, the earliest examples of picketing at Hadfields show the police operating within the terms of a 'contract with the crowd' and according to a model in which 'picketing was definitely non-violent; it rarely involved displays of force; it stayed within the law; and its principal instrument was peaceful persuasion' (Hartley *el al*. 1983, 56).

By the time of the March picket, the tenuous basis of accommodation between pickets and police had broken down. The single most important change was in the pickets' attitudes towards the police, following the way they felt they had been treated at Sheerness. Any possibility that they might have retained a distinction between the local and national police force was removed by the presence at the March picket of contingents of officers from outside the area. The police had become a generalized rather than a specific category, seen through their role in the strike as a whole rather than through its local forms. The police rank and file came to the situation 'cold', with their expectations of violence high. Thus those influences which had served to minimize disorder on both sides during February had been removed by March and the result was disorder on the picket line.

Summary

A variety of conditions served to promote the generally peaceful picket of Hadfields during the steel strike. The following were especially important, though they are not ranked in any order of priority:

1 The definition of the dispute as a routine industrial dispute shared by both sides
2 Co-operation between the organizers and the police, ensuring that generally neither side sought to take advantage of the other
3 The use of local police with local links, family connections in the area and accountability to the local community. All this gave them an interest in containing the situation and not allowing it to escalate into violence
4 Clear lines of command within the police, with senior officers in control at all times
5 A willingness on the part of the police to allow realistic picketing to take place, overlooking minor infringements of legality in the interest of maintaining peaceful relations

6 Adherence by the majority of participants to a set of principled norms of behaviour in which the boundary between the permitted and the forbidden was clearly demarcated.

The above conditions are symptomatic of the high level of accommodation that existed between the pickets and police at Hadfields. This accommodation was temporarily ruptured during the mass pickets of 12 and 14 February and broke down completely on 14 March, when each of the six conditions listed above was reversed.

In retrospect, the experiences of the South Yorkshire steel-workers at Sheerness in 1980 were similar to the subsequent experiences of Yorkshire miners entering Nottinghamshire in 1984. The violent mass picketing of 12 March may be viewed as a portent of the type of violence soon to be witnessed at Orgreave. There the total lack of accommodation between the two main groups of protagonists became obvious to the whole nation, though the reasons for it did not.

5
The picketing of Orgreave, May–June 1984

Background

The events at Orgreave occurred within the context of ever-worsening relationships between pickets and police, outlined in chapter two on the NUM rallies. The activities leading up to the mass picketing of the coke works began with a sudden decision by the local British Steel Corporation management to increase the supply of coke to their Scunthorpe steel works above the quantity already agreed with representatives of the ISTC and the NUM. The corporation claimed that the increase in supplies was a necessary measure, since the use of poorer quality coke had damaged one of the furnaces. However, a senior ISTC official saw government interference as the impetus to break the agreement (*Yorkshire Post* 31 May).

Overview of events: May

Members of the Yorkshire Area NUM began unofficially picketing the Orgreave coke works on 23 May. According to one South Yorkshire miner:

They'd started running coke out of Orgreave the previous week. We heard about it from lads who'd inform the South Yorkshire strike centre at Silverwood whenever they saw any coal or coke moving. We went to see what was happening. On Wednesday, pickets who'd returned from Nottingham heard about it and five hundred went to Orgreave. The police penned us up against a wall. Some lads got through onto a golf course that runs by the road and bricked lorries as they came off the motorway.   (Quoted in Callinicos and Simons 1985, 101)

On the second day, 24 May, a thousand pickets were matched by equal numbers of policemen. Whilst relations seemed generally amicable, the police and pickets engaged in a trial of strength as the afternoon coke convoy arrived. Two miners were hurt in the scuffling and stones and lumps of wood were thrown at the police. There was no further picketing of the works on the following day. The first flashpoint occurred on Sunday 27 May when the NUM President, Arthur Scargill, arrived to join the picket.

At first, Scargill was refused entry by the police but, after further discussion, was allowed to visit the workers. When Scargill reappeared, a crowd of pickets gathered around him. Almost immediately, the police formed a wedge to clear the roadway, knocking over the miners' leader and several other pickets in the process:

> The police claimed at the time that it was the pickets, solely, who had done the pushing and that the police response was to push back. Now in my view, that's not an accurate record of the event. . . . The order to disperse the pickets onto the pavement was ridiculous in the context of what was going on, and that's what caused resentment. And, yes, when pushed, the miners did push back, there's no doubt about it. The police, no doubt, had a right under law to push people onto the pavement. They had a legal justification, but they had no sensible justification. Even some of the bobbies at the back of the wedge were looking round and wondering what the hell they were at.   (Policewatch observer, in interview)

The damage had been done. Later that evening, most television news bulletins concentrated on this incident. Scargill reacted by accusing the police of brutality and called upon all NUM members to rally at Orgreave in massive numbers in the declared hope that they would emulate what had happened at Saltley in 1972. This reference in itself may have been provocative, since it is generally accepted that the Saltley debacle represented a public humiliation for the police (Allen 1981, Crick 1985). This may help to explain why Assistant Chief Constable Clement seemed so determined that 'there is no chance that this will be the Saltley of 1984. The plant will remain open until British Steel decides otherwise' (*Yorkshire Post* 19 June).

The following day was Bank Holiday Monday and there were no deliveries of coke, but on Tuesday 29 May police and pickets gathered outside Orgreave in their hundreds. The Yorkshire Area NUM had actually directed its members to fall back on Orgreave only if they were prevented from reaching their picketing targets elsewhere. In the event, it was where most of them ended up.

Pickets began arriving at Orgreave very early in the morning. By about 7 a.m., two large groups had been formed: one directly opposite the main gate, and the other some 500 yards up the hill towards Handsworth, where they were being held back by a line of police. About thirty minutes later, those pickets opposite the gate were charged by police officers – some on horseback, some on foot, and others with dogs. The pickets responded angrily. Some objects, mostly pieces of wooden fencing, were thrown in retaliation. The police tactic was successful in forcing them back on to a car park, where they were hemmed in by a cordon of officers two deep. At least one observer felt that this contributed to tension and restlessness among the crowd (Policewatch Daily Report 29 May).

Just after 9 a.m., both groups of pickets obtained their first view of the convoy, at which point those most distant from the plant engaged in a concerted push against the police lines. However, it quickly became apparent that the police had the upper hand. Whenever it seemed that the pickets were about to penetrate their ranks, reinforcements were immediately sent up to hold the line, or failing this, 'snatch squads' were sent in with orders to 'take some prisoners' (Coulter *et al.* 1984, 96).

The pickets were frustrated. They were being effectively prevented from carrying out any form of picketing at all and would clearly be unable to close the plant:

> It got, like, futile after a while. There was a feeling of powerlessness. They wouldn't let us peacefully picket. We couldn't go down to the barrier and talk to the lorry drivers and we couldn't push the buggers around 'cos they'd got the measure of us. That's when the stones came out.
>
> (North Derbyshire miner, in interview)

The police's immediate response to this situation was to spread a line of riot officers, equipped with white crash helmets and body-length perspex shields, right across their ranks. This ploy may have unwittingly encouraged an even heavier bombardment of stones. The sudden appearance of these officers drew spontaneous descriptions of 'Zulus' and 'like something out of Star Wars'. Some pickets were provoked, others panicked. Many started to throw stones.

Whilst the stone throwing was in progress, two police transit vans reversed down the road to the rear of the pickets, momentarily boxing them in. Some fifty to a hundred pickets immediately responded by surrounding the vans and smashing all their windows. This was the signal for mounted police officers to charge into the crowd. Very soon this pattern, of pickets throwing stones and the police charging in on horseback, became routine.

Three times during the afternoon of 29 May the mounted police charged into the ranks of pickets. Each time mounted policemen were followed by short-shield units on foot. 'It was your look out if you couldn't run. They should have charged you with that: "unable to run". That was the only crime that some of them committed' (North Derbyshire miner, in interview).

In this context, the stone throwing became increasingly prevalent:

> What other form of defence has a miner got if a policeman's charging at you with a riot shield, horses, using dogs, truncheons and whatever – and can get away with it, as we've seen. When you've got your backs to the wall, what else are you going to do? I'd like to ask the police, if we'd got riot gear, truncheons and all that, and they'd got nothing, would they throw stones? (South Yorkshire miner, in interview)

On the following morning of 30 May, Arthur Scargill was arrested on the charge of obstructing the police and the highway, whilst leading a small group of miners towards the coking plant. Superintendent John Nesbit, the officer who arrested Scargill, later recalled in interview that:

> It was a spontaneous thing. I had many people to move and they had in fact started to go down the road. I think that Mr Scargill was trying to make the point that he didn't want to move and he was going to stand and encourage people to stand where he wanted them. But I wanted to make it clear to him that I considered him no different from any other demonstrator. Had Mr Scargill moved, and had he gone down the field where he was directed, then that would have been an end to the matter.

Prior to Scargill's arrest, the number of pickets gathered at Orgreave was quite small in relation to the previous day. However, hostilities were resumed on almost as great a scale when the afternoon convoy arrived. It is difficult to imagine that the day's violence was entirely unconnected with the police's decision to apprehend the NUM President (Lloyd 1985, 66).

Overview of events: June

At the beginning of June, the level of picket-line violence at

Orgreave decreased. Between 7 and 17 June, there was no more than a token NUM picket at Orgreave, but on 18 June, a secretly organized mass picket took the police completely by surprise. This element of surprise had implications for the police response, as the Chief Constable subsequently explained in interview:

> On 18 June, we got information from all over that people were going to come to Orgreave. So our numbers there varied throughout the day because we never knew how many were going to come. These guesstimates are difficult to make . . . it's only when the people arrive that you get a chance to understand the numbers . . . so the gathering of resources was very fluid. We'd be bringing in people who'd been, perhaps, initially deployed in Humberside, suddenly bringing them up in a van, parking them up, dragging them out of the van and saying 'we want you to do this'. And it was extremely difficult, because we wanted to make sure every officer we put out was properly briefed, but the very nature of the circumstances dictated that we couldn't do that. It was a practical impossibility.

Early that morning, scores of pickets were virtually un-opposed as they entered the coke works and later had to be flushed out by police reinforcements, which included dog handlers. With the arrival of the morning convoy, the pickets started to push against the police lines, during which time a police riot shield was captured and eventually set alight. Mounted police officers immediately chased the pickets involved and this symbolic object was successfully retrieved.

For the rest of the morning and most of the afternoon, things remained peaceful. However, just when it appeared that the day's hostilities had concluded, a small group of young pickets made an inept attempt to roll a huge tractor tyre towards the onlooking ranks of policemen. Most of the police remained still but some officers rushed out, giving the impression of a false start in an athletics race. Stones were immediately thrown at them. As a response, 'police in full riot gear who had been stood down shortly before, after standing for hours in blazing sunshine being taunted by men basking in the weather, were hurriedly recalled' (*Sheffield Morning Telegraph* 19 June).

The order was given for police officers on horseback and on foot to advance on the pickets. Then occured some of the worst violence during the whole picketing of Orgreave. In the space of four successive advances, the police chased pickets across railway lines, up the streets of the nearby village and into private gardens. Chief Inspector Tony Clement claimed that he 'had no alternative but to drive the pickets into the estate. I had to protect my men from the hail of stones that were causing serious injuries' (*Yorkshire Post* 19 June). However, the pickets we interviewed complained of gratuitous violence by the police, a view supported by several Policewatch observers who characterized their behaviour as 'out of control' (Policewatch Daily Report 18 June).

When the police eventually regrouped, the pickets responded by engaging in a form of activity which was widely portrayed as 'criminal' in the mass media, but which others present at the time felt to have its own logic:

> They built a bloody great barricade and it was flaming. They'd effectively managed to stop the police charges by building that barricade. I mean, I saw that as a defensive move. People say that it was terrible, but basically that put an end to the police riot. (Policewatch observer, in interview)

Analysis

The public image of Orgreave was of an orgy of violence, endorsed by the police view that a hooligan element the worse for drink had taken over. The Assistant Chief Constable in charge of operations gave his interpretation of the 30 May events to the press:

> He said miners had left after the morning convoy, gone to public houses and then returned. 'They come back and the violence gets greater. That has been a feature of the picketing, if you can call it picketing, in this strike.' He added that the police had seen 'politically-motivated' people 'egging the miners on'. (*Yorkshire Post* 31 May)

The previous day, he had blamed Arthur Scargill:

> This picket line for the last few days that I have been in control has not had any violent animosity towards the police. That has appeared in the last two days. Mr Scargill has appeared here in the last two days. (*Yorkshire Post* 30 May)

The ingredients of this view are familiar and seem to figure in most police accounts of public disorder. Violence is attributed to a combination of drink, irresponsible leadership, and outside agitators. There seems little concrete evidence of the influence of the latter. Drink is known to lessen inhibitions and the appearance and attitudes of Mr Scargill were not designed to lessen the intensity of conflict. In our view, however, the explanation of why and how an initially peaceful picket was transformed into a series of violent confrontations requires a deeper level of analysis.

The initial question is why the mass picketing of Orgreave was able to take place at all. The police had previously shown themselves to be very effective in preventing mass picketing of this kind elsewhere, by stopping pickets *en route* and closing approach roads to the venue. It may have been that the location of Orgreave in the Yorkshire coalfield would have made it difficult to restrict the movement of pickets given that so many would come from nearby. It may also have been that the numbers expected would have been so large that the police would have been unable to police both the movement of pickets and their assembly at Orgreave.

Whatever the police decision and the basis for it, the effect was to lead miners to believe in retrospect that they had been led into a trap. Not only had Orgreave been left open, but alternatives had been closed off. 'To make sure that the men did fall back on Orgreave, the police tightened their road blocks on the Yorkshire/Nottinghamshire border' (Coulter *et al.* 1984, 5). By contrast, pickets endeavouring to reach Sheffield encountered no such physical obstruction (Beynon (ed.) 1985, 19).

The view that Orgreave was a set-piece confrontation, 'theatrically managed to publicly teach the miners a lesson' (Coulter *el al.* 1984, 5), is one shared by most of the miners we have interviewed:

> Orgreave could never have existed. This is why I say the police wanted a confrontation. There are only three roads leading into Orgreave. Now, in some of the towns we've visited, there are eight roads, and every road and 'scrub' road and side track is policed. Everybody got through to Orgreave. All ten thousand.   (South Yorkshire miner)

Whilst it is impossible to establish the validity of this theory, there is strong evidence that the views of the most senior police officers at Orgreave were in accord with those of the government. As Assistant Chief Constable Tony Clement (the director of the police operations) later explained to a local radio reporter:

> We have been committed to getting into work people who want to go into work, and if that takes every man in South Yorkshire Police Force and the surrounding police forces,

that's what we shall do. That is our job. These people have a right to go into work. They have a right to do what they are doing and no one is going to stop them by unlawful means.

(Radio Sheffield 29 May)

Clement was later to express the fear that

If the pickets here win by force, the whole structure of industrial relations, and policing, and law and order, and civil liberties is all gone. We cannot afford for people who want to go to work to be prevented by force.

(*Daily Telegraph* 19 June)

Orgreave seems to have been identified by the police as the show-down with the miners, the outcome of which would indicate the future progress of the whole strike.

As for the events at the scene itself, there is still no clear picture. The miners' account is that they were deliberately provoked by the police. Prevented from picketing, their inevitable frustration was bound to lead to acts which the police could use as a pretext for dispersing them. For them, throwing stones was a largely defensive measure, both an attempt to defend the right to picket which they felt had been taken away from them, and a defence against punitive action by the police.

The police explained their own conduct as equally defensive. According to the Chief Constable in interview, they acted against the pickets only when provoked:

You need to put sufficient policemen in there to withstand the pushing . . . That's exactly what we did. And then the problem comes with the stone throwing. When the pickets are not achieving their objectives in that manner, they then use other means and start throwing stones. So, therefore, you bring police in with long shields in order to be able to withstand that sort of thing. And then, when they start rushing and the crowd gets bigger, then you get the injuries. You've only got to see the videos of injuries simply caused by two large groups of active men coming together with force. Then the horses are put in to release that pressure, but once you start, once the pickets themselves say 'We're not getting anywhere, we've got to do this', then you're on the road to escalation which is extremely difficult, from the police point of view, to prevent.

If the sequence of cause and effect remains obscure, the role of specific actions which deepened resentment is easier to identify. The introduction of riot shields was to the police a sensible precaution against a likely bombardment of missiles, but to the pickets a statement of intent and an invitation to throw things. The use of mounted police seems to have had the effect of heightening the crowd's anger in ways similar to the use of dogs earlier on. Again, the police account argues this to have been a response to the situation. Assistant Chief Constable Tony Clement has emphasized that this tactic simply took the form of a 'sudden inspiration' when he sent in a line of eight mounted officers to rescue six stranded policemen:

> To see the effect those horses had on them, the way they backed off and scattered, it immediately suggested that if you were about to be overwhelmed, the horses could be invaluable. At no time had I envisaged using them in that way.
>
> (Quoted in Sunday Times Insight Team 1985, 99)

Other witnesses, like this local radio reporter, felt that the tactic was planned:

> Like a military manoeuvre, the police swept into action. They say it was a coincidence, but it was moments before the lorries came out. But I remember looking up and suddenly seeing two lots of horses sweeping in from the left and right simultaneously on the pickets. It was like a scene out of war, a battle. They swept in, the police went forward. The miners obviously didn't realize what had hit them. They surged backwards and it obviously took a couple of minutes before they realized what was happening. And they got back under control and the hail of stones and rocks, knives and other things, started to rain down on the police.   (Radio Sheffield 29 May)

McCabe and Wallington are quite clear that

> as the official police film of the encounter makes clear (contrary to the image of much media coverage), there were no 'scenes of violence' before mounted officers rode into the pickets and drove them away from the police line. Only after they had been attacked in this way did the pickets retaliate.
>
> (1988, 76)

This and other moves do appear to have been premeditated. As subsequently became clear at the trial in Sheffield of fourteen pickets charged with riot at Orgreave – all of whom were acquitted – the police tactics used there followed closely those recommended in the secret manual 'Public Order Tactical Options' drawn up by the Association of Chief Police Officers (ACPO) in the wake of the riots of 1980–1. They included the charging of the crowd with truncheons and the incapacitating of ringleaders 'by striking in a controlled manner with batons about the arms and legs or torso so as not to cause serious injury' (McCabe and Wallington 1988, 50). Their effect was wholly provocative, as was the rhythmic beating on shields – recommended by the manual – which greeted the return of the mounted police.

The events of 18 June indicate that the police used the opportunity to vent all the feelings of resentment accumulated over the previous three weeks. It was no accident that on that day especially, South Yorkshire officers were in charge of men from fourteen different police forces. Superintendent Nesbit recognized the importance of this in interview:

> I think what you've got to understand is that people coming from the Metropolitan area, also Hampshire, Bedfordshire, have no conception of what the mining areas are about . . . and what industrial problems can arise from people being made unemployed because of pit closures. They tended just to see it as violent industrial disorder without, perhaps, fully understanding the problems of close-knit communities fearing for their futures.

The events at Orgreave were removed from a local context, with its potential for locally negotiated agreements between police and pickets, and inserted into a national arena of irreconcilable conflict. Orgreave was not seen as a local picket during an industrial dispute but a trial of strength in a politically charged struggle. The way it was policed and who policed it was similarly defined by national rather than local considerations. The conflict betwen the South Yorkshire police and the area NUM had been transformed into a confrontation between the state and the 'enemy within'.

Summary

In our discussion of Hadfields we noted a number of factors which helped to account for the relatively low level of police–picket violence. These included the definition of the dispute, the liaison between picket organizers and police, the organization of the police, their attitude to minor breaches of the law, and the extent to which police and pickets shared a definition of behavioural norms. On all of these criteria Orgreave was different. Indeed various elements of the situation constituted a recipe for widespread disorder. Among these we may include:

1 The use of a variety of different police forces, differently trained and equipped, with no local connections or accountability
2 A policy of rapid turnover of police, preventing continuity of police tactics and precluding the development of relationships between police and pickets
3 Confused lines of command within the police, with conflicts of responsibility between local and visiting forces, and failure to control adequately the behaviour of junior police officers
4 Determination on the part of the police to prevent any meaningful picketing, enforce the letter of the law, and use force against the crowd
5 An absence of any agreed norms of behaviour as to what should be permitted or prohibited
6 A lack of organization and clear strategy on the part of the pickets
7 The use of strategies involving surprise.

The above factors are symptomatic of the fundamental lack of accommodation that existed between the pickets and the police. In its absence, the police resorted to riot control tactics which inevitably escalated the violence. In the next chapter we compare and contrast Hadfields and Orgreave to identify the factors predisposing any industrial picket to greater or lesser disorder.

6
Understanding picketing disorder

Comparison of case studies

Before considering the nature of and reasons for the differences between Hadfields and Orgreave, it is worthwhile considering the similarities. These may help to explain how and why the two outcomes were not inevitable.

Both disputes resulted from government policies to 'rationalize' public sector industries. Both occurred in one of the areas of Britain which was to bear the brunt of this strategy. The possible consequences for the economic devastation of South Yorkshire may have been less obvious in 1980 than they were in 1984 but both groups of workers were attempting to defend their livelihoods. Neither was a routine dispute about wages or conditions.

Both instances involved the picketing of workers not directly involved in the dispute. Though some Hadfields workers were members of the ISTC, they did not see themselves as party to a dispute about the reorganization of the public sector. At Orgreave the targets were lorry drivers working under contract. Hence in both cases picketing extended beyond the immediate boundaries of the dispute.

The two unions involved each had strong traditions of solidarity, having conducted such disputes successfully in the past. Their members were mainly young, wholly male and working-class, with some preparedness to use violence if necessary. In both instances, there is some evidence that small groups of pickets were looking for trouble and were prepared to initiate it by 'bricking' lorries. If anything, there is more evidence of this at Hadfields than at Orgreave. At both Hadfields and Orgreave, pickets committed acts which went beyond the bounds of normal picketing and were in breach of the law. Police and pickets were engaged in trials of strength no less at Hadfields than at Orgreave. As St Valentine's Day showed, the potential for violence could have been realized at Hadfields more often than it was.

' According to these limited criteria – of what was at stake, who was involved, the objectives of the picketing action, the latent possibility of flashpoints developing – Hadfields and Orgreave were quite similar. Yet the outcomes were different. While few in Britain can now remember that there was a national steel strike, much less what happened during it, the scenes of violence at Orgreave were witnessed on television by the whole nation and have become one of the dominant images of picketing in the 1980s.

Table 6.1   Arrests at Hadfields and Orgreave

Hadfields(1980)		Daily total	Orgreave (1984)		Daily total
January	8	6	May	24	13
	9	3		25	7
	10	3		26	8
February	11	2		29	82
	12	13		30	32
	13	10		31	10
	14	22	June	1	19
	19	1		4	1
March	1	75		5	1
				6	23
				18	93
Total		1			289

The number of arrests on each occasion turns out to be an unreliable index of the extent of disorder. There were almost four times as many police and pickets at Orgreave as at Hadfields but, as table 6.1 shows, there were only twice as many arrests: 289 compared with 135. These figures reflect the decreased viability of arrest when such large numbers are involved, which itself may have encouraged the police to mete out a good deal of summary justice at Orgreave. More indicative of the scale of disorder were the charges selected by the police. Offenders at Orgreave were charged with more serious offences including those of riot. Statistics of injuries were less liable to distortion. Only one policeman and two pickets were reported as having been injured during the whole of the Hadfields picket. At Orgreave, twenty-eight police officers and fifty-one pickets were notified as injured on 18 June alone, and many more pickets were undoubtedly treated elsewhere.

Orgreave cannot be explained by the general level of violence in the miners' strike, since this is a circular argument. Rather it has to be seen as the climax of a tendency for industrial picketing as a whole to become disorderly. This pattern can be understood as the result of four sets of factors: the political context, policing strategies, the attitudes of the pickets, and the consequent pattern of picket–police interaction.

First, *the political context*. In 1980, the Conservative government had been in office for less than a year. Its plan to restructure the steel industry was one of its earliest economic initiatives. The strike would therefore be resisted by the government but primarily because of its economic implications. The steel workers stood in the way of progress. This narrow view of the strike was limited by, amongst other considerations, the fact that the government had not yet created a new legal status for trade unions and picketing. As the climbdown of 1981 showed, the government was not yet ready to take on the NUM.

By 1984, the government was in the first year of its second term of office. It had succeeded in shifting the whole political culture to the right. Reform of the trade unions had been achieved through making secondary picketing a civil offence, enabling the courts to sequester the assets of recalcitrant unions. The inner-city riots of 1980–1 had confirmed and widened the support for the government's law and order policies, including greater powers for the police. The plan for coal was not only important to the government's political credibility, it was also central to its long-term energy policy, in which privatization and nuclear power were to take a larger role.

In such a context, the miners' strike was successfully represented as a political as much as an economic issue. The miners were identified with undemocratic behaviour at several different levels: the refusal to hold a national ballot, the revolutionary political ideals of the leadership, and the alleged use of violence to attain their objectives. In sum, whereas the conflict in the steel industry in 1980 had a distinct political context, its primary definition remained that of a 'normal' industrial dispute, if a threat to the government's economic strategy. The political context of conflict in the mining industry in 1984 provided a wider and deeper definition of it as a national political strike, threatening the very basis of democracy.

These themes were taken up with enthusiasm by the largely conservative national press and unwittingly reflected in the broadcasting media. They helped to consolidate the support for the government which had been evident in the recent General

Election. That the public had little sympathy for the miners was evident from national opinion polls commissioned by the media. Our own survey of the Sheffield public conducted at the time showed that locally there was a hard core of support for the miners (Critcher *et al.* 1984). But away from the mining areas most people were reliant on the media for their understanding of the issues and the events of the strike.

This setting of a political tone by the government and the orchestration of a national public opinion over and above regional loyalties, had its most perceptible effects on the police. There is now irrefutable evidence that the government had prepared for the strike. So had the police. The inner-city riots hastened reforms already in progress in the organization and ethos of the police, towards an emphasis on confrontational styles of policing.

The *attitudes and organization of the police* are the second set of factors which differentiate Orgreave from Hadfields. We have already seen how senior officers identified with the government view of the strike, albeit couched in the legal terms of upholding the right to work. National public opinion, as represented by government, was allowed to ride roughshod over local sensibilities. This was bound to affect police strategy. As we have seen, the police at Hadfields were highly sensitive to any effect their actions might have on local opinion, in the immediate and the longer term. If, as Jefferson and Grimshaw (1984) suggest, the actions of senior police officers are aimed at an audience of the powerful, then the expressed demands of that audience, and its political composition, had changed significantly between 1980 and 1984.

Changes in the police perception of their role were reflected in their organization. At Hadfields, the force used was mainly local, with outside officers kept in reserve. It was essentially a local operation with an integrated chain of command maintaining a conciliatory tone. Junior officers' desire to confront the pickets was kept in check. Minor, and sometimes quite major, infringements of the law were ignored in the cause of maintaining order. Arrests were made with discrimination and largely for specific offences. In handling the crowd, established methods of control, the cordon and the wedge, were predominant. In general, policing was reactive and controlled.

At Orgreave, it was quite different. Though South Yorkshire officers were in overall charge, they were in effect commanding a national police force co-ordinated through the National Recording Centre. The decision to prevent the pickets from realizing their objectives by any means was tantamount to a *carte blanche* for the full panoply of riot control: snatch squads, horses, dogs, and riot shields. In general, policing was proactive and uncontrolled. It was neither inevitable nor disinterested.

> The two days of really serious conflict at Orgreave need not, in our view, have happened if the police had used their common law powers to prevent the movement of lorries on the days concerned. All too clearly, however, the political implications of doing so would have been a sufficient deterrent for any but the most courageous or foolhardy chief constable. In effect, the memories of Saltley demanded a return match and the question of policing priorities did not arise.
>
> (McCabe and Wallington 1988, 134)

These differences in police methods alone might have been enough to determine *the attitudes and organization of the pickets*, our third differentiating factor. But there were other influences. The pickets at Orgreave were already frustrated by the limited successes of the mass picketing strategy, the refusal of other NUM areas to come out on strike and the extent of police powers ranged against them. Now they were frustrated by not being able to get anywhere near the coke lorries. Their leadership endorsed the strategy of mass picketing and the tactics which accompanied it, appearing in person to express support. However, there was no master plan; the behaviour of the pickets at Orgreave was, contrary to media claims, largely improvised. If some had premeditated ideas about what they would do, many more acted in the heat of the moment to what they saw as police provocation.

At Hadfields, the attitudes and organization of the pickets were quite different. Although the union had been split, this was more between a leadership reluctant to strike and a rank and file, in South Yorkshire at least, wishing to take action. The pickets were locally led, well organized, and disciplined. Their goal of getting fellow ISTC members at Hadfields out once more was also potentially more attainable than preventing non-union lorry drivers sub-contracted by British Steel from leaving Orgreave. Nor, until Sheerness, did the Hadfields pickets harbour any resentment against the police, perceived as observing the ground-rules of industrial disputes.

So – fourthly – *the interaction between police and pickets* was qualitatively different at Hadfields. Effective consultation between picket leaders and police was backed up by deliberate fraternization on the picket line. The bounds of acceptable behaviour were tacitly agreed and mechanisms were available to redress grievances on either side. At Orgreave, there was no such negotiation. The union leadership accorded the police as little legitimacy as the police accorded them. What the police regarded as the provocation of Arthur Scargill's visit to the picket line was complemented by the perceived provocation of his subsequent arrest. Instead of fraternization, there was verbal and physical abuse; instead of plans being disclosed in advance, there were attempts to catch the opposition off guard. Any limits on acceptable behaviour were abandoned in favour of unlimited scope for violent action and retaliation.

Thus, on each of our four criteria – the political context, police organization, the attitudes of the pickets, and the dynamics of police–picket interaction – Hadfields was conducive to order while Orgreave was not. This is to argue more than that Orgreave happened during the miners' strike and Hadfields during the steel strike. Even given this context, police and pickets at Orgreave might have behaved differently and achieved some sort of accommodation. The police decision not only to keep the pickets away from the plant but to hem them in with no lines of retreat seems in retrospect a crucial factor. Whether or not the pickets were led into a trap, they certainly felt and acted as if they had been. The sheer numbers of police and pickets increased the likelihood of disorder, as did the element of surprise used by both sides. But such factors are themselves indications of the break-down of accommodation, since both can be limited through negotiation.

No one set of contextual or interactional factors can be isolated as the ultimate cause of disorder. They are all interconnected. Changes in the ethos and organization of the police, whilst given specific impetus by the inner-city riots, occurred in a political context favourable to the extension and militarization of police powers. Pickets' perception of the police cannot be divorced from the assumed collusion between police, National Coal Board (NCB), and government. A more 'moderate' union leadership might never have embarked on the strike in that form, but sooner or later there was bound to be industrial action against pit closures.

Negotiation was impossible because the prevalent framework of interpretation precluded the possibility of compromise or negotiation. In that sense, all picketing disorder is political. It is an expression and reflection of the immediate and wider political context, where the meaning of the strike is defined, the lines of conflict drawn, and the range of powers to be used are delimited.

The behaviour 'on the day' may well be significant in determining whether disorder does actually take place but the potential for it lies in how the particular situation has been interpreted and contextualized. We may see more clearly how context and situation interact by considering other recent examples of mass picketing.

Industrial disorders 1972–87

In historical terms, Hadfields represented the end of a phase in industrial disputes. Orgreave was the harbinger of change. In his historical review of the policing of industrial disputes, Geary (1985) suggests that in the post-war period in Britain, industrial picketing had become even more routinized and orderly than it had been in the 1920s and 1930s:

> From the end of the Second World War until the 1970s there was, aside from the Roberts–Arundel strike of 1967, hardly any disorder associated with industrial disputes . . . the strikes of the 1970s were remarkable for their general lack of violence.
>
> (Geary 1985, 114)

This remained so, despite an occasional reversion by pickets to tactics which had been discredited in the inter-war period, including 'obstruction of the police and the highway, damaging lorries and even intimidating workers' (Geary 1985, 115). While police activities had begun to incorporate limited use of Police Support Units (PSUs) and snatch squads, they were more likely to engage with pickets in ritualized pushing and shoving near works entrances.

By the 1980s, this situation had changed. The 1984–5 miners' strike is flanked on either side by disputes involving the National Graphical Association (NGA), first at Warrington in 1983 and then at Wapping in 1986–7. A pattern emerged, in which the structure maintaining order during mass picketing established in the previous sixty years was breaking down.

The comparison between the miners' strike of 1972 and that of 1984 is instructive. Clutterbuck (1977) has remarked on the remarkable restraint shown by the police at Saltley in 1972, who declined to use the extreme force necessary to keep the coke depot open. Twelve years later, the unthinkable had become the likely pattern of the future. The turning point was Grunwick. Starting as a dispute over a sacked worker, it quickly became an issue of union recognition, attracting support from trade unionists, ethnic organizations, left-wing groups, and even a cross-section of Labour MPs. On the first day of the mass picket, however, it became obvious that the police were no longer going to act with restraint and intended to eschew negotiation with the organizers in favour of mass arrest of any who stepped off the pavement.

Some commentators, such as Dromey and Taylor (1978) and Rogaly (1977), have suggested that it was this initial police action and its coverage by the media which escalated the conflict at Grunwick. The violence which subsequently occurred remained localized, intermittent, and brief (Weir 1977). Nevertheless, the daily arrival of the works' buses transporting non-strikers into the factory invariably provoked confrontation.

On 23 June 1977 Arthur Scargill, then Yorkshire President of the NUM, led a delegation of miners to Grunwick. At Saltley, five years before, he had been left well alone by police. At Grunwick he was arrested on charges of obtructing the highway and the police (of which he was later acquitted). One miner, asked to compare Grunwick with Saltley, replied: 'There's no comparison. I was at Saltley gates and it was a child's picnic by the side of this' (quoted in Dromey and Taylor 1978, 123).

Clutterbuck points out that the arrest of Scargill and another NUM leader, Maurice Jones, was not to be identified as the most significant event that day. The focal point of media interest was a young police constable struck on the head by a bottle and seriously injured. Newspaper and television coverage pictured him lying on the pavement with a pool of blood by his head. Such publicity, argues Clutterbuck, 'had a dramatic effect and marked another turning point in the dispute' (1977, 214). The effect was to encourage the organizers to avoid picket-line violence. Subsequently the Association of Professional Executive Clerical and Computer Staff (APEX) General Secretary, Roy Grantham, endeavoured to limit the number of pickets outside Grunwick to 500, while the strike committee publicly denounced the violence. The level of confrontation immediately declined, only recurring on the 'national day of action' on 11 July and the final mass picket of 7 November.

The potential for violent confrontation revealed at Grunwick reappeared during the 1983 picket of Eddie Shah's *Warrington Messenger* plant, in a dispute over a closed shop. The NGA staged a weekly mass picket on the night Shah delivered his papers. However, the pickets were kept well away from the lorries by a mass police presence, including many from surrounding forces. According to Geary, the situation remained relatively orderly until the night of 30 November. A mass picket of 4,000 people was pushed back to make way for the delivery vans. When they resisted,

> the police called up reinforcements who seized union banners and confiscated the pickets' public address system. At this point some stones and bottles were thrown, a senior officer warned of possible baton-charges and a squad in full riot gear appeared. Missiles continued to be thrown, a policeman yelled, 'Come on, let's get these bastards' and the riot squad drove into the crowd, splitting it in two. Stoning intensified and barricades were set ablaze. At the end of the day 43 people were injured, including 25 police, and 73 arrested.
>
> (Geary 1985, 135)

Scraton argues that police tactics were provocative and politically motivated. 'From the outset of the dispute it was clear that the police intended to side with the employer in their selective enforcement of law on the picket line' (Scraton 1985a, 158). Significantly for the importance of the political definition of industrial disputes, Shah was portrayed 'not only as a champion of the law but as a defender of the right of workers not to unionise' (Scraton 1985a, 158).

A variation on this portrayal of the employer as the defender of freedom and trade unions as agents of tyranny was evident in the protracted dispute between News International, owned by Rupert Murdoch, and the NGA, the National Union of Journalists (NUJ), and the Society of Graphical and Allied Trades (SOGAT) in 1986–7. Rupert Murdoch's company had built a new printing works at Wapping, equipped with the latest newspaper technology, supposedly for the production of a new London evening paper once agreement with the unions had been reached. When the plant was ready, management moved the printing of all the group's newspapers to Wapping, claiming that negotiations between management and unions had broken down. The Electrical Electronic Plumbing and Telecommunications Trade Union (EEPTU) helped to recruit and train new workers, signing a 'no-strike' agreement in return for virtually excluding the traditional print unions from the plant. The inevitable result was a mass picket at Wapping, aimed both at those working there and at the lorries used to distribute the newspapers, owned by a company in which Mr Murdoch had a financial interest.

From the beginning the police had no doubt as to where their duty lay. Workers and lorries were to be allowed free passage and hence the pickets would have to be moved to allow this to happen. Some pickets tended to resist, others were literally unable to move because they were hemmed in by police. Nightly there was more or less violent confrontation. According to a *Guardian* reporter, the objective of mass picketing had become indivisible from antipathy towards the police:

> The mood of hatred towards the police among some groups of demonstrators was tangible. Unlike 3 May, the previous worst night of violence, there was little attempt to blockade the plant, or indeed to push through the police lines by force of numbers. (*Guardian* 26 January 1987)

Some protestors overturned a lorry which had carried a jazz band at the head of an organized march to the plant and tried unsuccessfully to set it alight. Others stoned the police, who responded by sending in riot squads with batons drawn. As more missiles were thrown,

> The line of riot shields opened up and roughly twenty mounted police galloped out, some to the left and some to the right, scattering demonstrators in all directions. Many protestors fell under the hooves as police forced the crowd back down the road. (*Guardian* 26 January 1987)

These were scenes reminiscent of the miners' strike. So too were police definitions of the right of access to roads immediately around the plant. Not only potential pickets but local residents had their movements restricted. Road blocks were erected, and members of the public were required on pain of arrest to supply their names and addresses and explain their presence. Cars parked on the route of the convoy were arbitrarily removed, Greater London Council (GLC) byelaws restricting the movement of heavy lorries after dark were ignored, and even traffic signals were altered to enable lorries to progress without stopping (NCCL 1986).

Warrington and Wapping, as well as the miners' strike, occurred after the inner-city riots of 1980–1. The strategies being designed to handle community disorder could be generalized to other kinds of disorder. Proactive policing was becoming the order of the day. Picket behaviour which might have been tolerated a decade before was now being defined and treated as criminal activity. Several factors seem to have been important in encouraging this development.

One was the increased politicization of industrial disputes. In all the above instances, pickets could see themselves as part of a wider political and economic struggle rather than a limited sectional dispute. At Grunwick, the issues of union recognition and the position of black workers widened the terms of the debate. At Warrington, the closed shop was a general union principle and it was recognized that Eddie Shah's pioneering use of new technology represented a long-term threat to the existence of printing workers' jobs. At Wapping the involvement of Rupert Murdoch and his tactical manipulation of his myriad interests extended the dispute from the issues of new technology and the role of the EEPTU to one about ownership and control of the media. In each case, the perception of the picket as an act of political principle could be and was reversed. At Warrington and Grunwick the 'right' of workers not to join a union if they so chose was upheld against the 'tyranny' of the closed shop. At Wapping, a more general notion was evoked, that the print unions were seeking to hold back progress necessary to the survival of the newspaper industry.

Such processes of politicization tend to strengthen police resolve, since they see the situation as having breached the boundaries of ordinary industrial disputes. Kahn *et al.* suggest that the police will be more uncompromising where a dispute 'is not straightforwardly about terms and conditions of work' because this threatens their ability to act impartially between capital and labour (1983, 88). This perspective is reinforced if such a dispute draws into the picket 'outsiders' whom the police do not see as having any business there, other than to use the situation for their own ends.

In such circumstances, the police feel that the composition of the crowd and its size undermine their ability to negotiate:

> At the heart of the police notion of the normal picket line is an event whose scope and form they can negotiate. Normality both resides in, and is to be judged by, the extent to which pickets and police can negotiate how the picketing is to be conducted. (Kahn *et al.* 1983, 89)

Hence the police will be more liable to make arbitrary demands of the crowd and to react punitively if co-operation is not forthcoming. Important here is the fact that discretionary powers of arrest may be used more widely if the situation is felt to be going beyond the rules of normal picketing. The chances are increased that

> the senior officer on the spot feels that 'something isn't quite right' or 'something is going to happen'. Such feelings do not lead to a deliberate policy to make arrests, but rather to a decision to take firm controlling action and if necessary arrest those who will not co-operate. (Kahn *el al.* 1983, 93)

At Grunwick, Warrington, and Wapping, as at Orgreave but in contrast to Hadfields, the police refused to negotiate, issued ultimata and attempted to forcibly disperse the crowd. The differing dynamics of these incidents can be used to construct a model of disorder.

Towards a model of industrial disorder

In table 6.2 we present a comparison of what we take to be the factors determinate of order or disorder at our own two case studies and the three other instances considered. It is clear that, whatever their official line may be, the attitudes and thus strategies of the police are strongly influenced by the political climate. When politicians and the media evoke a definition of an industrial dispute as involving a basic principle of democracy, this clearly invites the police to enforce the law in ways which accord pickets minimal rights. At Grunwick, the fact of a Labour government rather muted this definition, which remained low-key during the 1980 steel strike. By the time of Warrington, the definition is becoming harder. The miners' strike serves to make this interpretation readily available, so that at Wapping the questionable activities of News International can conveniently be overlooked in a general appeal to the rights of 'progressive' employers to use whatever means are necessary to introduce new technology and break union power. This politicization of disputes, as well as their occurrence in London, draws in those who wish to support the picket but are not themselves directly involved. This merely confirms the police view that this is no longer a 'normal' industrial dispute and disinclines them to liaise with the organizers, who are in any case less able to control such a heterogeneous picket. Such factors are likely to predispose both sides in the conflict to confrontational attitudes. The mechanisms which we understand to maintain order in principle, and which in practice largely did so at Hadfields, are lacking. If this analysis is correct, it would seem that peaceful mass picketing is now virtually impossible without a series of concerted efforts by both sides which the current political climate renders nigh impossible.

Thus it is both an empirical and a theoretical observation that picketing in the 1980s, in so far as it is likely to take place at all, is likely to remain disorderly. This is, it should be emphasized, a comparatively recent development and requires explanation as an historical trend. Geary (1985, 148–9) has produced a model documenting these changes in police–picket relations, which seem to represent a reversion to the pattern dominant around the

Table 6.2   Factors affecting disorder at mass pickets

Key characteristics	Hadfields (1980)	Orgreave (1984)
Definition of dispute		
Dominant political viewpoint	Routine industrial dispute (jobs/wages)	Politically principled (a 'threat to democracy')
Police		
Composition	Local police force (outside forces in reserve)	Various police forces deployed
Tactics	Cordon and wedge	Cordon and wedge; snatch squads; shield units; mounted police; dogs
Discretion	Technical offences overlooked; minimum arrests	Technical offences punished; maximum arrests
Organizers		
Attitude to violence	Disavowal	Tacit approval
Capacity to control pickets	Capable	Probably capable
Pickets		
Composition	Local ISTC; a few 'outsiders'	NUM pickets from nationwide
Interaction		
Liaison/co-operation	Formal consultation; few surprise tactics	No consultation; surprise tactics by pickets
Presence of norms	Agreed set of norms limiting behaviour	No recognition of limits of behaviour
Characteristic behaviour	Ritualistic pushing and shoving	Ill-tempered pushing and shoving; pickets throwing objects; police charges; use of batons

turn of the century. Pickets have supplemented the ritual of pushing and shoving with the stoning of police and destruction of property. Mass pickets have displaced the largely small-scale and symbolic picketing of the immediate past. Union officials tend to be unwilling or unable to control their members' behaviour. The police have reintroduced batoning as the main method of controlling pickets, a technique used before the Second World War but abandoned after it. The drawing of truncheons has become as routine as the sight of riot shields.

Grunwick (1977)	Warrington (1983)	Wapping (1986/87)
Politically principled ('right not to belong to a union')	Politically principled ('right not to belong to a union')	Politically principled (unions obstructing technological progress)
Local police force, but SPG deployed	Local police force with outside reinforcements	Various police forces deployed
Cordon and wedge; snatch squads	Cordon and wedge; snatch squads; shield units	Cordon and wedge; snatch squads; shield units; mounted police
Inconsistent reaction to technical offences; some arrests	Technical offences punished; maximum arrests	Technical offences punished; maximum arrests
Disavowal Incapable	Disavowal Probably capable	Disavowal Incapable
APEX members nationwide; high proportion of 'outsiders'	NGA members nationwide; smaller proportion of 'outsiders'	Print union members (principally local); many 'outsiders'
Initial consultation; surprise tactics by police Ill-defined norms limiting behaviour Ill-tempered pushing and shoving; pickets roughly arrested	No consultation; surprise tactics by police No recognition of limits on behaviour Ill-tempered pushing and shoving; use of batons by police	No consultation; surprise tactics by pickets No recognition of limits on behaviour Ill-tempered pushing and shoving; pickets throwing objects; police charges; use of batons

Geary is less concerned with this very recent change than with explaining the decline in industrial disorder which preceded it. He argues that in the sixty years after 1915, the overall level of violence in industrial disputes in Britain progressively declined. He cites three factors to explain this trend. The first is a process of constitutionalization. The political alliance between the unions and the Labour Party tended to make union leaders, at least at national level, anxious to avoid any behaviour by pickets which could be used to discredit the alliance. 'It is no coincidence that the emergence of the Labour Party as a major political power occurred more or less at the same time as the decline of serious industrial disorder' (1985, 119). The police in turn were constitutionalized by becoming subject to much greater control from the centre, which, often to the chagrin of junior officers, stressed sensitivity to public opinion. 'The centralisation process has functioned to constrain police reaction to industrial disorder and has motivated the development of relatively non-violent tactics such as the cordon and the wedge' (Geary 1985, 125).

Such forms of constitutionalization were predicated upon the need for both trade unions and the police to appeal to public opinion for validation of their actions. This was a result of the second factor affecting the development of orderly disputes: the media, especially television. Geary suggests that, contrary to popular belief, the presence of cameras normally acts to decrease the likelihood of violence. Neither side can afford to be seen initiating violence. 'There is no doubt, then, that the increased visibility of public order policing has functioned to reduce violence' (1985, 131).

The final factor helping to lessen violence came in the form of what Geary terms the democratization of civil liberties. He argues that public expectations of civil rights had increased and that these had been defined and maintained by the existence of a civil liberties lobby and its ancillary advice services. Observation, analysis, and criticism of police conduct all became possible in a way they had not been before.

> By the late 1970s industrial confrontation had become a sophisticated political game in which two sides, police and pickets, battled for public opinion . . . both sides attempted to achieve their conflicting objectives without losing public approval. This meant that violence beyond mere pushing and shoving was generally regarded as counter-productive in strike situations.   (Geary, 1985, 133)

The problem with this argument is that, as we have seen, the 1980s seem to have begun to reverse the trend towards order and reverted to a pattern typical of much earlier historical phases. In his brief discussion of this, Geary pays much attention to the ways in which 'hard-line' policing has been a strategy encouraged by government. Citing speeches made by the Attorney-General and the Home Secretary early in the miners' strike, he argues that 'such public statements, together with private communications, clearly left police chiefs in no doubt as to what was expected of them' (1985, 144).

While not denying the importance of this factor, we would want to go further to consider the role of the pickets as well as the police and to put law-and-order strategies into some sort of political and economic context. We can do this by reconsidering those factors which Geary argues to have become conducive to order, to see if any changes in them can help explain the apparent resurgence in industrial disorder.

The constitutionalization of the trade union movement has clearly been reversed in the last ten years. It is not the fact so much as the nature of the Conservative government which has brought this about. The Trades Union Congress (TUC) has been excluded from those processes of consultation which it had come to expect from government. Further, the legal as well as political status of the movement has been severely curtailed. The alliance between the trade union movement and the Labour Party, on which Geary places so much emphasis, has never been an easy one. Time and again, most obviously in the miners' strike, party leaders' consciousness of public opinion has led them to express support for the principles of a union's case but to disavow any industrial action to secure their objectives. Thus any union embarking on major industrial action is likely to find itself isolated by the rest of the trade union movement and by the most influential figures in the Labour Party.

The constitutionalization of the police may well have initially led to softer policing but that seems to have depended on government attitudes. Since the Conservative Party came to power in 1979 there has been clear political encouragement for tougher policing, especially of crowds. This shift in the direction of central control towards a more coercive stance has reinforced the declining sensitivity of the police to their immediate constituencies. Events are taken out of the local context of community and inserted into the national context of the state. Hence any potential local resistance to the new tactics emanating from the centre is muted. If the police have been constitutionalized, this has been in the service of an increasingly coercive state.

Geary's second factor, the visibility of police–picket interaction to the public via the media, seems overstated. The conservative-dominated national press has always sought to give more or less qualified support to police activity, even in the face of such tangible evidence as the death of Blair Peach. The decline of investigative journalism has further confirmed the apologetic role of even the liberal press. The role of the broadcasting media is more complex. The niceties of industrial relations seem to elude them in their quest for instant pictures and brief résumés, in newscasts at least. Though current affairs programmes play a slightly different role, there is evidence of a bias against understanding the grievances of strikers. There is, in the dominant media view, no such thing as a good or even justifiable strike. Geary's argument was that because of the media role as witnesses, violence on picket lines would diminish. It could equally be argued that, from Grosvenor Square in 1968 to Orgreave in 1984, media misrepresentation of the motives and attitudes of demonstrators and pickets has served to heighten a sense of grievance and discredit peaceful means of protest. The attacks on television camera crews during the miners' strike indicated how the presence of the media can attract violence, since their version of events is not to be trusted.

The democratization of civil liberties which Geary identifies as his third factor is suffering the same fate as the permissive society which spawned it. In numerous ways, especially those relating to police powers, the rights of the citizen have been curtailed, climaxing in the sustained attack on the jury system, in which senior police officers have played a leading role. In such a context, civil liberties organizations continue to function but in an increasingly circumscribed fashion. The Policewatch observers at Orgreave, from whom we derived some of our evidence, demonstrate the point. That they were there at all is a tribute to the traditions of civil libertarianism. That the police seemed to take no account of their presence indicates the extent to which they have been politically marginalized.

The audiences for police conduct have thus changed. A hard-line government, able to make its wishes clear without controlling the police directly, the media giving overt or tacit support to the police, the decline in civil liberties and the means to attain them; these comprise a changed political context.

We may now look back at the 1960s and 1970s and suggest that the accommodation in police–picket relations which then seemed to prevail was directly dependent upon political conditions of consensus and economic conditions of relative affluence. In such a context, the police could represent themselves and be seen as neutral arbiters of the law, willing to negotiate the conditions under which order was to be maintained. However, when industrial disputes are increasingly protests against the prospect of unemployment and pickets are actively defined as enemies of the state, then interpretation of the law is no longer subject to compromise. Order is not to be constructed through negotiation but imposed by force.

Thus order and disorder in industrial action, itself triggered by economic circumstances, is highly sensitive to the prevailing political atmosphere and the availability of effective means of action other than mass picketing. Just as demonstrations are expressions of political belief by those who feel other methods of protest to be inadequate, so the mass picket is an expression of industrial will by those who feel it is their only effective form of expressing and enforcing solidarity.

Mass picketing, then, is an attempt to compensate for lack of legitimated power. The use of the law to delimit the right to picket is thus a limitation on trade union power. The 'space' which was there for police and pickets to negotiate has been closed off. The right to work has been given predominance over the right to picket effectively. The intention, here and elsewhere, is to give the police power to define the activity and even the existence of a crowd as unlawful. Since mass arrests are presumably unviable, this power is in practice likely to be interpreted as the right to disperse crowds, if necessary by force. It is difficult to think of a more obvious prescription for disorder. Unless the law does deter the assembly of mass pickets, we are likely to see them gather, refuse to withdraw, and then be forcibly dispersed by the police.

What Weir said about events at Grunwick indicates how the problem of disorder arises from a conflict over rights and the very different ways these are defined by capital and labour:

> two traditions are in conflict: the individual middle-class tradition which believes that freedom resides only in the law; and the labour movement's belief that working people's rights and freedoms lie in their readiness to take collective action to assert them. Whatever the law has said, pickets have always tried to restrain strike-breaking workers from crossing the picket line and are always likely to do so.   (Weir 1977, 657)

Part three

Community disorders

Introduction

In this part we present two case studies which we decided, for reasons explained earlier in the introductory chapter and further explored in chapter nine, to bracket together as 'community disorders'. The first concerns a confrontation between black youth and the police in a Sheffield city centre precinct known as the Haymarket in the summer of 1981, during the period of major disturbances in London, Birmingham, Manchester, Liverpool, and Leeds. We came to study this incident in the autumn of 1983 and we thus had to reconstruct the events of two years previously. We initially used newspaper reports, mainly in the *Sheffield Morning Telegraph* and the *Sheffield Star* supplemented by briefer accounts in the *Guardian* and *The Times*. We were then able to obtain evidence produced in court consisting of signed statements from eight black youths, three of whom were arrested and charged, twenty eye-witnesses not themselves involved, and five police officers. Subsequently we interviewed ten participants, including six of those arrested, four youth workers, and three defence solicitors. We also sought interviews from the police but they declined to co-operate. These formed the basis for our synopsis and analysis of events.

The other case study is of two disorders occurring in mining communities close to Sheffield during the miners' strike. Both consisted of a series of street confrontations with the police over fortnightly periods. In Maltby, near Rotherham, such incidents occurred during the first two weeks of June 1984. In Grimethorpe, near Barnsley, similar incidents took place in the first two weeks of October in the same year. We researched these events within three months of their occurrence. In both instances we interviewed members of the local community who had been present during the disturbances. In Maltby we conducted thirty-three such interviews, in Grimethorpe seventeen.

These incidents were also discussed in separate interviews with the Chief Constable of South Yorkshire and his Deputies. The Superintendent in charge at Orgreave was also in command at Maltby, so was able to give us his version of events there as well. We also interviewed the local solicitor who defended residents appearing in court. Signed statements of witnesses were received from South Yorkshire County Council and the Yorkshire Area NUM. We not only used accounts presented in the regional press but were able to interview journalists from the two Sheffield papers and the local *Rotherham Advertiser*.

Chapter seven recounts and analyses the events at the Haymarket, and chapter eight those at both Maltby and Grimethorpe. Chapter nine compares our own case studies with other instances of community disorder. We examine the riots in Bristol in 1980 as recounted by Joshua *et al.* (1983), in Brixton in 1981 as enquired into by Lord Scarman (1981), and in Tottenham in 1985 as represented in the Broadwater Farm Inquiry (1986). We then attempt to develop a model generally applicable to such community disorders.

7
The Haymarket, Sheffield, August 1981

Background

In the centre of Sheffield in August 1981, there occurred in a shopping precinct a violent confrontation between police and black youths. A relatively minor incident, it lasted only an hour or two. Most injuries received were slight, damage to property was minimal and media interest ephemeral.

This was a flashpoint which failed to develop largely, we shall suggest, because of the immediate context in which it occurred. The national context was apparently one conducive to disorder. Disturbances had taken place in other major cities during that summer. Often, as in the Brixton riot four months before, they had begun with just such an incident between police and black youths. However, this general context had not been reinforced in Sheffield by the kinds of local factors found in areas where disturbances occurred. Relations between the black community or the local authority and the police had not recently broken down. No recent incidents between the two groups had nurtured a sense of grievance. There were no special police operations directed at black districts, which in any case were less visible and segregated than in other cities. Hence one reason for the containment of the disorder was the way the racial and policing situation in Sheffield failed to reproduce the kind of volatile local context to be found elsewhere. The incident remained an isolated one. It had repercussions, but widespread disorder was not one of them. In what follows we consider why disorder did not escalate. We want to demonstrate both how a routine piece of police action developed into a group confrontation and why it was ultimately contained.

Overview

On the afternoon of Saturday 15 August 1981, two police officers

115

were summoned to a small public balcony known locally as 'the Gallery', overlooking a pedestrian precinct in Sheffield's Haymarket. The officers were acting in response to a complaint by a middle-aged white woman that she had been spat upon by black youths. The officers warned the thirty or so black youths gathered there to behave themselves. An instruction to turn down the volume on their 'ghetto blasters' was complied with. The officers then left.

Shortly afterwards two different officers arrived and also ordered the music to be turned down. The youths protested. One of the officers attempted to confiscate a cassette player. The youths resisted. The other officer slipped away unnoticed to radio for help. Meanwhile, the first officer was punched. He grabbed his assailant, but the other youths moved in to release him. A violent struggle ensued, broken up when a civilian with two Great Danes came to the officer's assistance.

Police reinforcements soon arrived. According to one (white female) witness, a total of twelve police cars or vans arrived within minutes of the first arrest and eight more subsequently. As police officers climbed the twin staircases leading up to the Gallery, some black youths stood their ground, while others tried to escape.

As one youth tried to descend the stairs, he was met by police officers coming in the other direction. Refusing to return to the Gallery as ordered, he was arrested and handcuffed to the railings. A friend who intervened was also arrested and fastened in the same position.

By now, the youths were enraged. As the confrontation escalated, a policewoman caught hold of one youth, only to be set upon by four of his friends. Several items of her clothing were torn. At this point, police dogs were introduced and the Gallery was cleared. The youths quickly regrouped in the shopping area downstairs, shouting abuse at the police. A build-up of traffic occurred as the crowd was swollen by new arrivals. A police inspector repeatedly asked the crowd to vacate the area. When he was ignored, the command was given for the police to move in and make further arrests, whereupon further violence took place.

Among those arrested was a youth worker who claimed to have been attempting to defuse the situation by appealing to the police inspector to exercise more restraint. He was frog-marched to the van, one officer allegedly holding him by the testicles. It was estimated (*The Times* 17 August 1981) that as many as 500 people were involved in the incident at its height. Twelve of the seventeen people arrested were charged, with offences ranging from obstruction of the highway to assaulting a police officer.

South Yorkshire Police subsequently claimed in an internal report from their Community Liaison Section that it was their decisive reaction which prevented the disturbance from becoming more serious. Local youth workers agreed that the police did manage to disperse the crowd but stressed that it might still have reformed again. This was prevented by an agreement that the police would make obvious their intention to withdraw, reached with a senior officer who arrived late on the scene.

Analysis

A single complaint about spitting had led to seventeen arrests, none for the original incident. Clearly, the event had escalated beyond anything that might have been expected. The whole situation was initially routine. The Gallery was a favoured haunt of black youths on Saturday afternoons. There was no indication that their behaviour had been anything out of ordinary for the time and place.

The black youths claimed the police to be at fault in handling the situation insensitively. Chaining two youths to the railings was seen as an act of wilful humiliation. The introduction of dogs was resented. The peremptory nature of the police orders to the crowd were seen as victimization of black people. The youths did not see that their conduct had justified such a reaction.

In the absence of a detailed police account, we must hypothesize about their motives. The youths were clearly a public nuisance. A complaint had been received from a member of the public. The youths had failed to comply with reasonable requests from officers called to the scene. A policeman had been assaulted and a policewoman attacked. A hostile crowd had gathered and had to be cleared to prevent further trouble and restore order.

If we are to choose between or go beyond these incompatible accounts, three sets of factors in particular need to be taken into account: the general context of that summer, the sequence of the interaction, and the ways in which the confrontation could be and was seen in terms of conflicting claims to rights.

The riots which had been taking place in other cities could not have escaped the attention of those involved in the Haymarket incident. What Cohen (1973, 77) terms 'media sensitization' may have influenced some of the eye-witnesses to the confrontation, who perceived the black youths as threatening. One shop assistant said (in a written statement to police): 'I could sense an undercurrent of atmosphere that there was going to be trouble.' Another felt that 'they appeared to be gathering for some purpose'. A restaurant manager echoed these sentiments: 'The first thing that struck my mind was that they were there inviting trouble.'

There were more black youths present in the Gallery than normal; it was after all a warm and sunny afternoon. The perceptions of the onlookers may have been sensitized by what they had seen and read of riots elsewhere. This colouring of perception was literal, according to the black youth worker we interviewed:

> One of the difficulties with black kids, I think, is that people – like if you get a group of football supporters with scarves on, they get identified as a gang – they tend to lump them all together as a 'gang' just because they're black. In actual fact, they were just scattered.

One of the defending solicitors drew attention in interview to the claim that the first officers to arrive were not from Sheffield, having been called in to relieve the pressure on the local force caused by a local football match:

> You didn't get the community bobbies who man this particular area, who get to know the kids, who go every Saturday, who have a personal relationship with them and could say 'Look, just cool down; let's ease this out with no arrests', and so on. You got all sorts of people arriving, thinking 'Right! This is the Sheffield riot!'

Some of the youths claimed that police officers made comparisons with recent riots in Liverpool (Toxteth) and Manchester (Moss Side), references which would not have been lost on the youths themselves. While disavowing any intention to riot, their willingness to resist what they saw as police brutality against black people seems likely to have been informed by the knowledge that such grievances had been articulated with dramatic effect elsewhere.

It is thus quite feasible to suggest that, had this incident not occurred in the wake of the riots of 1981, both sides would have been less willing to allow the situation to escalate. There were nevertheless a number of features in the event itself which served to increase the likelihood of disorder.

One was the physical setting. The Gallery is essentially no more than an elevated corridor. This confined the disorder but made withdrawal or dispersal difficult. Black youths leaving the area were perceived as attempting to evade arrest. Once the police had blocked off the staircases, no escape was possible. The youths only had the alternatives of capitulating or resisting; hence the appropriation of shoes on racks outside shops as missiles. The dispersal of the youths to the streets below enabled them to congregate and created a traffic hazard. Thus the police felt obliged to clear the whole area, in which they succeeded but not before meeting further resistance.

Given this physical location and the sensitivity of those involved to any potential for riot, any error of judgement or provocative action by the police was likely to have severe consequences. The first pair of officers seem to have taken a tactful line, but the second pair adopted a more confrontational approach. The *Sheffield Star* (17 August 1981) reported claims that they had called the youths 'niggers' and referred to reggae as 'jungle music'. One of the arrested youths argued in interview that they were deliberately provocative: 'They came straight out: "turn your stereo down". They started slapping the tape recorder. Not right. They wanted trouble, man.' It was also claimed that one of them was a cadet and hence inexperienced in handling such situations.

The attempt to confiscate the tape recorder was one of a number of actions which served as an 'intensifier'. In such situations, actions and events take on a particular symbolic significance: they are seen as conveying messages about how the two sides perceive each other. A ghetto blaster is not the functional equivalent of a transistor radio. It is for many a black youth his most prized possession, an extension of his self and his black culture. As Hebdige has suggested:

> It was through music, more than any other medium, that the communication with the past, with Jamaica and hence Africa, considered vital for the maintenance of black identity, was possible. The 'system' turned on sound; the sound was intimately bound up in the nature of the 'culture'; and if the system was attacked the community itself was symbolically threatened. It thus became hallowed ground, territory to be defended against possible contamination by white groups. Police interference was, of course vehemently resented.
>
> (Hebdige 1979, 39)

More directly provocative to each side in turn were the chaining of the two youths to the railings, the attack on the policewoman, then the use of police dogs and the arrest of the youth worker.

In court, the arresting officers justified the handcuffing in terms of preventing those arrested from becoming violent. The defending solicitors suggested that the action was calculated to 'serve as an example to the others' and to show that the police were in command of a 'potentially explosive situation' (*Sheffield Star* 25 November 1981, *Sheffield Morning Telegraph* 27 November 1981). In her closing speech one of the solicitors referred to the handcuffing as 'the modern equivalent of placing someone in the stocks'. She could equally have cited other historical references to black people in chains.

The attack on the woman police officer was apparently interpreted by the police as justifying retaliatory action. In a formal statement one of the black youths recalled that:

> When I saw the dogs, I said to the officer who was standing nearby that they could not set the dogs on us. He replied that what had happened to the woman police officer had not been right either.

The arrest of the youth worker, not a noted trouble-maker, confirmed to the black youths that the police were acting indiscriminately. That he was frog-marched to a police van merely confirmed the sense of police aggression. By this time, both sides were attempting to score minor victories in humiliating the opposition, egged on by their supporters. According to a student eye-witness, 'there were several coloured girls stood around the edge of the troubles, shouting encouragement to the coloured youths and cheering when some broke away from the police'. As Southgate (1982) has emphasized, the fear of loss of face in such a situation is exacerbated by the presence of onlookers. Neither side can afford to be seen to be losing.

The struggle between the black youths and the police had its immediate causes but it can also be seen in wider terms. It was in part a struggle over space, over who had the right to be in the shopping precinct and on what terms. The black youths felt they had a right to be in the shopping centre and to play their music. To the police such a right was dependent on no nuisance being caused to the public at large. On a smaller scale, this is reminiscent of discrepant interpretations in other contests over 'black space', such as that which led to the Bristol riot:

> The riot was racial in that it began as a clash between black people and white policemen on a piece of black territory. It was a clash of cultures: a West Indian life-style of cannabis smoking and illicit drinking versus a white British view that condemns such behaviour.   (Kettle and Hodges 1982, 30)

The search for places just to be themselves has not been confined to black youth. One analysis of white working-class youth cultures argues that such subcultures function to 'win space for the young, cultural space in the neighbourhood and institutions, real time for leisure and recreation, actual room on the street or street corner. They serve to mark out "territory" in the localities' (Hall and Jefferson (eds) 1976, 45).

Ever since 1976, the Gallery had been one such focal point for disaffected youth, both black and white. Gradually, black youth had colonized it as their own. The subsequent rise in complaints by shoppers and traders of theft, spitting, obstruction, and the throwing of missiles by black youth led the police to conclude that the youths were, in the words of the internal police report, 'rendering the area a place where the ordinary public were afraid to frequent'. For the youths, the Gallery represented a sanctuary, their unruly behaviour a survival mechanism in the face of an otherwise hostile white society.

Over time, an accommodation had been reached between the youths and the police officers who habitually patrolled the precinct. It depended upon each side recognizing that each other had rights. The police tacitly recognized the youths' right to be there. The youths recognized the policemen's right to respond to complaints and to request limitations on behaviour. In the context of the summer of 1981, and as a result of actions taken on that day in August, that informal agreement was ruptured and the latent difference of interests made manifest. But the confrontation, like the previous agreement, was local in its ambit. Why the disorder was contained requires as much consideration as the reasons for its original occurrence.

It would appear that for an action or event to be regarded as symptomatic of a wider set of grievances, as the 'last straw', there has to be some relationship between a physical and social sense of community and a perceived threat to its interests or identity. In Sheffield in 1981 the black sense of community did not primarily derive from a war of attrition with the police. The opposition to the police on the day was more of a reaction to the specific situation than an opportunity to settle scores with an established enemy.

It has been argued that community disorder is more likely to be prolonged when it functions as 'an invitation to act out long-suppressed feelings' than when it represents an intense reaction to a specific instance of police brutality (Spiegel 1969, 334–5). If this is so, the Haymarket fracas lacked the wider dimension. As one arrested black youth put it to us in interview: 'Brixton and that lot had nothing to do with it. You know, better living standards, and all that? No, man. This was just police brutality.'

Sheffield's black community seemed to lack the generalized sense of grievance against authority as a whole evident in other major cities. This is partly attributable to the dispersal of the Afro-Caribbean population throughout several areas of the city. As Mackillop (1981) points out, there are identifiable areas with relatively large black populations, but there are no concentrations of wholly black communities in one particular inner-city area or council estate. Sheffield has no equivalent of St Paul's, Toxteth, Handsworth, Brixton, or the Broadwater Farm Estate.

It is possible that the activities of an 'anti-racist' local authority may have eased the black sense of powerlessness, though this was also the case in cities where rioting did occur. Black youth may have experienced the same kinds of deprivation as their counterparts elsewhere but they did not have a more general sense that their whole community was under siege, as Reicher (1984) argues to have been the case in Bristol.

This is not to say that relationships between the police and the black community were always harmonious. Mackillop (1981, 40) referred to 'a profound suspicion of the role and activities of the police at all levels of West Indian society in Sheffield'. As long ago as 1976, there had been a bonfire night confrontation between police and black youths in Endcliffe Park (*Sheffield Morning Telegraph* 6 November 1976). In July of the following year there occurred the 'Burngreave Affair', when several white men were arrested for protesting about what they alleged to be the beating of a black man by the police in the street (Cannon 1982). Subsequently the men were awarded compensation by the police.

These were however isolated incidents rather than a coherent pattern. Youth workers tended to acknowledge that South Yorkshire police adopted a racially sensitive policy, allowing Afro-Caribbeans to police their own shebeens and invariably liaising with community leaders prior to sensitive operations. Thus while there was a general suspicion of the police amongst Afro-Caribbeans, especially the male youth, there was no sense of the whole black community being permanently victimized by police activity. If there was nowhere in the city like Brixton, there were no police activities like Operation Swamp, which helped to trigger the Brixton riot of 1981. Nor was there a 'Front Line'; the territory in dispute was not physically or culturally central to the black community. By July 1987, the *Sheffield Star* reported a familiar controversy over police initiatives against drug trafficking in the Burngreave area, suggesting that Sheffield might begin to produce the patterns of police–black confrontation on the streets evident elsewhere. But in 1981, this had been less evident.

This was one of the reasons why the confrontation was always potentially containable. It was nevertheless important that the 'intensifiers' discussed earlier as contributing to the disorder were balanced by a 'pacifier' which helped to restore order, in the form of the truce eventually agreed between the police and black leaders.

This helped to establish a general accommodation between the police and the black youth which up to that point had not been evident in the Haymarket fracas. This may be why, of all our case studies, this was the one the police did not wish to discuss with us. From their point of view, it may have been best forgotten. Their initial treatment of the youth worker, for example, does not seem to have been in accord with their usual practices. What had been established as the norm for policing black communities in Sheffield was otherwise significantly different from that prevalent elsewhere.

Summary

Both the context and the content of the Haymarket fracas prevented it escalating into wider disorder. Compared with other cities, the history of police–black relations had been less conflictual and produced fewer incidents to nurture a sense of grievance. There was less reason for the incident to be seen as symptomatic of broader conflict. Nor was the immediate issue, of the right to frequent and play music in a busy shopping precinct, one which could mobilize a whole community in defence of its rights. The police had not invaded black territory.

Thus while disorder did occur, it was quickly contained, despite those actions which acted as 'intensifiers' of the level of immediate conflict. The success of the 'pacifier', in the form of a truce negotiated on the spot, depended in part on the wider context of police–black relations and the credibility eventually given to intermediaries. Despite sharing some characteristics with flashpoints elsewhere – a dispute over territorial rights, resentment at police intervention, immediate black solidarity – the disorder did not spread. The flashpoint sparked but it did not ignite. The environment was not conducive to a fire.

8
Disorders in Maltby and Grimethorpe, 1984

Background: Maltby and Grimethorpe

Some similarities have been observed between the experience of black communities prior to the disorders of 1981 and the experience of several mining communities during the more recent coal dispute. One account stresses how, in common with many black people,

> miners also found that their communities were subject to virtual states of siege, their villages occupied by large numbers of police. Freedom of movement outside their immediate communities was severely restricted, while even within mining towns and villages, striking miners and their families found their ability to move around subject to the control of the police. In addition, virtual curfews were imposed by the police with anyone on the streets liable to harassment and arrest.
>
> (Gordon 1985, 165)

Against this type of background, minor incidents involving small numbers of policemen and local inhabitants became the triggers for larger disturbances occurring in many mining towns and villages (Coulter *et al.* 1984, Kaye 1984). In the South Yorkshire communities of Maltby near Rotherham, and Grimethorpe near Barnsley, local miners were arrested, police stations were attacked, and there were repeated confrontations between the police and local people. Here, we focus on the so-called 'riots' in Maltby and Grimethorpe, try to explain why disturbances of this nature occurred, and then consider the validity of comparisons with inner-city disturbances.

Overview: Maltby

Late in the evening of Friday 8 June 1984, an incident occurred at closing time outside a club in Maltby that was to spark off successive weekends of violence in the town.

The Caledonian Club, known locally as 'the Cally', was founded in the 1960s by Scottish miners who had recently moved to Maltby and it soon acquired a reputation for the boisterous behaviour of the mainly young miners who frequented it. At lunchtime on the Friday in question, a Chief Inspector called at the club to inform the steward that residents of the neighbouring Blyth Road had complained about the level of noise, damage to their gardens, and other instances of rowdy behaviour.

The police version is that officers responding to further complaints at closing time that evening were subjected to verbal and physical abuse and that a police car bringing reinforcements was stoned. The miners allege that two pairs of police officers were awaiting a small group of six miners and their wives and girlfriends as they left the Caledonian. They maintain that the officers pushed and taunted them, saying 'It's about time you bastards got back to work.' A fight ensued.

Afterwards, four of the miners thought to have been involved in the incident, including a local NUM offical, were singled out for arrest as they queued for a meal in a Chinese take-away. All were taken to Maltby police station where they claim to have been mistreated:

> As I was going in, I came to the desk and asked to go to the toilet. When I came back, an officer said to me 'Have you been to the Caledonian?' and when I said 'No' he slapped me round the ear. My ear made a buzzing and ringing noise. . . . One of them said he'd seen me at Coleridge Road. He said there was a choice of charges, grievous bodily harm or smashing police car windows. I said I was not guilty and one of them hit me on the nose. It started to bleed. . . . I was interviewed twice and during the course of both interviews I was hit at least six times. I later discovered that I had a perforated ear-drum and a blood-clot in my ear.   (Maltby miner, in interview)

The police state that on the following evening, Saturday 9 June, two of their officers responded to yet another complaint from Blyth Road, where local miners were said to have been gathering stones from nearby gardens. These officers are said to have come under immediate attack. The miners' version is again rather different. They say that, as they were walking home from the Caledonian, a police patrol car made a rapid U-turn in the road and mounted the kerb as it approached, forcing them to jump into nearby gardens for their own safety. The driver is alleged to have said 'That'll stop you bastards picketing' (quoted on BBC1 Look North 18 June 1984). According to this account, two police transit vans immediately arrived. As many as thirty officers leaped out and seven of the fourteen miners present were arrested with some force:

> One grabbed hold of me and started hitting me about the head for no reason at all. I think he just went crazy. My head was pouring with blood.   (Maltby miner, in interview)

The miners insist that these officers were wearing Greater Manchester insignia, though the police were adamant that they were local officers. Once again, prisoners complained about their treatment whilst in police custody:

> They threw me into a cell which was about one and a half inches deep in urine. They crammed every prisoner in there. They wouldn't let them go to the toilet, so they just had to do it on the floor. They just threw me in there and that's where I lay all night.   (Maltby miner, in interview)

Members of the local NUM strike committee claim that for the remainder of the evening Maltby residents were stopped by police and told to go home. They further allege that the main roads in and out of the town centre were effectively sealed off by the police.

Finally during this first weekend, on the evening of Sunday 10 June, three local men were arrested in the town centre and charged with being drunk and disorderly. A local butcher witnessed most of the incident.

> Two policemen in a patrol car pulled up alongside of them, did a U-turn and stopped on the other side of the road watching them. The youths quickly dispersed in two directions. When the three youths going down the High Street were opposite the YEB, the patrol car flew alongside them. Out jumped two policemen and roughed up the three youths who didn't seem to know why. Then two seconds later came a mini-bus full of policemen and dragged the youths, still claiming their innocence, off to the station. If they had committed a crime or been caught damaging property, they certainly needed arresting, but they seemed innocent to me. This was seen by most of the lads at the take-away who went to the police station to protest. I don't know what went off in there but I only saw two come out. Just as they were coming out of the police station gate, the mini-bus full of policemen came back and one of the policemen

caught one of the lads with his shoulder. The lad asked what it was all about and he was promptly thrown back into the police station by his hair.

(statement to South Yorkshire Police Authority)

A small group of men went into Maltby police station to protest that the arrests had been made without any justification. There was an argument and insulting gestures were exchanged. The men were themselves arrested and charged with obscene behaviour.

There were no further disturbances during the course of the following week. However by Friday 15 June, several rumours had emerged: that police intended to impose a curfew on local residents, that police patrols were being increased, and that police reinforcements from outside forces were on standby in anticipation of a confrontation. Local NUM sources claim these emanated from reliable sources, though the police subsequently denied them all. The local *Rotherham Advertiser* seemed to believe them since it ran a sensationalist headline on 15 June: 'Cool it plea to avoid bloodbath'.

Fearing a major confrontation to be imminent, members of the Maltby strike committee contacted a number of journalists and Labour councillors. The Chairman of the South Yorkshire Police Committee, Councillor George Moores, was amongst those who visited local pubs and clubs urging the local residents to remain calm. The senior officer in charge of the local Maltby force, Superintendent John Nesbit, emphasized how at the time he went

> to great lengths to explain to them that there were no foreign officers in the Maltby area. It's fair to say that I gave an undertaking that there would be a very, very low-profile policing and that police officers would not be on open display.
>
> (interview)

However, shortly before midnight on Friday, between twenty and thirty men and youths gathered outside Maltby police station and aimed stones at its windows. Some police officers tried to chase them off, but quickly retreated on finding themselves outnumbered. Two police officers were then cornered in a bingo arcade by several youths. Though they managed to escape, the arcade window was smashed. Soon afterwards, more than a hundred people began stoning the police station. This time police reinforcements arrived and there were running battles for three quarters of an hour. Sixteen people were arrested, several shops had their windows damaged, and some were looted.

It has since been claimed that innocent people were arrested as they stood and watched the mayhem. Others complained that for the rest of the night local people were denied access in and out of the village, sometimes directed to take longer routes home as certain roads were closed to the public. As one miner quoted in a national paper put it, 'This town was under siege the other day. There was no road out of Maltby' (*Morning Star* 18 June 1984).

The police justification for such action was straightforward:

> Following that unfortunate incident when a large amount of property was damaged and looting took place, I felt that the low-profile policing had not had the desired effect, and with the Chief Constable's approval, I had a large number of officers then in the Maltby area.
>
> (Superintendent Nesbit, in interview)

On the following Saturday night, there was a general expectation that the violence would recur. A *Sheffield Star* reporter recalled to us being warned that going to Maltby was to risk her life. Rumours of a police curfew from midnight remained rife. It was thought that the police had closed several roads; at least a hundred police were known to be either on patrol or standby. Between 9.30 and 11 p.m., the police constantly dispersed groups of youth congregating at Queen's Corner crossroads, the town's main axis. The secretary to Rotherham's Trades Council suggested in interview that the police 'were keen to let it be known that they were in control, and that anything that smacked of disrespect for law and order was going to be stamped on'.

But by closing time, there were too many people at the crossroads for the police to move on. Some had come less to cause trouble than as a matter of principle:

> The feeling around the village was: 'we're not going to be in for twelve'. And a lot of ordinary people, not just miners, said 'Bugger it, if we want to be out on the street at midnight, we'll be there.' And there were seven hundred people on the street corner.
>
> (Maltby miner, in interview)

In such an atmosphere words were exchanged. The police were called 'Maggie's boot boys', 'fascists', and 'cowards'. Exactly what led to the outbreak of trouble is disputed. According to an NUM offical, the police commanding officer, Superintendent Nesbit, was talking into a two-way radio ensuring that his men were in position when as he was doing that, a miner walked past him and said something about 'It's just like a fascist state with you buggers here all the time'. And Nesbit just turned round and said 'Get him!' Then it all broke loose. The lad was struggling to get away and a lot of youths on the corner started stoning. . . . Then, within seconds, there's van loads of police screaming round the corner and they were all over the bloody place; there were bricks and the lot going through the windows . . . and looting took place. (interview)

However, Superintendent Nesbit felt that the confrontation had already begun before he became personally involved:

There were three or four hundred, I would estimate and I was in the High Street talking to some old ladies and explaining to them, when we heard this chant, this roar, and young people appeared on the flat roofs adjacent to Queen's Corner. They were armed with milk bottles. And they began to throw bricks and milk bottles. I was speaking to these old ladies and asking them to go away when I was struck in the face by a youth. I subsequently arrested him. I then called for reinforcements we had standing nearby. (interview)

During the ensuing free-for-all, police dog-handlers were brought in to clear the area and transit vans were driven on to the pavement in an attempt to disperse the crowd (*Sheffield Morning Telegraph* 18 June 1984). The superintendent had his nose broken. Eventually the police formed a line across the road and gradually pushed the crowd further into the village. Once again there were complaints about the indiscriminate and brutal nature of many of the twenty-nine arrests made that night.

Analysis: Maltby

What happened on that second weekend has to be seen in the light of the previous week's events. The miners interpreted the original police action as a concerted attempt to undermine the effectiveness of Maltby as a picketing centre:

I'd say that the motives of the police were quite simple. We've got hard core of pickets in Maltby. I wouldn't say we'd get a hell of a lot of the membership picketing . . . but we've probably got one of the best records in the area for actually getting to the target. And I think they were trying to split us from the community and trying to put pressure on us. I think they openly provoked trouble on that first night.

(Maltby NUM branch official, in interview)

Within this version, the harassment of those leaving the Caledonian was a deliberate act of provocation, since, 'if you want to cause trouble all you have to do is to visit a club or pub on a Friday night, especially if you're a police officer' (Maltby miner, in interview). Memories of the confrontation at Orgreave were also still fresh:

I think the type of tension in the police–picket relationship is something connected to Orgreave. When you see dogs let loose and people charged with horses, you relate that to police activity and you know that, if instructed to do so, the police in Maltby would probably do the same.

(Maltby NUM branch official, in interview)

The Chief Constable of South Yorkshire also acknowledged the importance of Orgreave, but stressed its significance as signalling the failure of the strike.

I accept completely that there is a tremendous amount of frustration building up in the community. The strike is dragging on and their efforts to close Orgreave have not been successful. Because the police are endangering that success it builds up frustration against the police.

(quoted in the *Yorkshire Post* 18 June 1984)

In interview, he expanded on the theme that Orgreave had encouraged extreme behaviour from miners.

Now, Maltby wasn't a great deal of distance from Orgreave, and I'm quite sure that a lot of those involved were also involved on the picket line. But what I would describe it as, was a sort of lessening of the standards of behaviour which people normally apply, and this is always the problem when you get public disorder. There is, within the individuals involved, a belief that what they are doing is not frowned upon as much as it would otherwise be. Normal standards of behaviour are relaxed to the extent that they feel it is in order for them to throw stones at the police station. . . . But by what standards of behaviour are they allowed to break shop windows? I don't know.

Others cited a rather different context for the events, pointing to a recent history of confrontation between the police and local youths, what the secretary of the local Trades Council referred to as a 'long history of heavy-handed police tactics against youths in the village'.

Whatever the importance of such events or of Orgreave, the

incidents of the first weekend were in themselves enough for local feelings to be running high.

I think it's very relevant that, during the week, a great number of people in the village were incensed by the actions of the previous weekend. They felt that the police had been heavy-handed. They felt that the police had acted without any justification. They felt that the police were abusing their powers and had assaulted people during the unnecessary arrests. (Defence solicitor, in interview)

Local people had also heard allegations about the mistreatment of prisoners in custody and of the involvement of the Greater Manchester Police. Some of them had recently had the novel experience of police telling them when and which way to go home. There were fresh rumours that local publicans and chip shop owners had been told to close early at the coming weekend to help enforce a curfew. In such a context, it is not surprising that an interchange between a local youth and a senior police officer proved to be a flashpoint since it symbolized the underlying tension.

The police attributed a good deal of the trouble on the second weekend to elements other than the local miners, Referring to the active role of a 'small minority', a Police Federation spokesman talked of opportunist thugs and hooligans who were 'hitching a ride' on the miners' strike (quoted in the *Daily Telegraph* 18 June 1984); a local superintendent accused a lot of criminally minded people who were 'hell-bent on creating trouble' (BBC1 Look North 18 June 1984); according to the Chief Constable, those responsible 'came from a particular group who are determined to be active and determined to abuse the police' (quoted in the *Yorkshire Post* 18 June 1984). Super-intendent Nesbit singled out skinheads for the blame.

The Maltby strike committee dissociated themselves from the damage to the shops of those local traders who had helped the local community during the strike. They also referred to the involvement of 'outsiders'. But, as with attempts to blame trouble on outsiders after other instances of public disorder, it seems likely that most of the perpetrators were drawn from the local community. What happened in Maltby seems to resemble the pattern identified by Reicher (1984) for St Paul's in Bristol in 1980 of two separate riots, one directed specifically against the police, the other an opportunist expression of anger against authority in general, with the smashing of shop windows a mixture of frustration, defiance, and opportunism.

Overview: Grimethorpe

On Wednesday 3 October 1984, several van loads of police officers surrounded the Grimethorpe colliery wastage tip with the intention of clearing the area of local men, women, and children who were 'coal picking'. According to local residents, the police and local Coal Board managers had previously during the strike overlooked this practice, choosing to confiscate only large amounts of coal that were suspected of being intended for sale rather than domestic consumption. The events of 3 October marked a sudden departure from this policy.

Local people allege that the police raids were repeated on the Wednesday and the Friday of the following week. No arrests were made, but those on the tip complained of being manhandled by police officers who they said were from the Greater Manchester force. Twenty-two people were arrested during two similar raids on Sunday 14 October. The police seized a variety of bicycles, motorcyles, and wheelbarrows being used to carry the coal. Allegations of brutality were made against members of the Metropolitan Police.

On the following morning (Monday 15 October) more trouble occurred, this time on the colliery premises. Lorry drivers preparing to take Grimethorpe coal to local coking plants and the police protecting them were stoned by local men. When the police ran for cover, a mechanical shovel was captured and quickly set alight. Wrongly believing that several Police Support Units were positioned on standby behind the local police station, the residents then converged upon the unmanned building and smashed in several windows before leaving.

Later in the afternoon, the men returned to the police station to find a female police sergeant and a male police constable supervising repairs to the building. They were immediately chased, the sergeant being caught and beaten. By three o'clock the village was effectively sealed off by riot police, but a number of youths were not deterred from stoning the colliery buildings an hour later.

There was no further trouble until the public houses emptied for closing time. Violence occurred as police officers pursued local men through the village. The police claimed that this was in response to complaints that gangs of youths were systematically breaking shop windows in the village High Street (*The Times* 17 October 1984).

Grimethorpe residents deny that this was the case. They saw the window breaking as an angry response to police action rather than a cause of it. It is alleged that one such incident took place as a group of local men, mostly miners, were standing outside a public house waiting for their wives and girlfriends to join them. They claimed the police attacked them.

> They just charged – say, ten or fifteen of us. Not causing any trouble, just waiting for my wife. I tried to get back in the pub. I was clubbed from behind, dragged up the road, kicked, punched, into the police station. I was hit in the face, had my face pushed into a desk, doused and God knows what else – all in a matter of five minutes.   (Grimethorpe miner, in interview)

Local women complained of obscenities levelled at them by the police and the nature of many of the arrests they witnessed:

> Policemen started shouting to us: 'How much do you charge, love?' and 'You look alright for a fiver; we know where you get your money from'. . . . And I shouted back that I'm not a prostitute. They more or less laughed, and my husband said 'Come on, we're going home.' And, as we were walking down the street, we witnessed an incident where a lad was arrested. A police van came up the street – I would have said speeding, but I can't estimate it because I don't drive. It stopped just a few yards at the back of us. And this young lad was walking down the street with his hands in his pockets. The van doors were half open. The police got out, just ran across the road, grabbed this young lad and he was knocked to the ground. Several of them were kicking him and two were hitting him on the back with truncheons. We ran down and were shouting at them to get off him, and one called me a 'slag'. Another called me a 'whore', and they told me to fuck off back to our houses or else it'd be us. They picked him up, threw him in the van, and drove off.   (wife of Grimethorpe miner, in interview)

The South Yorkshire Police Committee subsequently organized a public meeting in Grimethorpe on 17 October. Local people made a series of complaints about police misconduct. On hearing these complaints, George Moores, the Chairman of the South Yorkshire Police Committee, made the well publicized remark that individual policemen 'come into the force as nice, decent, peaceful chaps. We send them to training centres and they come out like Nazi stormtroopers' (*Sheffield Morning Telegraph* 18 October 1984). The Deputy Chief Constable of South Yorkshire also attended the meeting, where he expressed the hope that some local residents would be prepared to admit that they were 'not entirely blameless'. Nevertheless, he professed himself 'not happy to hear all that I have heard', and apologized for excesses on the part of his officers (*Sheffield Morning Telegraph* 18 October 1984).

However, the Deputy Chief Constable later insisted in interview that his comments at the meeting should be seen in their proper context:

I think first of all, it was the first time in England anyway, that a policeman has been put in a position of finding himself confronted by a crowd of maybe four or five hundred, in a hostile environment, with members of the Police Authority seated on a platform behind him. Tremendous media interest: I went to a number of meetings in other villages which never received a mention. Tremendous interest in this because of what happened in Grimethorpe. The accusations levelled against the police, which were unanswered by anybody, were absolutely devastating. . . . If I had just stood up and said 'this is a load of lies', I do believe that the situation in Grimethorpe would have been considerably worse – not just for me and the Chief Superintendent in plain clothes at the meeting, but for those who had to police Grimethorpe the next day. Anyway, I was given an opening. You may remember that Grimethorpe police station had been under siege and that stones had been thrown. I remember one lad saying 'David slew Goliath with a stone', to tremendous applause and cheers. That gave me the opportunity to stand up, to tremendous booing throughout the hall. I was asked to do so by the Police Authority members who were probably in sympathy with the miners as well. I was able to quote back a little biblical phrase, 'blessed are the peace makers'. What I said was 'I've listened and shuddered at many of the things said about police officers. For anything they have done wrong, I unreservedly apologize. But I would hope that there are some here and now who would say that they themselves are not entirely blameless.'

Now, if you analyse those words, all that I am apologizing for is anything which had been done wrong or what they think had been done wrong. Now, I went on, and this wasn't picked up as much by the press, and said that, at the same time, I would ask you to look at yourselves and ask if you have anything to reproach yourselves for. Then I had a hearing. I said that the Chief Constable didn't intend for Grimethorpe to dissolve into a lawless society; it was not in the interests of anybody. I hoped that it would return to the happy village it had once been, with more emphasis on its band-playing than its present problems. I had a full hearing then and sat down to applause. It was quite spontaneous.

In retrospect, he was unimpressed by the various accusations of police brutality:

> Many of the things I'd heard at other meetings before. There seemed to be an almost predictable round of accusations, which would contain such things as: policemen without numbers on; calling women sluts; policemen who were clearly soldiers because of the way they marched; policemen chasing unarmed youths and girls through the streets; policemen wearing helmets and visors; policemen wielding truncheons; policemen arresting ordinary people who were doing absolutely nothing. Virtually anything which could be verbally hurled at the police was being hurled.   (interview)

Clearly, the police account and that of local residents remained incompatible. The specific details of incidents were being recounted and interpreted in terms of the events of the past fortnight and the seven months of the strike.

Analysis: Grimethorpe

Fundamental to the police version of events, as given by the Chief Constable, was the argument that the actions of the police on 14 October were merely a pretext rather than a justification for disorderly behaviour. This was said to the press at the time. 'A certain element in the community are taking advantage of the current tensions and frustrations and indulging in behaviour not normal in pit villages' (*The Times* 18 October 1984).

Local residents gave no credence to this view. They interpreted the raids on the coal tip as a vindictive attempt at reprisal by the police for recent clashes on the picket line at Woolley Colliery near Barnsley. Supplementary to this account was the view that the police were colluding with the NCB management to prevent coal picking in order to demoralize the miners by cutting off supplies of fuel as the winter approached.

The Chief Constable felt he had no choice. Once the legal owners of the coal tip had made a complaint about theft, the law had to be enforced. He also thought there was something in the view that taking coal from the tip had reached an unacceptable level. That any action would be identified as police repression was likely, but the alternative was to fail in the first responsibility of a police officer, to enforce the law:

> There was no way that the police were not seen as being on the side of the NCB. There was no way we could avoid that . . . if

police action was seen as starving them back, there is no comment I can make on that except to say that if people are committing offences, the police have got to react to it. And if, in reacting to it, those who are committing those offences say 'They are trying to starve us back to work', there is nothing I could say which would remove that thought from their mind. . . . If somebody had said to me 'Is it going to exacerbate the situation, arresting people for stealing coal?', I would have said 'Yes, there is no other way. No other effect can it have'. But, at the same time, if you are there and your office is to uphold the law, you can't decide that you are not going to uphold the law of larceny simply because it is going to cause a bit of trouble. (interview)

Strict enforcement of the letter of the law thus conflicted with a customary, if technically illegal, community right. By originally turning a blind eye to the practice of coal picking, as they had done during previous miners' strikes, the police and the NCB were tacitly acknowledging the miners' right to the coal. The raids on the local tip were looked upon as a serious violation of local custom and practice. When judged from this angle, the stoning of NCB property and the attacks on the local police station may be looked upon as a community response to an infringement of their rights. Even so, it is unlikely that this response would have been quite so determined had the police not adopted so rigid a view.

The defence of a series of rights was one validation of the opposition to the police evident on Monday, 15 October:

The lads were just pissed off with it. The police were stopping us from picking our coal. So, when somebody said 'There's three van loads of riot police round the back of the police station', we said 'Let's go and get them instead of waiting for them to come and get us.' (Grimethorpe miner, in interview)

Some symbolic significance was also attached to the assault on the woman police sergeant. More so than anyone else, she personified the police attitude towards the community:

She'd been on the tips on the previous raids and she was giving it that she was God Almighty, that nobody frightened her. And she was clubbing the kids and women around. And any arrest that was made that day, she was going up to the men and trying to ridicule them. (Grimethorpe miner, in interview)

Given what they would have seen as a general break-down of

law and order, it is likely that, as with the Maltby disturbances, the police tactics of Monday 15 October constituted an attempt to recover control of the streets. There are signs that the police attitude was greatly affected by the recent attack on the woman officer. One Grimethorpe resident recalled a brief conversation with a police officer at the height of the disturbances:

> I said to him, 'Why have you come to Grimethorpe? Why have you done this: We don't want this on our streets.' And he said, 'Well, you did our policewoman, and now we've come to get you.'   (wife of Grimethorpe miner, in interview)

Summary: Maltby and Grimethorpe

In the simplest sense, the Maltby and Grimethorpe riots were acts of community resistance in the face of what local people interpreted as deliberate attempts at intimidation by 'invading' police forces. In both cases, members of the local community saw the police raids on their villages as an attempt to undermine the effectiveness of the strike, whether by preventing picketing at Maltby or cutting off unofficial fuel supplies at Grimethorpe.

A perceived infringement of fundamental community rights was common to both cases. At Grimethorpe, villagers objected to being denied a right to pick coal, established by custom and practice. At Maltby, local citizens complained that they were no longer allowed the right to walk the streets of their village freely.

Rumours about the imposition of a police curfew at Maltby and the involvement of 'outside' police forces at both villages fuelled resentment towards the police. The credibility of such rumours was enhanced by residents' own experiences of encountering road blocks or of being instructed to return home. The reputations of particular police forces had been established on the picket lines, as had a general suspicion of the police as a whole.

The involvement of outside forces, lacking any commitment to long-term community relations, would help to explain allegations of indiscriminate arrests and the excessive use of force. According to Lloyd (1985, 69), the type of incidents reported at Maltby and Grimethorpe 'point to punitive expeditions by PSUs, suggesting either that discipline was breaking down or that senior police officers were permitting them to go and beat hell out of the communities'. Statements by Maltby residents even imply that officers were acting under the strain of long hours spent on picket duty at nearby Orgreave. Police accounts emphasize the role of certain elements within the community using the tensions generated by the strike as an excuse for hostility towards the police. Our evidence suggests more widespread animosity on the part of local residents. The retaliatory attacks on police stations and patrolling police officers were perpetrated by local youths and regular pickets intrinsically hostile to the police, but such activities had at least tacit support amongst local people as a whole. The Chief Constable of South Yorkshire complained of behaviour that was not normal for mining communities. The abnormality of the community's behaviour could equally be interpreted as a response to abnormal policing.

A desire for retribution following attacks on the police stations and fellow officers may have played some part in determining the magnitude of the police response in both communities. However, it is more likely that the primary motive was to restore their authority by regaining control of the turf. There can be little doubt that the paramilitary-style police operations on 16 June at Maltby and 15 October at Grimethorpe were intended as a corrective to temporary break-downs of law and order. These operations were highly successful from the police point of view, though this may have been to the considerable cost of long-term community relations.

9
Understanding community disorder

Comparison of case studies

We suggested earlier that the incidents we have examined in this section could be both classed and analysed as 'community disorders'. A stress on such similarities runs counter to more obvious differences: that the Haymarket incident was the outcome of racial conflict, while those at Maltby and Grimethorpe were the outcomes of industrial or class conflict. That comparable effects were produced does not necessarily imply similarities of cause.

We do not wish to deny the real and substantial differences between these situations and their contexts. Rather we want only to suggest that understanding of such events requires us to compare what otherwise seem to be quite different types of incident. As we argue in the conclusion, this does not mean accepting that what is common to them is the psychology of collective behaviour. We need to see any particular incident in several different ways. It can be compared with others involving exactly the same sort of group but can also be compared with those involving different groups temporarily or permanently occupying a similar social, political, or physical location. Mining villages are not inner-city areas. Their traditions, experiences, and inhabitants are quite different. Yet in the instances we have examined, there are comparable processes at work in producing disorder in these very different kinds of communities. The task is therefore to recognize both the similarities and the differences.

At the level of detailed analysis, the contrasts between the incident at the Haymarket and those at Maltby and Grimethorpe are striking and obvious. For the Haymarket fracas, the crucial context was the set of relationships established between the police and the Afro-Caribbean community. For Maltby and Grimethorpe, the context was the rupture of the relationship between mining communities and the police resulting from experience of the strike. In the two villages, perceptions of police–community relations had been sharpened by recent picket-line confrontations at Orgreave and Woolley. No such incident had happened between police and black youth in Sheffield. In Maltby and Grimethorpe, the police presence was interpreted as an 'invasion' of mining communities. No black youth could feel that the Gallery 'belonged' to him the way the miners and their families could feel they owned the streets of their villages.

Such differences in the contexts of the incidents were matched by differences in their dynamics. At both Maltby and Grime-thorpe, rumours spread about the activities, intentions, and composition of the police force. Except for shop windows, the targets singled out for attack by crowds had symbolic significance: the police station in Maltby, the colliery buildings in Grime-thorpe. In the Haymarket, there were no rumours about the police, only witnessed events. The only symbolic target identified was a blue uniform. Even shop windows were left largely intact.

However, such differences in context and dynamics do not necessarily suggest that we are dealing with different classes of events. Change in a relatively few variables would bring the Haymarket fracas much closer to the Maltby and Grimethorpe 'riots'. A recent incident as a felt sense of grievance, the location of the original incident in a black café or community centre, rumours about what the police had or hadn't done; had all these been present at the Haymarket, parallels with Maltby and Grimethorpe would have been more obvious.

Even in their actual form, there are some substantial similarities between the three incidents. In all, the police claimed to be responding to a complaint from a member of the public: a passer-by about spitting in the Haymarket, local residents about noise and nuisance from the Caledonian in Maltby, the National Coal Board about theft from the coal tip in Grimethorpe. In each case, the police response included a specific act which precipitated the disorder. In the Haymarket it was the attempt to confiscate the tape-recorder, in Maltby the confrontation outside the Caledonian, in Grimethorpe the harassment of coal-pickers. Again in every instance, resentment was fuelled by subsequent police actions. In the Haymarket, the handcuffing of prisoners to the railings, the use of dogs, and the arrest of the youth worker were seen as provocative acts. In Maltby and Grimethorpe, provocation took the form of massive police presence on the streets, arbitrary arrest, and verbal abuse. The attempted imposition of a curfew in Maltby was the ultimate provocation.

The police in turn seem to have been provoked by specific actions of the crowd. At both the Haymarket and Grimethorpe, junior officers at least seem to have been particularly incensed by attacks on women police officers, justifying instant retaliation. What was said by a policeman to a Grimethorpe miner's wife in explanation of saturation policing ('you did our policewoman, and now we've come to get you', p.137), was almost identical to the reply of another officer to a black youth protesting about the use of dogs in the Haymarket ('what happened to the woman police officer was not right either', p. 120).

This cycle of provocation and retaliation was a common dynamic of all three events. In each case, attempts were made to reach an accommodation. At the Haymarket, attempts by black youth workers to negotiate with the police were initially rebuffed, though finally accepted. At Maltby, an approach by local councillors produced an offer by the Superintendent in charge to reduce the visibility of the police, a concession which proved too little and too late. In Grimethorpe, there was agreement to hold and attend a public meeting, where the Deputy Chief Constable's apparent apology was accepted as an act of contrition. The rather different outcomes to the negotiation process should not disguise the similarity in the mediating role performed by community leaders.

In wider terms, what was at stake was similar in each instance. They were all about territory. In Maltby and Grimethorpe, the streets of the village were the territory at stake, with the coal tip in Grimethorpe as a second contested space. In the Haymarket, the struggle was over access to a walkway in a shopping precinct. Thus in every instance, the police were perceived to be depriving members of the community of the right to be present in a particular place at a particular time. The police were also seen to have an ulterior motive: racial harassment in the Haymarket, breaking the strike in Maltby and Grimethorpe.

All these similarities suggest that these apparently different events can be understood in substantially the same terms. The resemblance is even greater at a more abstract level. For each in its own way represented a conflict of interests between a set of traditional rights valued by a community and a police commitment to uphold the letter of the law. At the Haymarket, the right of black youths to congregate in a public shopping precinct found opposition in the police view that their conduct was likely to cause a breach of the peace. In Maltby, the rights of miners and their wives to be in and around pubs and take-aways after dark was opposed to the police view that they were a noise and a nuisance which could be used as cover for criminal activity. In Grimethorpe, the long-established tradition of picking coal from tips, which had survived during every previous strike, was redefined by the Coal Board and the police as a common act of theft.

In each case, the community's definitions of its rights did not accord with police interpretation of the law. In the absence of a Bill of Rights (see p. 197) and in the presence of massive discretion granted to the police in interpreting and enforcing the law, potential for such a conflict of interest exists in each and every community in Britain, however defined. The circumstances under which noise becomes defined as a nuisance, the presence of people on the streets as an invitation to crime, or the perks of a trade as an act of theft, are left entirely to police discretion. In each case, measures other than heavy policing might have been used. Compromises might have been negotiated. The failure or refusal of the police to follow these strategies is not unique to the cases we have examined. In the distant and the recent past, the police and their equivalents have encountered such situations and their decisions have sometimes failed to avert public disorder.

Towards a model of community disorder

The incidents we have analysed are relatively minor compared with the riots which took place in the inner cities of England after 1980. These riots were regarded as unprecedented, without equal this century. Perhaps they were, though we need to know more about the ill-documented history of public disorder between the two World Wars to be sure.

The racial dimension of these riots is often thought to be a wholly new influence. But race riots also have a history, if a largely unwritten one. Joshua *et al.* (1983) have demonstrated how there was, early in the twentieth century, a tradition of white riots against the presence of small numbers of black seamen in English seaports. The first 'race riots' were not perpetrated by black people but against them. The trend extended into the post-war period, to the 1958 Notting Hill riots and beyond. Joshua *et al.* suggest that such riots were subsequently displaced by more individualized attacks on black people, emergent in the 1960s as 'paki-bashing' and persisting in the widespread racist attacks in London today.

From the early 1970s, white racist attacks provoked defensive action by black communities, involving opposition to a police force increasingly seen as an agency of institutionalized racism. In

London especially there were a series of minor disorders indicating this new spirit of black resistance, notably those surrounding the Notting Hill Carnival in 1975 and 1976. In retrospect, these can be seen as precursors of the more serious disturbances to follow in 1980, 1981, and beyond.

There is now a voluminous literature on the riots, especially those in Bristol, Liverpool, Birmingham, and London. We are not in a position to review all the arguments. Many of them focus quite properly on the specifically racial factors underlying the situation of black people in inner-city areas, their economic and social position, experience of living in deprived areas, and increasingly acrimonious relationships with the police. We do not wish here to imply that these are in any sense unimportant. Whether the incidents were 'race riots' or not, they clearly had a racial dimension. To discuss them without acknowledging this racial dimension is akin to dicussing the incidents in Maltby and Grimethorpe without reference to the miners' strike. We have consistently argued that police–community relations always take place in a context, both local and national.

However, we do wish to abstract certain features of thse disturbances from their full context for the purposes of our analysis. Our objective is to see whether what we have identified as crucial elements in the relatively small-scale confrontations in the Haymarket, in Maltby, and in Grimethorpe have also been present in the larger and more specifically racial disorders which have taken place elsewhere.

Since we need a sample of such disturbances and because some are rather better documented than others, we have chosen three riots: that in April 1980 in Bristol, as recounted by Joshua *et al.* (1983); that in April 1981 in Brixton, for which we draw on the report of Lord Scarman's official inquiry (1981); that in Tottenham in October 1985, using the report of the Broadwater Farm Inquiry chaired by Lord Gifford (1986). We shall also consider separately the Handsworth riot of September 1985, which turns out to be distinctive in particular respects. Each of the reports on the other disorders represents an attempt to construct an account of what actually happened on each occasion. They are rather different in kind. Joshua *et al.* have produced an interrogation of official accounts, with only limited access to witnesses. Scarman's is a 'liberal' establishment view, heavily reliant on the accounts of the police. The more radically-minded Gifford inquiry was hampered by police refusal to give evidence. Each is thus a partial view, but also the most detailed and comprehensive account available. With these caveats in mind, it is nevertheless possible to construct a plausible outline of the sequence of events and their immediate context which led up to and shaped the course of disorder.

In every case, we find that police–community relations had undergone a significant deterioration in the period immediately prior to the riots. Such deterioration had occurred at official levels of police–community liaison. Recent incidents had served to symbolize this breakdown and provided a framework in which to interpret subsequent events. In this respect, though not necessarily in others, such riots are similar to those examined by the Kerner Commission in the United States in the 1960s:

> Violence was generated by an increasingly disturbed social atmosphere, in which typically not one, but a series of incidents occurred over a period of weeks or months prior to the outbreak of disorder. With each incident, frustration and tension grew until at some point a final incident, often similar to incidents preceding it, occurred and was followed almost immediately by violence.
>
> (Kerner Commission 1968 in Evans 1975, 20)

Unlike our own case studies, police action in the three inner-city areas was not initiated in response to any specific complaint by a member of the public. More proactive police activities were involved: a stop and search of a motorist in Brixton; a traffic offence and subsequent search of a house for stolen property in Tottenham; a raid on a café suspected as a distribution centre for drugs and alcohol in Bristol. In the context of inner-city policing, though scarcely anywhere else, these are routine procedures. That they are routine has tended to make their eruption more puzzling. We quoted in our introduction to the book Lord Scarman's evident inability to explain why such an everyday act as the search of a black man for drugs should spark off violent confrontation. The point is that they are only everyday in a certain context: they are the routines of policing black communities. Hence it may be their very typicality, rather than any abnormality, which allows them to be seen as symbols of police harassment. This symbolism is reinforced when, as happened in each case, a black person is seen to have been mistreated and hence to personify the fate of black people at the hands of the police.

For this symbolization to be seen and acted upon, it seems that there have to be specific and visible instances of police behaviour which can be defined as illegitimate. At Tottenham, resentment was felt initially at the circumstances in which a middle-aged

West Indian woman, Mrs Jarrett, died during a police search of her home. Further resentment was felt when police closed off the estate at a time when people wished to return to the police station to renew their demonstration. At Brixton, such incidents included police treatment of an injured black youth, the launch of 'Operation Swamp' – an attempt to use saturation policing to stamp out street crime and drug-dealing – and the aggressive arrest of a bystander who intervened in the search of a car. In Bristol, a whole series of events seemed to worsen rather than improve the situation: the handcuffing of the arrested café proprietor, the influx of police and their lingering presence in the area, the introduction of dogs and riot shields. Such actions serve to intensify the level of conflict, and invite response from the gathering crowd:

> a communicative process . . . occurs at the scene: as rumours are exchanged, alternatives mooted, objects thrown, the crowd responds with apparent approval or disapproval; people cheer, laugh, boo, shout or remain silent; it is these reactions that create the emerging norms.   (Sullivan 1977, 81)

Direct or indirect police provocation of the crowd was in all three instances complemented by crowd provocation of the police. In Bristol, police cars were attacked and one was set on fire. In Brixton, a bus was driven at a police line and ambulances and fire engines were attacked. In Tottenham, where the police subsequently showed most signs of feeling provoked, a serious injury to a patrol man, petrol bombs, gunshots, and, most of all, the murder of PC Blakelock, all acted to confirm the vigour of police response.

At various times in all instances, there were attempts at mediation which failed, largely because senior police officers failed to accede to the demands made by community leaders and refused to discuss or disclose their next moves. That territory was at stake is obvious: the crowd was attempting to wrest control of the streets from the police. The withdrawal of the police in Bristol was seen as a significant defeat and one unlikely to happen again, judging from Chief Constables' immediately declared determination not to tolerate what they called, in a phrase significantly derived from Northern Ireland, 'no-go' areas.

However, in mainland Britain, it is less the actual control of the streets which is contested but the form such control should take. The essence of the conflict is over who has the right to be on the street on what terms and under whose conditions. Couched by the protestors as 'freedom from police harassment', it is an objection to what have become the routine practices of policing inner-city areas. This is both a specific and a general grievance, since it amounts to a claim for equal citizenship. The police as representatives of the state are seen to be denying full rights to one section of citizens. The police justification for such action is that it is necessary to enforce the law, especially in respect of drug offences, theft, and street crime. Such an interpretation can become a validation of hostility towards all members of ethnic minorities as potential criminals.

> The economic alienation of young black people gives rise to a culture with a propensity to crime. The police make the initial connection between race and crime; the niceties of the links between deprivation, racial discrimination and delinquent behaviour do not concern them. In this environment, whatever racist sentiments exist within the police force are reinforced. The activity of policing the inner city with high crime rates and a high proportion of black youth, in the context of a more 'military' style of policing . . . reinforces and fosters racist sentiments among police officers.   (Lea and Young 1982, 13)

The exclusively legalistic view of policing inner-city communities was evident in the Police Federation's reaction to the implementation of the Police and Criminal Evidence Act, arguing that it would restrict police initiatives and lead directly to a rise in street crime in Brixton (Radio 4 World at One 27 November 1986). The police want the power to stop and search suspicious, mainly black, people in inner-city areas. The black community wants the right to go about its business without being arbitrarily stopped and searched by the police. The right of a section of the public not to be harassed by the police is in direct conflict with the duty of the police to search indiscriminately for evidence of crime. In this condensed and symbolic form, black people are asking to be treated as normal citizens rather than as potential criminals. The police demand to be able to act upon what they regard as suspicious behaviour. As long as these two claims to rights cannot be accommodated, then routine police operations in the inner-city will continue to be potential flashpoints.

When, where, and how much disorder erupts cannot be predicted with any certainty. Too many variables are involved. Lord Scarman, for example, clearly felt that various rumours circulating about police malpractice contributed to a build-up of resentment (1981). In Tottenham immediately after Mrs Jarrett's death, there were also rumours that there was to be a riot. How important such rumours are, whether they are a cause or effect of heightened tension, seems difficult to establish.

What can be established, from our own case studies and brief consideration of these wider events, is a set of preconditions for community disorders in general, of which inner-city riots are one extreme form. These are presented in table 9.1. It is our contention that this table is comprehensive and includes all the factors identified as significant in our own case studies of community disorder and authoritative analyses of other major instances. It does not and cannot specify their relative importance, nor indicate any particular patterns of cause and effect. It does, however, go beyond mere description to provide a working model of those situations and their dynamics which may lead to community disorder. Like all the models in this book, it is handicapped by the lack of data on negative examples where, despite every indication of the potential for it, community disorder does not in fact take place.

Moreover, while these categories of factors can be successfully applied to the events at the Haymarket, in Maltby and Grimethorpe, and at Bristol, Brixton, and Tottenham, they still only constitute an ideal type to which any specific incident only approximates. This can be seen by the unevenness with which the model can be applied to the Handsworth riot of September 1985. The events there, as recounted by the committee set up by Birmingham City Council and chaired by Julius Silverman (Silverman 1986), did not conform to the pattern our model would lead us to expect.

There is, for example, controversy over the state of police–community relations immediately before the riot. Lord Scarman, amongst others, had drawn attention to the apparent success of the policy of community policing introduced into Handsworth during the early 1970s. Some dissented from its effectiveness at the time, while others suggested that it had been progressively abandoned after 1981. Relations between police and black youth were scarcely harmonious but there is no specific evidence that they had recently deteriorated. Two drugs raids on the Villa Cross public house in May and July 1985 had caused some resentment amongst black youth, though other sections of the community had endorsed them. The police report on the disturbances stressed that their local 'tension indicators' had not identified the possibility of disorder, especially as the Handsworth Carnival had gone off without major incident the day before the trouble began.

If the immediate context of the Handsworth disorders remains

Table 9.1 Factors affecting disorder in communities

Key characteristics	Bristol	Brixton	Tottenham
Police–community relations	No information	Permanent tension; collapse of liaison committee	Latent hostility; collapse of liaison initiative
Recent incidents	No information	Treatment of injured black youth	Stop and search on 1 October
Initial complaint	Police initiative *re* drugs/alcohol	Police initiative *re* drugs	Police initiative *re* car tax and theft
Precipitating police action	Raid on Black and White Café	Search of man and car for drugs	Jarrett search; sealing of estate
Acts fuelling community resentment	Use of handcuffs, dogs, and riot shields; influx of police	Operation Swamp	Police attitude to Jarrett death; racist abuse
Acts fuelling police resentment	Attack and burning of police cars; storming of café	Attack on firemen and ambulances	Injury to PC Cabon; murder of PC Blakelock; petrol bombs; guns
Territory at stake	Black Café	Streets of Brixton	Broadwater Farm Estate
Symbolic targets	Police cars	Police cars; all property	Police lines; estate shops
Rumour	No information	*Re* fate of injured black youth	Of impending riot
Alleged outsiders	No information	'Strangers' and petrol bombs	Four 'unknown' white men
Negotiation and accommodation	Failed attempt by Superintendent to talk to crowd	Friday meeting; intervention by councillors	Meeting at Tottenham police station; rebuff of black leadership
Community rights vs. law enforcement	Freedom from police harassment vs. laws relating to drugs and alcohol	Freedom from police harassment vs. laws relating to drugs and street crime	Freedom from police harassment vs. laws relating to motor vehicles and theft

Haymarket	Maltby	Grimethorpe
Relatively harmonious	Some disharmony then conflict of strike	Conflict of strike
None	Orgreave picketing	Woolley picketing
Passer-by *re* spitting	Local residents *re* noise and nuisance from pubs	National Coal Board *re* theft
Attempted confiscation of tape recorder	Confrontation outside Caledonian pub	Arrest of coal pickers
Handcuffing of prisoners to railings; use of dogs; arrest of youth worker	Instigation of curfew; police on streets	Arrests at tip; police on streets; abuse of women
Attack on policewoman	Attack on police station	Attack on policewoman
Shopping precinct	Village streets	Coal tip; village streets
None	Police station; shop windows	Colliery buildings; shop windows
None	Curfew; police reinforcements; mistreatment of prisoners	Vanloads of police
None	Manchester police and skinheads	Metropolitan police
Eventual withdrawal	Blaming outsiders	Deputy Chief Constable's 'apology'
Right to be in shopping centre vs. breach of the peace	Right to be on streets vs. breach of the peace	Right to pick coal/be on streets vs. theft

confused, it is not even clear which actions precipitated them. On 9 September, a routine police inspection of illegally parked cars outside the Acapulco Café resulted in the arrest of a man on suspicion of possessing a stolen vehicle. A crowd gathered and police reinforcements arrived, but withdrew when the man was taken away. Some witnesses alleged that a black woman was pushed over when she tried to intervene but she has never been properly identified. An alternative report on Handsworth from the black community (Report of the Review Panel 1986, 6) suggested that it was enough for black people to believe the police habitually capable of such an action for it to become a source of grievance. If that is so, then we are dealing with events which do not require the status of fact to become flashpoints.

At 7.30 p.m. of the same day, an emergency call summoned fire officers to the derelict Villa Cross building, originally a cinema and subsequently a bingo hall. A fire was discovered but as the firemen fought the blaze a crowd of youths gathered and began to stone them. The police were called as more groups of youths began to congregate along the Lozells Road. Looting and arson broke out. The police, initially outnumbered, were forced to fall back. More shops were looted and buildings set on fire as the rioting developed. Two Asians were killed in their post office and many more residents were injured, some seriously. Order was not restored until four o'clock in the morning. The next day, further violence followed the visit of the Home Secretary to Handsworth and sporadic looting took place over a larger area than had been covered by the previous riot. Meetings were held between the police and community leaders. Eventually, calm returned.

What we cannot find here is a cycle of intensifiers, actions by police or public which fuel the resentment on each side. The alleged police assault of the black woman was not the immediate cause of the disturbance which seemed rather to lie in the reaction of the youths to the arrival of the firemen at the Villa Cross. Whether the fire had been started deliberately and for what purpose is impossible to determine. The police did not forcibly remove the crowd and were in fact forced to retreat, so their specific actions cannot be regarded as provocative.

It does seem that the Villa Cross building had become a kind of symbol of what was happening to the community. Plans to convert it into an amusement arcade had been opposed locally. The council were unable to intervene, since no change of use was involved. It is not possible to know whether it was set on fire because it was the Villa Cross or because it was empty. Looting and arson were similarly indiscriminate. Nobody can decide whether Asian shopkeepers were victimized because they were Asian or because they were shopkeepers.

There is no evidence of rumour spreading amongst the crowd. Some youths were seen to be directing the crowds but only the police subscribed to the view that this constituted an organized criminal conspiracy. Local negotiations could not have been seen to have broken down since they were prevented by the speed and intensity of events. Finally, while some of the prior activities of the police might have been seen as attacks on community rights, there was no equivalent of the lingering police presence in Bristol, of Operation Swamp in Brixton, or of the cordoning off of the Broadwater Farm Estate.

Julius Silverman concluded that:

> The general evidence, course and story of the Handsworth riots are very close and similar to the history of riots in Brixton and other places. It would in my view require very strong evidence to show that this was a different phenomenon to Brixton. (Silverman 1986, 73)

Yet, as he subsequently notes, many of the detailed characteristics were different, even unique, especially that most of the rioting did not have the police as its target. Handsworth as a deprived, multi-racial community does bear a striking resemblance to St Paul's, Brixton, and the Broadwater Farm Estate. The form of the community disorders in each place was very similar. But the dynamics of the Handsworth disorder seem to be different.

For those who subscribe to academic or lay views that the 'mentality of the mob' takes over, such differences are unimportant since riotous crowds have by definition no logic or rationale for their actions. To look for a pattern amongst chaos is pointless. A quite alternative view, held by Silverman himself, is that the dynamics of community disorder are less important than the context of deprivation which induces it:

> the really important matter for the future of Handsworth is not who struck the match which set Handsworth alight, but the evidence of the social conditions, the mass of hostility, frustration and personal violence which still exist in Handsworth and other Inner Cities. What should society do about these? (Silverman 1986, Foreword)

Neither an emphasis on a mob mentality nor a stress on social deprivation would necessarily acknowledge the usefulness of seeking to construct a model of disorder. We would want to defend our project at the very least on the grounds that such an analysis can help to identify policies which might in the future avert community disorders. The most important clearly lie in the area of political and economic justice but others centre on the role of the police as it affects such communities in general and particularly around potential flashpoints. Viable strategies include the need to mediate through and negotiate and consult with community leaders; the importance of being seen to make concessions to community feeling; the avoidance of unintentionally and intentionally provocative acts. Policing should be informed by a balance between 'law' and 'order', between the powers of the police and the rights of the citizen.

There is nothing new in these suggestions. Almost every inquiry into community disorder, including that of Lord Scarman, recommended that policing should follow these lines. We have merely tried to indicate that what each separate inquiry identified as issues specific to one particular disorder are in fact characteristic of them all.

There are no obvious signs, that any of this has found its way into police thinking or training, much less into police practice. Rather, the view has been taken that the best thing to do about possible public disorder is to extend the tactical and technological repertoire of riot control.

This is not to lay the blame for these community disorders solely on the shoulders of the police, nor to suggest that real changes in police methods, were they to occur, would solve these communities' problems. The police operate in conditions which are not of their own making. They are not directly responsible for the structural location and cultural disposition of Afro-Caribbean youth in British society. They did not begin, though they had considerable control over the course of, the miners' strike. They did however make crucial decisions which affected the degree of disorder. In the euphemistic language of public inquiries, these would be described as unwise, ill-advised, errors of judgement. Yet more is at stake than consideration of police tactics. What we can identify, looking across this set of case studies and indeed all those we have considered, is the evolution of a clear police strategy. The lines have been and are being redrawn between the rights of citizens at demonstrations, on picket lines, in their home communities, and the intention of the police to uphold the letter of the law. This is a shift in the politics of policing, from policing by consent to policing by coercion. To understand why and how this has come about in relation to public order, we have to trace the links between the daily interaction between the police and the public on the streets of Britain and the whole political and economic development of contemporary society. To that task, our concluding section is addressed.

Part four

Conclusions

Introduction

Our conclusion falls into two chapters. In the first, chapter ten, we develop a working model of public disorder, as it has emerged from our consideration of the three types of disorder. This is then compared with the established sociological theory of Smelser (1962), the analyses of urban social movements by the Marxist geographer Castells (1983), and recent work by Moscovici (1985) on social representations within the perspective of social psychology. In chapter eleven we move on to matters of policy, arguing that the focal concerns of the police occupational subculture and increasingly repressive legislation have together dominated public order policy, to the detriment of any concern with the causes of disorder or with the civil rights of the citizen. Here we draw on such recent relevant texts as Brewer *et al*. (1988), McCabe and Wallington (1988), and Uglow (1988).

10
A model of disorder

The objective of this chapter is to develop and evaluate a model of public disorder. Such a model should in principle be applicable to a whole range of situations, allowing differentiation between types of crowds yet remaining sensitive to the special features of any individual instance. The extent to which we have managed to meet these criteria should become clear in the course of the discussion. We shall attempt to establish that, despite important differences between an organized political demonstration, an industrial picket, and a confrontation with the police on the streets of communities, the same kind of analysis is applicable to all of them. Nor do we consider it impossible to generalize from the miners' strike, despite its exceptional features.

> The conflict . . . was not that of any normal or routine industrial confrontation. It was on a different scale and contained quite a different order of priorities from any other dispute. It grew into an expression of anger, of bitterness and resentment bordering on civil war between different attitudes to work and life. (Goodman 1985, 79)

In our view, the miners' strike was less an aberration than the logical development of emerging forms of disorder found in industrial, political, and inner-city contexts, revealing their basic structure in particularly dramatic and visible form. The factors which weakened constraints on violence during the miners' strike were not unique to it. They can recur, and indeed have since recurred, in other contexts.

We therefore consider it legitimate to have treated incidents during the strike as in principle comparable to others occurring outside it. Our ultimate justification for the pairings and comparisons made must lie in the conclusions we were able to draw and the general propositons about disorder which stem from them.

One of our most important findings is that disorder is not a random occurrence in a unique set of circumstances. There is a common pattern, or dynamic, underlying apparently diverse events. This includes, on occasion, incidents which might be described as flashpoints in the terms with which we began this book. Yet what converts an incident into a flashpoint is not so much its inherent characteristics as the way the incident is interpreted at the time. This depends on the pattern of interaction in the particular situation but also on its immediate context, the cultural predispositions of those involved, the political definitions in operation, and the nature of what is at stake. Our rough concentric rings model of the genesis of flashpoints in our introduction (p. 22) has come to have the potential to reveal these processes, a potential it is now time to realize.

A model of disorder

The model we have developed is an attempt to theorize the factors found in our own and others' investigations to be crucial determinants of order and disorder. We have grouped these into six levels of analysis: structural, political/ideological, cultural, contextual, situational, and interactional. We use the term 'level' to indicate that the processes and structures involved are of qualitatively different kinds: the characteristics of groups are not derivable from those of societies, nor are social processes merely individual interactions writ large. We also include spatial and temporal factors which are not specifically social or individual in nature. This means that the levels cannot simply be treated as a checklist of factors to be added together.

Table 10.1 represents our model of factors structuring the occurrence or non-occurrence of public disorder. Its layout serves merely to condense and clarify the model and does not imply any chronological development or linear flow. Disorder does not 'begin' at the structural level and proceed through the others to the interactional level. Nor do we intend to imply that disorder is necessarily predetermined by the 'higher order' levels. We shall argue that disorder can be averted at 'lower' levels even where over-arching factors indicate the likelihood of disorder. Conversely, disorder can occur at the interactional level in the absence of predisposing factors at the other levels, although it is then less likely to spread. We begin with the most generalized level.

Table 10.1 Levels of structuration in public order situations

Order	Level
	Structural
Changes possible through social/economic reform	Material inequalities
Changes possible through political reform	Ideological alienation
State defined as legitimate	Relation to state
	Political/ideological
Protestors have access to political institutions	Marginality
Protestors defined as having rights	Legitimacy
Normal legal procedures	Sanctions
	Cultural
Local co-ordination of local force	Police composition
Latent and passive	Police solidarity
Mixed sexes and ages	Crowd composition
Heterogeneous temporary and moral	Crowd solidarity
Convergent and consensual	shared meanings
Differentially positive	Mutual typifications
	Contextual
Accommodating	Police–protestor history
Few or none	Previous incidents
No expectation of violence	Media sensitization
Concerted and productive	Pre-event liaison
	Situational
Overt and sensitive, organizers disavowing violence	Crowd organization
Reactive and low key	Police organization
Flexible application of law	Police objectives
Symbolic dissent from others' actions	Crowd objectives
Absent invisible or out of range	Targets for dissent
Specific and marked off	Spatial location
Minimal threat	Public property
	Interactional
Fraternization; selective use of minimum force	Treatment of crowd
Tolerance and respect	Treatment of police
Verbal attack	Treatment of targets
Making of concessions	Arbitration
Absent	Flashpoints

1 Structural level

The structural level refers to conflicts inherent in material and ideological differences between social groups and the extent to which they are resolvable within the existing social structure. *Material inequalities* of power and resources exist between class, gender, and ethnic groups. Conflict may arise if disadvantaged

---

Disorder

Demands for fundamental changes in social/economic order
Demands for fundamental changes in political order
State defined as illegitimate

Protestors disenfranchised from political representation
Protestors defined as threat to society or state
Extraordinary legal powers

Local co-ordination of nationally recruited force
Manifest and active
Exclusively male and youthful
Homogeneous permanent and personal
Discrepant and oppositional
Negative stereotyping

Conflictual and a source of grievance
Recent
Expectation of violence
Bogus or non-existent

Non-existent or ineffectual; organizers not disavowing
violence
Proactive and visible show of strength
Inflexible definition of legal obligations
Instrumental aimed at preventing others' action
Present visible and in range
Diffuse and unmarked
Potential or actual interference

Insults; indiscriminate use of maximum force
Hatred and abuse
Physical attack
Issuing of ultimata
Present

---

groups are unable to improve their position and thus have little stake in the existing institutions of political and social order. Structural conflicts are always mediated through the state, in its role as moderator of sectional interests. How these differences are resolved defines the type of state. In liberal democracies, some sort of consensus about means and ends is sought, whereas in authoritarian states, one set of interests is forced upon the whole of society. Such factors determine whether, and how, structural differences of interest appear in the political arena.

In contemporary Britain, economic recession and its political management have borne heavily upon specific groups and communities whose differences of interests with the state have consequently sharpened. Confrontations such as those between employers and workers or between police and black people are manifestations of such structural conflict. Hence what begins as a protest against proposed redundancies may be translated into a struggle over the future of whole communities; what starts as a spontaneous protest against police brutality expands into a struggle of black people against white society. In part, this happens because of the objective situation in which the group is placed. The material interests of both striking miners and black people have been directly counter to those of the state. But this also has to be recognized subjectively. Clearly not all striking miners and presumably no working miners perceived their interests in these terms. It is still not a universal perception amongst black communities.

Groups whose material situation is not disadvantaged may feel an *ideological alienation* from the state. Students and nuclear disarmers who are not personally the victims of inequality may feel that the state is committed to activities they find morally repugnant. Thus, whether the initial grievance is material or ideological, what is crucial is the group's perception of its *relationship to the state* and its front-line representatives, the police force. The conflict may change so that it is no longer one within the state but over the state. Once an industrial dispute, political demonstration, or spontaneous community action has passed this threshold, the potential for public disorder has increased. The extent to which dissent becomes disaffection from the state itself depends upon protesting groups' access to other means of opposition at the political and ideological level.

2 Political/ideological level

The political/ideological level refers to the relationship of the dissenting group to political and ideological institutions and their response to its activities. Where a group can express its dissent through established channels within the framework of parliamentary democracy, the political system will appear as in principle amenable to change and influence. The opposite case is that of *marginality*, where the group is, or feels, effectively disenfranchised, unrepresented by the system. The state appears to be immutable: a hostile institution over which they have no control. The political power a group feels itself to have is an important influence on its attitude towards the use of violence to achieve its ends or defend its interests.

Legitimacy refers to the ways in which the group's declared ends and the means proposed to achieve them are subject to ideological processes. Through the agency of the mass media, politicians and commentators will represent the dissenting group in a more or less favourable light. At its most positive, the right to protest and on occasion some recognition of the justice of their case will be acknowledged. At its most negative, what the group is trying to achieve and the means at their disposal will be portrayed as a threat to the fabric of society. While violence often appears as the reason for such labelling, it is more often a pretext for repeating a definition which has already been formulated and expressed. To dismiss protestors as hooligans, criminals, or crypto-communists is likely to further alienate them from all representatives of the state.

These processes can affect the way the law is enforced. Because of the constitutional peculiarities of the British police, discussed in chapter eleven, they are highly sensitive to overt or coded messages about how political elites expect a public order situation to be handled. Even normal legal procedures can be applied with greater or lesser rigour but it is also possible for elites to signal their endorsement of additional *sanctions* which extend police powers in extraordinary ways. Even before public order legislation which formally legitimated the extension of police powers, their effective expansion has been observable in inner cities and on picket lines.

The experience of protestors of political marginalization and ideological vilification may lessen their resistance to violence, just as the offering of a *carte blanche* to the police may lead them to be less wary of provoking crowds. Such responses need not be automatic, if other factors militate against disorder. One consideration is whether violence is culturally endorsed.

3 Cultural level

By 'cultural' we refer to all the ways in which groups of people understand the social world and their place within it, their definitions of the rules which do or should govern behaviour and how they define themselves and other social groups. The diverse cultures of ethnic groups, youth subcultures, particular occupations, and localities give rise to specific ways of defining situations and the behaviour appropriate to them. As such they provide a basis for collective mobilization and action. They also carry with them beliefs about the rights of individuals or groups. They foster certain characterizations of other social groups and expectations of how they are likely to behave in a given situation. If the groups involved have differing or incompatible definitions of the situation, appropriate behaviour, or legitimate rights, then the potential for conflict is increased.

Such cultural factors affect the possibility of public disorder since they shape how dissenters and police view themselves and each other, and thus the most appropriate forms of their interaction. We take as given here (though further explored in the next chapter) the existence of an occupational police culture based upon group solidarity, masculine presence, political conservatism, and preparedness to use force. In any specific situation, the way this culture finds expression is affected by the *composition of the police*. A large police presence, drawn from several different forces, with a diffuse command structure is less disciplined than a smaller contingent of local police under a tight chain of command. In the former situation, there is more likelihood that the *solidarity of the police* will move from latent and passive forms to manifest and active expressions of group identity in opposition to that of the crowd.

The crowd culture will vary with the nature and *composition of the crowd*. A crowd may be homogeneous in its composition, drawing on a permanent sense of its own identity derived from occupational, ethnic, or other forms of group membership. Individuals in such a crowd are more likely to feel that the crowd is an extension of their own social identity, experiencing and expressing a permanent sense of *crowd solidarity*. By contrast, members of a crowd which is heterogeneous in composition and temporary in its identity, may perceive their membership as partial and conditional.

Such perceptions have concrete effects upon the pattern of interaction between police and dissenters, affecting the possibility of protestors and police arriving at a set of *shared meanings*. Recognition of complementary rights, to protest or picket on one side, to uphold the law on the other, is rendered less viable by mutually antagonistic identities and outlooks. Meanings will become less convergent and consensual than divergent and oppositional. As a result of group solidarity *typifications* of others may collapse into stereotypes: all police officers are fascists; all demonstrators or pickets are communists; all police are racists; all blacks are criminals. When sexual and racial insults emerge, what might otherwise be disregarded as words spoken in the heat of the moment become insults to the integrity and identity of the group itself.

While discrepant perceptions of a situation may increase the likelihood of disorder, they do not make it inevitable. Participants in a potentially conflictual situation can still come to a compromise and accommodate each other's objectives. It is possible for police and pickets to evolve a set of agreed norms about what is acceptable on a picket line, a good clean shove being permissible whereas throwing bricks is not. Whether such accommodation is reached will depend on factors at other levels.

4 Contextual level

The context of potentially disorderly situations refers to the long-term and immediate set of existing relations between those involved, especially between the police and dissenting groups. Individual incidents are perceived and responded to on the basis of pre-existent relations between the groups. This *police–protestor history* will determine how far the police can claim an impartial role and the extent to which organizers can offer any guarantees about the behaviour of members of the crowd. Where there have been recent incidents between the two groups which remain unresolved and nurture grievances, both sides may anticipate the initiation of trouble by the other side, be prepared to respond in kind and not be averse to settling some old scores. *Previous incidents* often serve to symbolize relations between groups. They will have become part of each group's folk-lore and tend to make groups highly sensitive to real or imagined grievances.

This folk-lore will have been disseminated through the groups' formal and informal means of communication: daily conversation, rumour, magazines, formal meetings. The police force, trade unions, political organizations, and working-class communities all have their grapevines. Any conflictual context is also likely to have been picked up by the mass media. Depending upon their form, audience, and political stance, the media can exaggerate or minimize the possibility of conflict. The implications of such *media sensitization* for the behaviour of participants in general seems less easy to determine than the visible effect it has upon the organizers of the event. Their attitudes and those of the police to *pre-event liaison* will be structured by expectations of violence, stemming from their own perceptions and those of the media. An assessment that violence is a real possibility may have quite divergent outcomes on liaison. On the one hand, it can make both organizers and police anxious to avoid any repetition of events which have worsened inter-group relations. On the other hand, the police in particular may take the view that if there is a strong likelihood of violence, pre-emptive policing is necessary.

A highly sensitive context does not make disorder inevitable, any more than a relatively stable and conflict-free context guarantees the maintenance of order. Other levels come into play, not least the characteristics of the immediate situation.

5 Situational level

We use the term situational to refer to the spatial and social determinants of an event or incident. At this level, those immediately involved begin to have some control over the situation. From the point that the possibility of police–organizer liaison exists, then decisions are made by both sides which can directly contribute to order or disorder as outcomes. However, these decisions are not and cannot be taken independently of the overall definition of the situation derived from structural, political/ideological, cultural, and contextual levels. Definitions of the immediate situation are continuously informed by ideas of what is at stake, how political elites have defined the protest and protestors, the habitual perspectives of protestors and police, and their expectations of each others' conduct based on past experience. All these are, for example, present in the mutual assessment of sincerity and effectiveness which underlies police–organizer liaison.

The most beneficial outcome of such negotiations for the maintenance of public order is a commitment by the organizers to effective measures of *crowd organization*. Where the organizers not only disavow violence themselves but can be seen to direct the crowd's behaviour to the same ends, then the likelihood that the police will respond in kind is increased. Complementary forms of *police organization* tend to involve local command of local officers, adopting a reactive and relatively low-key style of policing, with reinforcements kept out of sight and agreements with the organizers about the location and activities of protestors. This is only possible where *police objectives* can be defined in ways which allow a flexible interpretation of the law. Minor infringements of the law may be overlooked in the interests of the wider objective of maintaining order. Where for any reason the police feel obliged to enforce a narrow and literal interpretation of the law, then policing is more likely to be proactive, involving a visible show of strength from the start.

The strategies adopted by the police will involve an overall assessment of the situation and its political consequences, previous encounters with the group, and of course an assessment of the crowd itself. The nature of what are seen to be the *crowd objectives* is a crucial determinant of policing style. If these are, or can be restricted to, the expression of symbolic dissent from the actions of others, then order may be more easily maintained. Where the crowd's objectives begin to become those of directly interfering with the activities of opponents, then protection of their legal rights may involve forcible restraint of the crowd's behaviour.

In such ways the organization and objectives of crowd and police affect the possibility of disorder. These take shape in a particular physical location. A crowd which begins as a symbolic group may adopt more instrumental objectives if *targets for dissent* are present, visible, and within range of the protestors. Even where such nominated targets are absent, it is possible for the police to become themselves the targets of protestors' activities. This is more likely where the police have to physically restrain the crowd. How such restraint can be exercised depends on the *spatial location* of the protest. If the crowd can be situated behind barriers and its movements predicted, then police action will be primarily designed to contain it. If such movement is not restricted, the police may have to move or disperse the crowd, especially if it is interfering with pedestrians or traffic, shops or the conduct of business. Discretion can be exercised even here: a road can be closed to traffic or protestors can be physically moved on to pavements to clear a way for vehicles and pedestrians.

Space can of itself be more or less conducive to disorder, since it structures the room for manoeuvre for protestors and police. Equally important is the way the space is perceived. The police view is likely to be shaped by a sense of the manageability of space and the protection of the *public* and *property* in general. Protestors are more likely to perceive space in terms of where they have the right to be and go. These potentially conflictual definitions of space may be sharpened or blunted by what happens between police and protestors.

6 Interactional level

This level involves consideration of the dynamics of interaction between police and protestors. These patterns cannot be understood apart from the meanings which those involved bring to and activate during the interaction, meanings which derive from all of the levels previously discussed. In themselves, however, patterns of interaction constitute signals of how each side perceives the other. Actions which more or less guarantee retaliation, such as throwing bricks at police officers or forcibly dispersing a crowd, are particularly strong signals that accommodation has broken down. They are as much effects as causes of the breakdown of order. Those involved rarely perceive the logic of each others' actions: 'suddenly bricks were thrown at officers'; 'the police charged us for no reason'. Such actions do have a rationale, however invisible to the other side. They are part of a pattern less obvious to immediate perceptions than subsequent analysis.

If it is not always possible to determine exactly who or what started it, why it starts is more specifiable. The turning point is when one side sees the actions of the other as unreasonable. What is defined as unreasonable on the day depends on what has gone on before. What is reacted to violently in one setting, with particular structural, political/ideological, cultural, contextual, and situational features, may evoke a less dramatic response in another. What is defined in one situation as a bit of pushing or shoving or as a routine arrest, may be interpreted in another as an attempt to break the police line or as brutal victimization of the innocent. Such definitions are not arbitrary; they have to be based on real actions. But these are always perceived in terms of the definitions concerning what is held to be fair and just within the 'rules of the game'. For the crowd, such rules may be very general, such as the right to stand in a certain area, or quite specific: the right to hand in a petition or to speak to lorry drivers. For the police, a certain amount of raucous behaviour by the crowd may be tolerated but only if held within specified limits.

There is then a breaking point, at which the *treatment of the crowd*, the *treatment of the police*, or the *treatment of targets*, is seen to breach the agreed norms of interaction, justifying retaliation in kind. One mark of this breakdown is the shift of insults from routinized general jeering to highly personalized abuse. Physical or verbal, such exchanges are interpreted symbolically as indicative of how each group actually feels about the other.

Incidents trivial in themselves can thus evoke a response which seems out of all proportion to their objective characteristics. They then set in motion a chain of response and counter-response, a spiral of mutual recrimination. They have become *flashpoints*. While almost any action may potentially act as a flashpoint, what seems to be important is their amenability to interpretation in symbolic terms. Flashpoints have to be, in the language of semiology, 'signs' which connote an underlying set of assumptions about each group's perception of the other. Hence the importance of physical or verbal attacks on women as markers of the lack of respect shown to a group when its most vulnerable members are abused. If leaders of police or protestors are attacked, that will be seen as undermining their authority and legitimacy. To become a flashpoint, incidents must contain elements which can be interpreted in this symbolic way in a general context which makes such interpretation viable.

There is still, even at this point, the possibility of *arbitration*. Our evidence and other studies provide examples of moments when leaders of police or protestors seek to make contact with the other side to defuse the situation. For example, concessionary gestures by the police, such as the release of an arrested person, can de-escalate conflict. But if either or each side issues ultimata, then one side has to choose to resist or back down. This is rarely achieved without the occurrence of disorder.

The interactional level is where disorder actually occurs. The other levels may make disorder more likely, but its occurrence can never be taken as inevitable. It is possible for disorder to be averted at the interactional level, even when the other levels suggest a propensity to disorder. It is also possible for almost any crowd otherwise predisposed to order to be incensed by a particular action directed against it, especially an indiscriminate one.

From the social scientific point of view, disorder, like all violence, is a form of interaction. It indicates that all other forms of communication have been exhausted and nothing is left but for the strong to conquer the weak. We have been trying to suggest why and how this happens. Explanation is rarely to be found in one single factor. Even where it is possible to identify one or several acts which started the trouble, this rarely of itself explains why such actions were initiated or how and why others interpreted and acted upon them. To understand why a 'spark' sets off a 'fire' we need to analyse the principles of combustion. It is not the presence or absence of an individual element which is important so much as how elements fuse and interact. Our model of analysis has been an attempt to identify not only the groups of relevant variables involved but also to specify the different levels of structuring and determination involved.

A *model of disorder*

Application of the model

The model's application to our case studies is summarized in table 10.2. All of the events contained some potential for disorder at the *structural* level. This is obvious in the case of the economic and class conflicts manifested in the miners' case studies and in the Haymarket fracas involving disadvantaged black youths, though less so in the case of the Thatcher demonstration. But even here, deep-rooted conflicts between the central state and more peripheral forms of political organization could have become a crisis of the state itself. It is not at this level alone that we are able to differentiate automatically between orderly and disorderly situations.

At the *political and ideological* level, further potential and actual differences between our case studies emerge. The established Labour councillors and trade-union officials who organized and led the coalition of interest groups in the orderly Thatcher demonstration had far greater political legitimacy, at least at the local level, than the politically marginalized black youth of the Haymarket incident or the miners and their leadership during the strike. The Grimethorpe public meeting showed how a local community could activate its relationship to politically legitimate leaders and temporarily overcome its marginalization. Otherwise, the miners were (mis)represented as a threat to democracy, in a way the steel strikers of 1980 were not.

Reaction to ideological attack is shaped by the protesting group's *cultural* resources and dispositions. In our discussion of demonstrations in chapter three, we noted how the class, age, and gender of dissenting groups affected their expectations about the 'right' form of protest and their treatment by, and reaction to, the police. Masculinity remains crucial here. Occupations based on male bonding tend to breed a certain 'machismo'; this is as true of the police as it is of miners. In Afro-Caribbean communities male pride is often at stake on the front line. Yet as we saw in cases other than those we have studied, a masculine culture alone does not guarantee whether a situation becomes disorderly. It can be held in check, as the behaviour of miners and police at the main part of the second NUM rally showed.

The *context* will predefine likely responses to conflict. The police seem as capable of nurturing grievances as the protestors, Orgreave being in part 'revenge' for Saltley. However, expectations can be altered by pre-event liaison between organizers and the police, as the second NUM rally in particular, but in fact every single example, showed. Media sensitization may heighten expectations of trouble or make those involved more anxious to aviod it. No protest is without this sort of context which shapes its development.

Planning may structure the *situation* of the protest. Physical layout, specific space which is being contested, and the visibility and symbolism of targets may all vary in each situation but remain constant as crucial factors. Two demonstrations in the middle of Sheffield, one by radical groups and the other by miners, may superficially be similar but on examination turn out to be significantly different in these situational factors. Picketing and community disorders reproduce the salience of these factors, where crowd and police behaviour define and reflect both the situation and its possibilities of action.

It is at this level of *interaction* that the flashpoint may occur. Previous levels may make its occurrence more or less likely but do not determine it altogether. The orderly and good-humoured police–demonstrator interaction of the Hadfields picket, the Thatcher demonstration, or the second NUM rally could have been disrupted by the kinds of provocative behaviour evident at Orgreave, at the first NUM rally, in the Haymarket, and on the streets of Maltby and Grimethorpe.

It is quite clear, as one of the lessons of the miners' strike and of the inner-city riots, that when conditions are propitious for disorder at every level, then its occurrence is more likely. However, it can also occur if only some levels are conducive to it. Specifying exactly what those are requires more extensive application of the model to refine it. One possibility is comparison of this model with others claiming dominance in the field.

Theorizing disorder

The theoretical status of the argument we have presented may be usefully explored by contrasting it with Smelser's influential theory of collective behaviour, to which our model bears a passing resemblance. Smelser defines collective behaviour as 'an uninstitutionalised mobilisation for action in order to modify one or more kinds of strain on the basis of a generalised reconsititution of a component of action' (1962, 71). This definition is only meaningful in the context of the structural–functional model of social action elaborated by Parsons (1951) which underlies Smelser's work. Society's existence is seen as dependent on its successful fulfilment of such functional imperatives as internal integration, task accomplishment, and so on. Social institutions

Table 10.2 Application of flashpoints model to case studies

Level of structuration	Case study		
	'Thatcher Unwelcoming'	First miners' rally	Hadfields
Structural	Economic/political conflict; regional, class, and sectional	Economic conflict/political disaffection; regional and class	Narrowly economic normal industrial dispute
Political/ ideological	Political legitimacy of organizers and most protesters; ideological marginalization but not vilification	Political illegitimacy of miners and leadership; ideological vilification	Semi-legitimacy of strike as 'apolitical'
Cultural	Cultural rejection of violence by mixed age/sex and predominantly middle-class crowd	Cultural acceptance of violence in some situations by male, working-class, mainly young crowd	Cultural acceptance of violence in some situations; male working-class mainly young crowd/shared occupational culture
Contextual	Pre-event communication between crowd organizers and police good; no recent local history of disorder	Recent police–picket clashes; widespread media vilification of miners and strike	Previously peaceful strikes
Situational	Situation defined as normal demonstration; physical separation of crowd from targets; no symbolic significance of venue; space not confined	Situation defined as conflictual; symbolic significance of NUM building for miners; physically confined space	Situation defined as routine picket; no immediate threat to public or property nor any symbolic space or targets
Interactional	Situational norm of non-violence; verbal exchanges good humoured; arrests perceived as justified; speeches and music to occupy crowd	Verbal exchanges ill-tempered; physical violence provoked retaliation; arrests resisted; no diversions for crowd; symbolic targets present	Mutual respect of pickets and police; absence of provocative behaviour; both sides restrained

Orgreave	Haymarket	Maltby / Grimethorpe
Political conflict/political disaffection; regional and class	Economic disadvantage/ political marginalization; racial, class, and generational	Political conflict/political disaffection; regional and class
Political illegitimacy of miners and leadership; ideological vilification	Political illegitimacy of young blacks and black leaders; ideological construction of blacks/youth as problem/threat	Political illegitimacy of miners and leadership; ideological vilification
Cultural acceptance of violence in some situations; male working-class mainly young crowd/shared occupational culture	Cultural acceptance of violence in certain situations by young male, black, and working-class crowd	Cultural acceptance of violence in some situations; male working-class mainly young crowd/shared community culture
Recent clashes on picket lines and roadblocks; extensive media sensitization and vilification; police tactics prepared in advance	Previous complaints from shopkeepers; media sensitization due to widespread urban riots of 1981	Confrontation on picket lines; complaints by NCB/local residents
Picket definition of situation as infringement of right to picket divergent from police definition of situation as illegal picket; physical space confined; symbolic targets (lorries) present	Situation defined as threatening by traders and police; rival claims to occupation of space; symbolic significance of venue; physically confined space	Residents' definition of situation as one of infringement of customary rights divergent from that of police; symbolic significance of communal space and of targets: police personnel and property and street locations
Flashpoints of appearance of lorries and arrest of Scargill; violence answered by violence	No shared behavioural norms; verbal exchanges conflictual; attempted arrest perceived as not legitimate; violence provoked violence	Flashpoints of arrests on streets and outside pubs and attacks on police stations exacerbated by verbal abuse; violence answered by violence

such as the family, schooling, and the political system, are analysed in terms of their functional role within the wider society. Human activity is also seen in functional terms: it is so organized as to ensure that the functional requirements of institutions and of society as a whole are met.

Parsons analyses human action in terms of four integrative elements in society: values, norms, mobilization into roles, and situational facilities. Values define the aims of the action; norms or rules of conduct regulate activity; interdependent roles guide it into socially appropriate channels; and situational facilities, including material and cultural resources available to actors, enable these processes to be realized in concrete action. Values stand highest and situational facilities lowest in a hierarchy reflecting both their importance in determining human action and their level of abstraction. Thus values are the most important yet least tangible of influences, while situational facilities are the most tangible but least important.

Each component has itself various levels of organization – seven in all – which again run from the most general to the most specific. For example, within the value component, a general value such as 'freedom' has to be translated at each level of institutionalization until it reaches that of the individual's beliefs and action. If changes occur at higher levels but are not translated into change at lower levels, strain will result. Collective behaviour is a manifestation of such strain and indicates an imbalance in the system.

Smelser adds to these complex frameworks six further determinants: structural conduciveness, structural strain, crystallization of a generalized belief, precipitating factors, mobilization for action, and social control. Each determinant contributes its own effect to the overall process.

> We conceive the operation of these determinants as a value-added process. Each determinant is a necessary condition for the next to operate as a determinant in an episode of collective behaviour. As the necessary conditions accumulate, the explanation of the episode becomes more determinate. Together the necessary conditions constitute the sufficient condition for the episode. (1962, 382)

These 'two sets of organising constructs: the components of social action and the value added process' (Smelser 1962, 383) are said to 'supplement' one another, accumulating a total set of conditions in which order becomes more or less likely. Each determinant has its own sequence. For example, the growth of a hostile belief goes in five stages: ambiguity, anxiety, assignment of blame/responsibility to agents, desire to punish those responsible, and a generalized belief in omnipotence. In addition, the precipitating factors have specific effects on the growth of such a belief in that they may confirm existing hatreds, introduce new deprivation, reduce opportunities for peaceful protest, and symbolize a failure for which responsibility must be assigned (1962, 249–51).

Table 10.3 Comparison of flashpoints with Smelser's model

Flashpoints model	Smelser model
Structural: conflicts of interest based on material differences in life-chances and access to economic/political resources	*Structural conduciveness:* physical and organizational facilitators/constraints, differing according to type of behaviour
Political/ideological: lack of representation; alienation from dominant political order; group vilified/presented as threat	*Structural strain:* conflicts of interest; means–ends ambiguities; normative malintegration; differences in values
Cultural: beliefs, values, ways of living constitutive of group identity based on class/locality/ethnicity/occupation, etc.	*Crystallization of belief:* generalized beliefs differing according to type of behaviour creating common culture spread by rumour, etc.
Contextual: previous episodes of conflict; formal/informal communication channels (rumour, liaison); media sensitization	*Precipitating factors:* incident or rumour of incident indicative of breakdown of relations; hostile outburst; sudden threat or deprivation
Situational: physical setting; organization of crowd/police; immediate objectives of crowd and police; presence/absence of symbolic targets	*Mobilization for action:* role/type of leadership; degree/type of crowd organization; ecological factors (distribution of disaffection/location of targets)
Interactional: violence towards symbolic targets; over-reaction to aggression; rejection of arbitration; breaking of situational norms	*Social control:* decisiveness of authorities; firmness of agents of order; commitment to law and order; redirection of crowd attention

Table 10.3 summarizes the main features of our model as compared to Smelser's. His model refers to collective behaviour in general rather than situations of actual or potential public disorder, so the table refers specifically to his category of 'hostile outburst' which includes riots and other instances of public disorder involving police–crowd confrontations.

At first glance, there are considerable similarities between our model and that of Smelser, to the extent that only a few ways of grouping and defining categories seem to differ. We specify six levels whereas Smelser's general model of social action has seven, and his specific model of collective behaviour has six determinants. The basic similarities between our model and Smelser's are that both:

1 are structural models in which social structure rather than individual or group factors is seen as generating disorder
2 are of general applicability to a range of instances of public disorder
3 involve multicausal rather than monocausal explanations
4 distinguish between general underlying conditions and more specific precipitating factors
5 see disorder as resulting from a combination of factors at different levels.

We differ, however, on the theoretical presuppositions underlying Smelser's model, the kinds of explanation to which it gives rise, and the policy recommendations which follow from it.

Smelser's commitment to the construction of a general theory of collective behaviour depends crucially on a concept – strain – meaningful only to those who see society as a self-regulating system. It is in practice less important than what he calls 'structural conduciveness'. Underlying roots of conflicts are taken to be less important than the characteristics of the situation in which potentially conflicting groups find themselves. This reverses our order of determination, where conflict at the structural level is a basic precondition for disorder.

Differences of labelling and ordering thus turn out to be substantial differences in how disorder is to be conceptualized and explained. This is further evident in the little emphasis placed by Smelser on the historical and political contexts in which disorder may arise. Different groups, situations, social contexts, and historical periods are collapsed into one generic category. The model succeeds in being both ahistorical and apolitical.

Nor does it pay sufficient attention to the details of interaction. Smelser counterposes the crowd, seen as unpredictable in its dynamics and predisposed to irrational behaviour, with a rational and disciplined state force whose only function is to control the crowd. The role of any kind of communication other than the directive is denied. Smelser refers to but does not analyse incidents which might be called flashpoints. Otherwise, interaction appears only as control exercised by the authorities.

Nor can we accept Smelser's advocacy of the 'short, sharp

shock' theory of riot control. 'When the authorities issue firm, unyielding and unbiased decisions in short order, the hostile outburst is dampened' (1962, 265). His prescriptions for avoiding disorder seem to us more likely to cause it:

(a) Prevent communication in general, so that beliefs cannot be disseminated. (b) Prevent interaction between leaders and followers, so that mobilisation is difficult. (c) Refrain from taking a conditional attitude towards violence by bluffing or vacillating in the use of the ultimate weapons of force. (d) Refrain from entering the issues and controversies that move the crowd; remain impartial, unyielding and fixed on the principle of maintaining law and order.   (Smelser 1962, 267)

How the agents of order are expected to prevent 'interaction between leaders and followers'\, let alone 'communication in general', remains obscure. The advice to troops and police to refrain from taking sides in controversies is admirable in theory, but ignores both the cultural predispositions of the agents of order themselves and the political context within which they are operating. Maintaining 'law and order' is assumed to be an unambiguous goal.

Smelser's crowd control strategies seem to us wrong in principle. They are derived logically from his model of disorder and thus reflect its inherent weaknesses. Because he removes interactional and interpretative process from his model, he is left only with the possibility of the cultural and psychological dispositions of the crowd – their hostility, aggression – as causes of disorder. That the agents of social control may also be susceptible to such pressures escapes his attention. The theoretical presuppositions of structural functionalism and the flaws in his model lead to the advocacy of policies which we would see as counterproductive, precisely because they are all based on a misconception of what disorder is, how it comes about, and how it might be avoided.

Kent State as a test case

Our differences with Smelser can be illustrated by brief consideration of a case study of the Kent State incident. This confrontation between students and civil guards at Kent State University, Ohio in May 1970 followed President Nixon's announcement that American troops had been sent into Cambodia. A planned demonstration by students was banned by the

State Governor. Students congregated anyway and began to taunt and stone the National Guard. Eventually the Guard attacked the crowd. Four students were shot dead and many more seriously injured. The incident provoked the first national student strike in American history, and intensified protest against the war.

Lewis (1975), who was himself present as a faculty peace marshal, has offered an analysis of these events utilizing Smelser's model. Lewis admits finding no evidence of some of Smelser's factors, such as the 'state of anxiety' in the crowd which should precede a 'crystallization of belief', but otherwise concludes Smelser's model to have provided a viable explanation of what occurred. We cannot agree with this evaluation and would argue that Smelser's model marginalizes, ignores, or misrepresents factors vital to the occurrence of disorder which our own model would succeed in highlighting.

Among these are factors included in Lewis's narrative but omitted from his analysis. We would lay much greater stress upon the structural conflict behind the protest, between a student-led anti-war movement and a Republican president and his 'silent majority'. The way this had been translated in the political arena into a defence of patriotism and the American way of life against communism abroad and its sympathizers at home would seem an integral part of the conflict, stressed by our emphasis on the political/ideological level. Such incompatibilities of interest and definition permitted the State Governor to issue an instruction to the National Guard that all assemblies, whether peaceful or violent, were to be broken up, an authoritative and unequivocal instruction to state forces to adopt an absolutist version of their legal responsibilities.

One of the most serious weaknesses of Lewis's account, as of Smelser's model itself, is the failure to explain the interaction between state authorities and the crowd. Lewis's justification for this absence is that few guardsmen gave evidence to the Scranton Commission, which was appointed to investigate student protest. This is a fatal flaw, one permitted by a model which denies any independent motives or action to the forces of social control. The 'machismo' and group solidarity of the National Guard would have provided a cultural clash with the radical values and lifestyles of the students and resulted in mutual stereotyping. The effect of this on the viability of any accommodation between the groups is tacitly admitted by Lewis who concedes that the National Guard's refusal to negotiate or liaise with the faculty peace marshals pre-empted one possibility of avoiding disorder.

Lewis gives too little weight to the report of the President's Commission on Campus Unrest (the Scranton Report (1970)), which emphasized the resentment felt by students at the invasion of their university 'turf' by the National Guard and the denial of their right of peaceful assembly.

Lewis's account does not seem to validate Smelser's model. Our own model, grounded in data rather than abstract theory, turns out to be a much better identifier of factors conducive to disorder, even for an event in another country and some time ago, for which we only have secondary evidence.

Structures and meanings

We do not claim to have solved the many problems which beset any attempt to model the processes which maintain public order or provoke outbreaks of disorder. In the introduction (pp. 10–12), we suggested that any adequate theory of disorder should be able to circumscribe its applicability, explain disorder as a distinctively group activity to which meanings are given, and be able to causally connect disorder to its specific economic and political context. We have somewhat tentatively delimited our area of concern by focusing on issue-oriented rather than issue-less disorder. We have also tried through our six levels of analysis to encompass both the broadest level of structural conflict and the narrowest of interactions where flashpoints occur. We have tried to indicate the kinds of processes which connect them. Yet problems remain in the basic definitions of the structural roots of conflict and the meanings given to the situation by those involved, which undermine attempts to interrelate them.

There is a temptation to see disorder as a simple reflection of structural conflict: inner-city riots reflect racial conflict, picketing disorders reflect industrial conflict, demonstrations reflect ideological conflict. All structuralist theories are open to this temptation. The French urban geographer Castells, for example, has attempted to construct a Marxist theory of urban processes, focusing on community organizations. His early work (1976), based on an Althusserian theoretical framework, defined three key components of the social formation: the economic, the political, and the ideological. In the last instance the economic determines which level is dominant at any given historical conjuncture, but not the precise form which it may take.

The 'urban' is seen as a terrain of struggles over the provision of housing, health, and other services, giving rise to protest movements of various kinds, such as tenants and neighbourhood organizations. The essential parameters of urban struggles are structural contradictions at the economic level, ultimately manifested in traditional class struggles at the point of production. Frustration at the failure of the system to produce socially necessary facilities creates tension, which if not defused by political means threatens the break-down of order.

The basic problems involved in this approach are precisely those of defining 'structural contradictions' and explaining how they generate motivated action. Contradictions in society may create conflict but, as Saunders pertinently asks (1981, 201), why do the same system contradictions give rise to 'wild' spontaneous reactions in one area, to organized political movements in another, and to apathetic resignation in a third? Other factors apparently need to be taken into account but the theory does not specify what these are or how they relate to underlying contradictions.

Similarly unsatisfactory is Castells' failure to explain how those involved in the 'urban struggle' perceive their situation, either in terms of formal ideological conceptions or everyday taken-for-granted cultural perspectives. In Castells' early Althusserian model – as in Parsonian structural-functionalism – human activity and intentionality are absent: they have no *raison d'être* other than to reproduce economic and social structures. For Castells, human actors are merely the 'support-agents expressing particular combinations of the social structure through their practice' (Castells 1976, 78).

This deficiency remained, despite Castells' later (1983) attempts to revise the theory, producing a more active definition of 'community movements' which 'fight to defend or create communities with a particular cultural identity arising from particular historic or ethnic sources' (cited in Lowe 1986, 34).

In his attempt to remedy the problems of Castells' model, Pickvance still has to retain a diffuse variable of 'general economic and social conditions'. He does, however, concede that an unresolved issue is whether the key explanatory variables 'are limited to "hard" structural features of societies . . . or whether they include "softer" structural features such as "cultural understandings"' (cited in Lowe 1986, 182).

Thus, although rooted at the other end of the academic spectrum from Smelser, Castells' work reveals the same problems. 'Structural contradictions' replace 'structural strain' but the definition is no clearer. Human action is still seen as reflective of underlying social structures rather than reflexive and purposeful. The difficulty stems from a top-down formalistic mode of analysis, beginning with society theorized as a totality and then trying to work down to largely hypothetical social situations.

An obvious alternative to such an approach is to start with actors' perceptions of their situation and analyse the meaning they attribute to their behaviour. An example of this approach is Moscovici's theory of 'social representations' (Moscovici 1981, Moscovici and Hewstone 1983), which appears to offer the possibility of linking sociological to social psychological processes. These representations have been defined as 'concepts, statements and expectations originating in daily life in the course of inter-individual communication' which constitute 'common sense "theories" about key aspects of society' (Moscovici and Hewstone 1983, 115). The activity of a group is explicable in terms of such consensually shared understandings of given situations. As Potter and Wetherell point out, social representation theory is not easy to describe. 'Moscovici's writings are fragmented and sometimes contradictory . . . and researchers have tended to interpret the theory in widely different ways' (1987, 139).

A number of studies using this approach have analysed accounts of the riot at St Paul's in Bristol during 1980. Litton and Potter (1985) found little agreement about the causes of the riot or about such key terms as 'racial', 'cuts', and 'amenities' used to describe its context. This finding may reflect the researchers' failure to distinguish adequately between the participants' accounts and those of other parties.

Three corresponding studies (Reicher 1984, Reicher and Potter 1985, Potter and Reicher 1987) highlight a strong degree of uniformity in the participants' explanations of their actions. Typically, such accounts emphasized the role of police 'brutality', 'harassment', or 'repression' in the creation of conflict and characterized the riot as a collective attempt to rid St Paul's of an 'illegitimate and alien police presence' (Reicher 1984, 13).

Significantly, the crowd members regarded themselves as 'representing the entirety of St Paul's in the sense of an independent community fighting for its right to survive . . . the notion of community was a real, albeit ideological, creation for participants' (Reicher 1984, 15). As Potter and Reicher (1987, 37) point out, this ingroup perspective encourages a reformulation of the event 'from a "riot" to "fighting back": a legitimate and rational action against the police, rather than a blind, irrational conflagration'. This contrasted with media and other external accounts which portrayed the riot as totally irrational.

Approaches to 'social representations' are as yet insufficiently coherent to warrant the title of theory. The source of such interpretations, and the forms in which they are collectively sustained, remain unexplored. Still less have any of these concerns been related to more sociological concepts of social structure and culture.

The problem of defining 'structure' and 'meaning' and their interrelationship is not confined to the study of public disorder but inherent in the social scientific enterprise of understanding human behaviour. Our model of public disorder cannot hope to resolve it and we claim no more than the ability of our model to encompass and interrelate more significant variables in the genesis of public disorder than any other we have encountered. It remains to consider its implications for the formation of policies designed to minimize public disorder.

11
Public order policy

The miners' strike was a watershed in the recent history of public disorder and its policing:

> The strike revealed changes and trends which had already happened or were underway before it began – in policing and the law particularly: the continuing movement of these trends appears as a theme both during and after the strike.
>
> (McCabe and Wallington 1988, 7)

A number of the events analysed or mentioned in this book mark a progressive escalation of the problem:

> A litany of names charts the changes in police strategy: Saltley; Red Lion Square; Notting Hill; Lewisham; Grunwick; Southall; St Paul's; Brixton; Toxteth; Warrington; Orgreave; Stonehenge; Handsworth; Broadwater Farm; Wapping . . . in the post war context they amount to a sea-change in the policing of disorder. New forms of organization, new equipment and a new readiness to deploy *de facto* riot squads trained in 'tactical options' indicates the deterioration in police–society relations and, perforce, the relationship between state and society.
>
> (Brewer *et al.* 1988, 32)

The issues raised range from particular actions by specific police officers in situations of actual or potential disorder through to the changing balance between the rights of the citizen and the powers of the state. In this chapter, we consider four central issues: police culture, public order law, the status of civil rights, and the constitutional position of the police.

The police occupational subculture

Accounts of the police occupational subculture (Skolnick 1966,

Manning 1977, Holdaway 1983, Reiner 1985) perceive it as a form of organizational reality or common sense which helps to categorize and thus make more manageable the people, places, situations, and encounters daily confronted by junior officers. While the police occupational culture varies in its precise forms and application, its basic premises are consistent:

> The culture of the police – the values, norms, perspectives and craft rules – which inform their conduct is, of course, neither monolithic, universal, nor unchanging. There are differences of outlook within police forces, according to such individual variables as personality, generation or career trajectory, and structured variations according to rank, assignment and specialization. The organizational styles and cultures of police forces vary between different places and periods . . . and . . . according to particular concrete situations and the interactional process of each encounter. None the less, certain commonalities of the police outlook can be discerned.
>
> (Reiner 1985, 86–7)

Both Reiner and Holdaway stress the pragmatic and anti-theoretical orientation of the police culture. The application of the law to concrete situations is preferred in a way which marginalizes political, historical, or psychological considerations. What Skolnick (1966) terms a 'cop culture' predefines tactical responses to difficult circumstances. Thus, as Holdaway (1983) points out, junior officers will feel familiar with all known 'sites of danger'. They are likely to arrive on the scene with the situation almost totally 'weighed up', in Manning's phrase (1977, 236), and once there will choose the 'recipe for action' (1977, 236) considered most appropriate. For example, Holdaway explains that 'an arrest is sometimes made in the hope that it will contain the conflict and etch the boundary of police tolerance' (1983, 39).

Southgate (1982) analyses how police action towards groups and individuals is predicated on a narrow set of typifications, especially of ethnic minorities. Though his research showed that the experience of policing black communities softened as many police attitudes as it hardened, Southgate concludes that overall the dominant view was 'unsympathetic' towards West Indians particularly, manifested in the use of such racist terms as 'bucks', 'coons', and 'niggers'. Smith and Gray (1985) emphasize that such hostility was not always evident in police officers' actual dealings with black people, understanding such language as the 'rhetoric' of a working group, helping to maintain collective solidarity. But when, as in the aftermath of the riots, blacks were identified as a threat, then racist attitudes were more openly expressed and allowed to govern action. Thus, the use of dogs to control black youths became the norm.

Such responses receive further endorsement from another aspect of police culture: its commitment to action, hedonism, and challenge. Holdaway reports that any calls for assistance were immediately broadcast to all officers both in cars and on foot, generating a sense of excitement. 'The prospect of a violent disturbance or a riot is certainly found interesting and exciting by many police officers' (Smith and Gray 1985, 341), though sometimes tinged with apprehension.

This positive evaluation of the prospect of action is rooted in the avowedly male and masculinist ethos which dominates the police subculture (Reiner 1985). Its particular emphases are on physicality, aggression, and heterosexuality. This ethos recognizes the frailty of respectable women but has a range of abusive terms, such as 'whores', 'slags', or 'filth' for women whose conduct or associations are thought to forfeit their right to respect (Scraton 1985b). Both violence and sexuality serve to define the male camaraderie of the force. 'Stories of fighting and violence tend to come up in conversation alongside, and mixed in with, sexual conquests and feats of drinking: all three combine together in a cult of masculinity' (Smith and Gray, 1985, 369).

The police nevertheless have a strong sense of their own role as moral custodians of society, which entitles them to respect from members of the public. Their person is particularly inviolate, so that any bodily interference with an officer results in immediate retribution to restore what Holdaway calls 'the virtual sanctity of the uniform'.

> For the lower-ranking police officer, the uniform he wears conveys an authority that he will not willingly see questioned or diminished. If a reduction of that authority is the price of neutrality as between one group of citizens and another, he will not normally pay that price.
>
> (McCabe and Wallington 1988, 82)

In any sort of confrontation the police have a particular status need to ensure that they come out on top (Bittner 1967). Notions of credibility and loss of face are clearly inseparable from the strong occupational commitment to authority, respect, and control:

> As police control of the 'turf' is effectively challenged and rioters gain control of the streets by default, the word may

183

> spread . . . that the rioters have 'beat the police'. Losing face,
> humiliated by their temporary defeat and with their profes-
> sional pride undermined, the police may have a strong desire
> for revenge and to show their efficacy.   (Marx 1970, 49)

These attributes have particular implications for the policing of
public order. The police reaction at all levels to perceived
defeats, as at Saltley in 1972 and St Paul's in 1981, seems to have
been two-fold: a determination not to let it happen again and a
desire to get their own back. This element of retribution was
evident in the community disturbances we studied, as were
instances of racist and sexist abuse.

It is when the police feel themselves and their office under
most challenge that the cardinal values of the subculture find
their clearest expression. In the drawing of the line between 'us'
and 'them', there is no room for other points of view to be
considered, much less understood. When this culture meets that
of the Afro-Caribbean community, the definitions of what
constitutes normal behaviour are totally incompatible.

Reiner observed similar disjunctions of perspectives between
police and pickets: 'What was absent from the policemen's
perspective was any consideration of the issues underlying
picketing. The relevant problem to them was public order' (1977,
55). In his later work (1985, 97), Reiner argues that the police
tend to share the broad political and legal ideals of the
'respectable' working and middle classes.

The inherent political conservatism of the police occupational
culture is uncompromising. The law is an absolute and those who
infringe it in any way should be summarily dealt with. Senior
officers who consider the political implications of their decisions,
or who become involved in bargaining, are regarded as soft
(Reiner 1977, 93). Rank-and-file officers declare their willingness
to fire plastic bullets but see senior officers as too timid to give
them the order (BBC2 The Queen's Peace 22 October 1986).

There is always a potential clash between the 'bureaucratic
reality' of senior and chief police officers and the 'highly
contingent and practical definitions of the lower ranks' (Holdaway ed. 1979, 7). The latter are liable to experience 'mounting
frustration and anger' (Manning 1977, 54) if senior officers fail to
respond immediately and with force. When the order is
eventually given, frustration and anger will find expression in the
vigour of police response. Junior officers are also likely to take
the absence of senior officers as an opportunity to deal with a
situation in the way they believe should be the habitual one.

The open and rigid nature of these attitudes should not be underestimated. In the absence of any control or discipline exerted upon it, the police occupational culture is itself conducive to disorder. From its perspective, order is not to be maintained by negotiation but imposed through force. Order exists when the police are totally in charge, disorder when for any reason their control is physically threatened. There is only one valid definition of the situation: that of the police. Any consideration of other perceptions and interpretations is redundant. What demonstrators, pickets, or members of communities think or feel is irrelevant. The only purpose of talking to people is to tell them what to do. In so far as other parties involved are considered at all, they are viewed through racial, sexual, and political stereotypes. The most important feature of interaction with such groups is not to lose face. The best reaction to a volatile situation is to effect an arrest, to show who's in charge.

Public order policing conducted on these principles would involve applying the law inflexibly, untainted by any gestures towards compromise. No attempt would be made to reach a formal or informal accommodation with the crowd. Superiority would be established by an imposing police presence and dictation of the crowd's activities. Any hint of disorder would produce an instant and indiscriminate police response. Physical or verbal mistreatment of officers would be responded to in kind, if necessary in numbers and with force. In short, left to itself, the police occupational culture would consistently provoke crowd disorder.

The theory of police organization is that this occupational culture is in practice never left to itself. It is constrained within a legal framework and directed by the supervision of senior officers, whose views are necessarily more sensitive. We have some limited evidence that such control can be exercised. At the 'Thatcher Unwelcoming' demonstration, officers were instructed to fraternize with the crowd and clearly did so. At the second NUM rally, senior officers intervened to avoid provoking the crowd. But on other occasions – Southall, Manchester University, Orgreave, Maltby, and Grimethorpe – senior officers were prepared to condone any method of achieving their goals. In other cases, the control was not exercised because no senior officers were present. Where police officers are led by sergeants, or at most inspectors, then the instincts of the lower ranks dictate police tactics, as in the confrontations which took place after the NUM rallies.

This specific belief in the efficacy of violence as a means of maintaining public order is integrally related to the dependence of the occupational culture on masculinity. Without understanding that this is a man's world, any view of police life is inadequate. The use of racial and especially gender stereotypes, the identification of self-worth with the showing of deference by others, the importance of not losing face, the belief that 'we're all mates in this together', are all specifically masculine ideals. There are no female equivalents. They are not unique to the police force and can be found in other subcultures. It is precisely when the police are confronted by groups who share this masculine ethos, such as miners and Afro-Caribbean youth, that disorder is most likely. The ends of the conflicting groups will differ, but their natural means of achieving them will be similar. In this specific sense, whatever else may divide them, the police are actually very like those with whom they are in conflict. They share masculine culture.

The ramifications of this cannot be pursued here but we can consider how the worst excesses of this masculine style might be controlled within the police force. Police training could be directed to unlearning the responses which the typical background and outlook of the police officer would produce in volatile situations. Whatever competence in riot control the modern police officer may need, this should at the very least be balanced by some training in riot prevention. Most generally, this should start with some attempt to allay the worst excesses of the racist and sexist stereotyping to which police officers seem to be prone. As Smith and Gray (1985) discovered, the current gestures towards this goal in training programmes do not survive the first few months in the company of serving officers. It may appear unreasonable to expect police officers to refrain from responding in kind when the subject of abuse, but if the objective is to defuse the situation, then this is what is required. It is depressing to hear, as we have done, police officers suggesting that the cultural problem with Afro-Caribbeans is that they have none.

The most viable tactics for dealing with crowds also require attention. We have suggested that, wherever possible, crowds should be allowed to police themselves, that serious negotiations should be undertaken with leaders, both beforehand and on the spot, that concessions which may appear to 'lose face' may gain the more important objective of maintaining order. The emphasis has to be on compromise and negotiation; we fear it is currently on conflict and authority. Force should only be used in the last resort and then selectively, not out of cowardice, but because the alternative is an escalating spiral of violence.

It is not our understanding that these are currently the emphases in what is a very brief period of police training (twelve weeks in 1988). This is essentially the conclusion of McCabe and Wallington (1988). They note that the strength of the police subculture makes attitudes difficult to change. The need to consult and negotiate with the parties to social conflict is one crucial basis for the maintenance of both public order and civil liberties. The alternative is 'policing . . . misguided in its failure to focus on the central objective of policing – the preservation of order – as a broad goal and its disregard for the civil liberties of all concerned' (McCabe and Wallington 1988, 140).

Uglow argues that the concept of order requires clarification:

> Order is not simply regularity, pattern, conformity, and tranquillity in everyday life; it is a more complex notion – the knowledge that person and property are protected not by patronage or physical might but by rights is a form of order which signifies the stability and health of constitutional arrangements. (1988, 84)

The police conception of order is quite different, based on the idea that 'in public, people should be routinely walking, shopping, or passing the time of day'. Almost by definition, the gathering of a crowd constitutes a threat to this version of public order since 'they disrupt the routine flow of people and vehicles' (Uglow 1988, 84). It is this idea, that public order is incompatible with the presence of any crowd, which is at the heart of recent public order legislation.

Public disorder and the law

The election which brought the Conservative government to power in 1979 was fought in part on a law-and-order platform. On a whole range of issues, the Conservative Party was committed to strengthening police powers to control public order situations. Football hooliganism, picketing, and inner-city riots were all subsequently defined as different manifestations of the same underlying problem of 'violence' and hence susceptible to the same legal and policing solutions. The results have been summarized by Brewer *et al.*:

> Taken together, the existing law in relation to terrorism, the recent Police and Criminal Evidence Act and the changes to public order law represent a quantum leap in police powers,

187

reinforcing the view that the British state is becoming more authoritarian. The public order law will mean that the police, besides being charged with the duty to keep the peace, will be enabled to mediate the already constrained ability to engage in protest and dissent on a much wider front. (1988, 31)

Since 1979, the government has instigated a number of reports and investigations producing a range of recommendations for the reform of public order legislation. These are summarized below following Card (1987). Among these was the Home Office *Review of Arrangements for Handling Spontaneous Disorder* (1980) which focused particularly on the law relating to public assemblies and to racial hatred. In the same year the House of Commons Select Committee on Home Affairs produced a *Report on the Law Relating to Public Disorder* which also looked at the 1936 Act's provisions covering meetings and processions.

Lord Scarman's report on the Brixton disorders (Scarman 1981) also evaluated the law on public disorder, considering it adequate in the main and not in need of reformulation. The Law Commission also investigated aspects of public order law, producing in 1982 a Working Paper on *Offences Against Public Order* and in the following year a *Report on Criminal Law: Offences Relating to Public Order*. Many of the proposals in these reports were incorporated into the government's own White Paper *Review of Public Order Law* in 1985, which provided the framework for the Public Order Act 1986.

The Act is divided into five parts. Part I deals with riots and other offences against public order, Part II with processions and assemblies, Part III with incitement to racial hatred, Part IV with provisions for crowd control at football grounds, and Part V with various miscellaneous provisions such as aggravated trespass (section 39). The three schedules which form part of the Act either repeal obsolete legislation or emend that still considered useful.

A discussion of the Act in its entirety is available in Card (1987). We wish only to emphasize how certain features of the Act designed to decrease the possibility of public disorder may actually increase it. Three considerations of this kind are: firstly, the increase in overall police discretion in interpreting and enforcing the law; secondly, the ambiguity of key sections on the offences of riot, violent disorder, and affray; and thirdly, increased police powers over the conditions under which demonstrations and marches may take place.

The extension of police discretionary powers takes little

account of the difficulty of making fine judgements in what by definition is a confused situation. For example, in order to be found guilty of riot, the accused should be among twelve or more persons who use or threaten violence for a common purpose, and whose conduct would cause a person of 'reasonable firmness' present at the scene to fear for his personal safety. The problems arising here are enormous. The major practical difficulty is that of correctly identifying the participants in a violent mêlée, which the new provisions resolve no more effectively than the old. The subsequent failure of prosecutions for riot following the Orgreave and Broadwater Farm disturbances attest to this difficulty.

Distinguishing between participants and bystanders is also likely to be a problem, since the boundaries for liability for riot are wide. Mere presence may be interpreted as providing encouragement of violence and those who do not themselves use violence may be defined as accomplices of those who do. As one commentator puts it, 'anybody who fails to dissociate himself effectively and rapidly when a riot develops will render himself liable to conviction' (Smith 1985, 20).

A further problem lies in the stipulation that the conduct should give rise to fear for their safety in a member of the public. It is not necessary for anyone actually to be present, or even that the activity should happen in a public place, since the Act also applies to private premises. The notion of the hypothetical bystander seems to give extensive latitude for the police to decide whether the conduct would give rise to fear. This criticism also applies to the new offence of 'violent disorder' and the redefinition of 'affray' since both involve reference to conduct giving rise to fear. The offence of 'violent disorder' differs from 'riot' in that only three people need be involved and a common purpose is not necessary. 'Affray' covers the threat of unlawful violence towards another and is aimed at incidents such as gang fights.

We can anticipate the likely consequences of such legislation on police conduct and its perception by others. Any law which leaves such wide scope for creative interpretation is bound to lead to both actual and perceived miscarriages of justice, which can only exacerbate the tensions which led to the outbreak of the disorder in the first place. Arbitrary arrest, even if carried out in good faith, may provoke crowd response.

The invitation to wider powers of police discretion is encouraged by the vagueness with which certain key offences have been defined. This is our second area of concern. The new offence of using threatening, abusive, or insulting words or behaviour is extended to private premises and no longer requires an actual or likely breach of the peace. The intention is to protect those subject to such behaviour whose response would not normally constitute a breach of the peace, such as the elderly or members of ethnic minorities. The danger is that merely tiresome behaviour may now be defined as falling within the scope of the Act. In fact, even a private argument in which abusive language is used and causes offence will now fall within the scope of the Act. Furthermore, under section 5 of the 1986 Act such behaviour may lead to arrest if carried out merely within earshot of a person likely to be caused 'harassment, alarm or distress'. As Card comments,

> It is certainly arguable that the elasticity of some of the terms in Section Five leaves the boundaries of the offence to be settled in particular cases by the police and the magistrates. The legislative techniques of drafting offences in vague terms and trusting that they will be enforced sensibly after the event is not one to be encouraged.   (Card 1987, 55)

Given the well attested tendency of the police to consider certain sections of the population as intrinsically suspicious and troublesome, it seems likely that these sections of the Act will come to be used as a means of controlling the activities of the young and/or black and/or unconventional.

The third area of concern arises from the provisions of the Act relating to demonstrations and marches. We again find an increase in police powers, this time over the conditions which organizers and demonstrators must fulfil in order to be allowed to proceed with their activities. These are not counterbalanced by affirmation of the rights of citizens to demonstrate and march in support of a cause or principle.

Under the 1936 Public Order Act there was no formal requirement to notify the police of a planned march or demonstration, though in practice organizers normally informed the police in advance. A Chief Constable had the right to impose conditions on a march, for instance to prescribe its route. In practice these powers were rarely invoked, the police preferring to negotiate informally with the organizers. The solution embodied in the legislation is to remove the space for negotiation by increasing police powers to dictate the conditions for a march or demonstration. Organizers are required to give written notice of their intention to hold such an event, normally six days beforehand. A march or demonstration may take place without the requisite notice but the organizers risk prosecution. Even where correct notice has been given, the police can subsequently ban the march under section 13, effectively rendering the event unlawful.

The process of negotiating conditions is already so fragile that it seems positively counter-productive to give the police total and arbitrary power to sanction marches or demonstrations, without establishing the right to demonstrate. It is not even clear that this will deter demonstrators and is much more likely to result in massed ranks of the police facing a crowd of demonstrators whose presence has been defined as illegal, as at Southall in 1979.

Other limitations on the right to march lie in the powers of the police under section 12 of the Act to impose conditions before the procession. Invested in the Chief Constable initially, such powers can be delegated to the senior officer present once the procession has begun to assemble or is under way. Again, our own research suggests that past attempts by relatively junior officers to intervene in the course of a march or demonstration are frequently resented, especially given the difficulty of communicating to large or moving crowds what the new requirements are, much less any logic which might lie behind them. The conditions which can be imposed are widesweeping, including not only the numbers and the route but also banners and slogans. Failure to comply with such instructions is a criminal offence, so their implementation will require a policy of mass arrests where demonstrators do not comply. More, rather than less, disorder would seem the likely outcome.

Among the considerations listed for the police to take into account when deciding whether or under what conditions a demonstration or march should take place are whether it may result in serious public disorder, cause serious damage to property or serious disruption to the life of the community, or have the purpose of intimidating others with a view to compel them to do something they have the right not to do or to prevent them doing something they have the right to do. All that is required is that the senior officer has a 'reasonable belief' that any of these may pertain. The police are thus given the power to make what can only be guesses, however well-informed, about the intentions or outcome of a demonstration. Such guesses have inherent legitimacy, even if subsequently proved inaccurate – as long as they were 'reasonable'. A possible outcome of these powers is the effective removal of the right to demonstrate from any groups which the police do not trust. Disruption of traffic would be grounds enough.

Only the police are empowered to make these kinds of

judgements; the involvement of local authorities is dependent on the endorsement of a Chief Constable, except in London where application will be made directly to the Home Secretary by the Commissioner for the Metropolitan Police.

This extension of unaccountable police powers over marches also applies to static demonstrations, termed within the Act 'public assemblies'. Defined as gatherings of twenty or more people in a public place wholly or partially in the open air, these were previously subject to no specific statutory controls, apart from local by-laws. The White Paper (1985) saw this as an anomaly, particularly as mass pickets and demonstrations were defined as sources of public disorder. There is to be no requirement of advance notice of public assemblies, but in most other respects the law is the same as that relating to processions. The power to determine numbers is likely to be the crucial factor, since this alone can undermine the effectiveness of a demonstration, as illustrated by police action against a continuous anti-apartheid vigil held outside the South African Embassy in London from 1986 onwards.

Similarly, the law now gives the police power to limit the numbers of pickets at a given location and to direct them where to stand, on the grounds that the purpose of the picket is intimidation, aimed at preventing the exercise of the right to work. This power was exercised *de facto* by the police during the miners' strike but had no statutory force, the reference to six pickets being contained in Department of Employment guidelines which had no legal status. However, pickets refusing to comply with such an instruction could be and frequently were arrested for the common law offence of obstructing a police officer in the execution of his duty or the statutory offence of obstructing the highway.

Thornton (1985) has argued that the legislation largely consolidates legal powers which already existed, but it is difficult not to see the new Public Order Act as the worst kind of politically motivated legislation, designed to appear to be taking action to resolve the problem of public disorder, without any concern to understand the processes underlying the maintenance of order. The *Code of Practice on Picketing* grotesquely oversimplifies the complexity of the problem in its claim that 'the main cause of violence and disorder on the picket line is excessive numbers' (Department of Employment 1980, 29) and plucks the figure of six out of the air as a reasonable number of pickets.

The basic nature of the new Public Order Act has been identified by McCabe and Wallington.

Many of the measures which the Act attests to be acceptable would, before the 1985 riots and the disturbances in 1985 and 1986 at and near Stonehenge, have been called illiberal. Without viable provision for redress of injustice or the prevention of abuse, that is what they are. The control by a senior officer of the size, location and duration of a public demonstration is a form of Riot Act which does not require any judicial imprimatur in the shape of a magistrate's presence or the order of a judge.   (1988, 117)

The basic error in the thinking behind the legislation is the belief that public order is something which has to be enforced. We have argued, and hold our own and others' case studies to validate, the view that public order is the outcome of a fragile consensus which has continually to be negotiated. Most disturbing is the cost to civil liberties of these and other proposed measures. The rights of suspects under interrogation are whittled down, the defence right to peremptory challenge of jurors and the defendant's right to silence are questioned, the jury system itself is under attack. Conspicuously absent from any of these discussions are the rights of the citizen over and against the powers of the state. That public disorder may be rooted in perceived infringements of those rights, and that one such contested right is in fact the right to protest, is not a concern of public order legislators. For those of us with a brief to understand the nature of public disorder, consideration of civil rights is fundamental.

Rights and the law

We have been suggesting that the Public Order Act of 1986 is political in origins and effects. It is in a wider sense an ideological move, in which the extension of state power is legitimized by a misrepresentation of the problem. Two steps are required in this process of legitimation. Firstly, there is the denial of any rational motive or possible justification for the disorderly behaviour. The participants are either politically motivated opponents of the state or their activities are simply a cover for the criminal element in society. The second step is to state that, even where the activities of dissenters are not actually illegal in form, they are illegal in effect because they interfere with the rights of 'ordinary' citizens. The very activity of picketing or demonstrating becomes objectionable because it undermines more inalienable rights such as the right to go to work or the right to free passage in the streets. Thus we are no longer presented with a contrast between order and disorder, based on a distinction between legal and criminal behaviour. Rather, the contrast is between rights of the 'ordinary' citizen which are taken to be self-evident and those of the protestors which have no inherent legitimacy.

Brewer *et al.* (1988) argue in a comparative study of state reaction to public disorder that there are in principle three possible responses: accommodation to the demands of the protesting group, criminalization of their motives and actions, or suppression of the form, and ultimately their right, of protest. The 1980s in Britain have provided much evidence of the latter two reactions and precious little of the first.

In the prevailing definition, order has become a question of the state and its functionaries assuming more power, if necessary at the expense of citizens' rights. This puts at risk the legitimacy of the state, which in democratic societies rests on its role as guarantor of citizens' rights. In a sensitive discussion of this issue, McCabe and Wallington concede the difficulty of defining precisely the scope of citizens' rights but further argue that:

> The assertion of the very existence of these rights, whatever may be the effect of their expression, provides the moral basis and indeed the only justification for the willing submission of citizens to the control of any government, autocratic or popular. Such a contract demands from citizens and government an understanding of the range of freedoms which, in a just society, should be accessible to all.
>
> (McCabe and Wallington 1988, 11)

Public order situations involve two sets of rights: the right to protest and the rights being protested about. That is why we have been attracted to the notion of issue-oriented riots, involving both these claims to rights. The immediate issue at stake may be the right to picket, the right to demonstrate, or the right to be on the street without being harassed by the police. There are great variations in the ways in which these rights are defined in any one situation. The right to picket may or may not be defined by pickets as the right to be present *en masse*, the right to stop and argue with anyone going to work, even the right to shut the gates. What happens in practice is that these rights come to be negotiated with the police. They have to be, since 'picketing is effectively conducted entirely at the discretion of the police' (McCabe and Wallington 1988, 34). The most extreme outcomes are those where the pickets outnumber and outwit the police, thus enforcing their rights over and above the law, as happened at Saltley in 1974; or where the police adopt tactics which effectively prevent any picketing, as happened at Wapping during 1986. At Hadfields, order was maintained by balancing the rights of the pickets against those still working by adopting a flexible interpretation of the law. By contrast, at Orgreave, the law was rigidly upheld in a manner which denied the right to picket and hence provoked disorder.

Crucial in this equation, and thus to the balance of public order, is the extent to which the police do and are seen to recognize the rights of pickets, demonstrators, or members of communities. Such recognition can never be absolute; it is always conditional upon rights being exercised within boundaries. These boundaries are not, however, immutable legal requirements but interpretations negotiated within the particular situation. This was recognized by Lord Scarman in 1974.

> A balance has to be struck, a compromise found that will accommodate the exercise of the right to protest within a framework of public order, which enables citizens, who are not protesting, to go about their business and their pleasure, without obstruction or inconvenience.   (Scarman 1974, 87)

Our own case studies of the 'Thatcher Unwelcoming' and the two NUM rallies indicate quite clearly the viability of this approach. Where order was maintained, this was because the right to demonstrate was conceded and the conditions under which this right could be exercised were negotiated in detail. Disorder resulted from an imbalance between rights and the law. At the first NUM Rally, the conduct of the miners recognized no legal limitations, which then had to be enforced by the police. In the incidents after each rally, the police on the spot adopted the view that the miners had no legal right to be on the street and therefore felt justified in attempting to remove them by force. Two of the most notorious instances of disorder at demonstrations in recent times, at Southall and Manchester University, arose when the police decided that the demonstrators had no right to be there and should be removed. In such situations a whole host of factors contribute to disorder: group loyalties, male codes of honour, a simple desire for revenge. These may appear at the time to be the prime motivations of those present. But an equally important motivation is a sense of moral outrage that rights are being infringed by arbitrary application of the law.

In our case study of Grimethorpe, that sense of moral outrage was evident in the street confrontations with the police and in the subsequent public meeting. For once, the local community had the ability to articulate its claim to rights, at least in retrospect. Elsewhere the sense of rights and the means to articulate them are more elusive. The connection between an incident or an issue and the disorderly reaction to it is often more tenuous. An inner-city riot may be a claim to the right to be free of police harassment, to smoke cannabis or drink alcohol, or to have access to decent employment and housing. Here the rights being mobilized are not, as at a normal demonstration or picket, specific to the particular situation but have more general purchase. One of the factors taking the miners' strike beyond the usual bounds of industrial conflict was that it came to involve larger claims to rights, the right to jobs for individuals and the right to an economic future for whole communities.

Unlike the American or European systems, the rights of the citizen are not codified as such in English law. Britain has not incorporated the European Convention on Human Rights into English law. The most recent attempt to instigate such a move, through a private members' bill in the House of Lords, was defeated. The technical arguments for and against such a move are complex. What is easy to identify is the current lack of legal standing for most of what are assumed to be civil rights. This applies to a range of issues. Contrary to popular belief, for example, there is no positive right to freedom of speech in Britain. Its exercise is hedged round by a whole web of laws of slander and libel, contempt of court, incitement to racial hatred and the notorious Official Secrets Act. There is not even a right to stand on the pavement; as many demonstrators and street vendors have learned to their cost, the offence of obstructing the highway can be extended to include just standing about. 'Rights' are a residual category in English law, reducible to the freedom to do what is not expressly forbidden. 'Legally, public "rights", whether individual or collective, rest on a fragile surface: they are residuary rather than positive freedoms' (McCabe and Wallington 1988, 78).

If such supposedly elementary freedoms have no legal status, it is not surprising to find more complex rights remaining undefined in law. There is no right in law to strike, much less picket, merely a limited immunity from prosecution under civil law of trade unionists engaged in industrial disputes provided that they are not contravening the law. The existence and scope of this immunity has been the form which the 'right to strike' has taken in the history of English law. Thus what are essentially arguments about the basic rights of labour cannot become questions of constitutional principle, since there are no such principles.

Apparently minor changes in the law and its administration can as a result effectively remove civil rights. Recent trade union legislation, under the guise of protecting innocent individuals, has been used to undermine the principle of the right to strike. Secondary picketing has been made subject to civil prosecution, the number of pickets restricted initially in a code of practice now in the Public Order Act, and strike ballots are now compulsory. Through such measures, the legal position of trade unions and the rights of their members are being radically redefined. There is no constitutional redress for such activity, since trade union rights have only the status which the law defines in largely negative terms: not what trade unionists have the right to do, but what under the law they may not do.

This is but the most obvious example of the absence of rights from the British constitution. Their absence has a specific effect upon the potential for public disorder. If rights are not legally defined, if the law is designed to restrict such rights without in any sense guaranteeing them, if the individual's rights are preferred to those of the group, then any collective attempt to secure rights is likely to run foul of the law. Moreover, the police are obliged only to enforce the law, not to counterbalance this with any inalienable rights:

> The enactment of a Bill of Rights based on the European Convention of Human Rights would make explicit many of the matters which are at best implicit in domestic law. This would make it easier for the police to accept the positive duty to recognize and safeguard those rights and freedoms which are of particular concern to civil liberties campaigners; in this way a clearer basis for a common commitment to civil liberties could be established. (McCabe and Wallington 1988, 15)

Instead of such a move, precisely the reverse has happened: the right of assembly is now to be subject to such stringent conditions as to be effectively denied altogether.

Thus public disorder, in the forms we have been discussing itself frequently a claim to rights, has been used as the pretext for legislation which severely limits the right to protest at all. The objective seems to be to get rid of disorder by prohibiting crowds from assembling. In so doing, collective claims to rights are denied by making their expression illegal. It is a crude solution to a complex problem. If it works, order will be maintained at the expense of rights. If it does not, then not only order and civil rights but the law itself, will fall into disrepute. So too will the

197

police, whose constitutional independence from the state is our final concern.

The police and the state

Policing of all kinds, and especially of public order, is inevitably a political act:

> Nowhere are the police political innocents: to claim otherwise is disingenuous. By focusing on public order, policing is clearly revealed as a political activity. Recognition of this fact may be more palatable to the passive observer of events in South Africa or Northern Ireland, but is no less true of Britain.
>
> (Brewer *el al*. 1988, 4)

As such, it is framed by the general powers and particular policies adopted by those with control of state power, since 'the state plays an important role in conditioning the styles of policing adopted by a force in particular circumstances, at different historical periods and when confronted with specific issues and threats' (Brewer *et al*. 1988, 280). It is this factor which leads Uglow to claim that 'the fundamental issue in any discussion of a police force is its relationship with the State' (1988, 17).

In the 1980s, public order policy has been presented by Conservative politicians and chief police officers as essentially reactive to new threats to public order. In some areas, such as football hooliganism, this argument has legitimacy. But in the issue-oriented disorders we have been considering, this argument misrepresents the extent to which the police have been put in the political front line. They have been required to control sections of the population who regard themselves as victims of the radical economic policies adopted by the government. As McCabe and Wallington (1988) and Brewer *et al*. (1988) suggest, policing by consent is no longer possible where conflict rather than consensus is the dominant mood in political life. However, policing does not merely reflect the state of politics: the police themselves have come to be political actors. They have been deliberately used and manipulated, most obviously during the miners' strike, as one powerful arm of a political offensive. Uglow makes the most credible explanation of changes in policing policy: 'the social and political polarization of Britain in the 1980s and the recognition that industrial and political stability would be hard to maintain at a time of high unemployment throughout Western Europe'

(1988, 13). Such a view is frequently portrayed as left-wing rhetoric but Uglow is a declared liberal, whose chief concern is with 'the changes in the constitutional balance between individual and state that the changes in policing are bringing about' (1988, vii). As Brewer *et al.* remark, 'the idea that the police act in political ways to enforce government policies is no longer confined to the tributaries of radical opinion: it has flowed into the mainstream of political life' (1988, 2). Their comparative analysis of public order policing in seven nations leads them to conclude that this tendency is not confined to Britain, since generally 'liberal states are becoming more suppressive and authoritarian in their strategies of order-maintenance' (1988, 235).

Those who view such developments with alarm need to develop alternative accounts of, and strategies of response to, threats to public order. Our whole book has been just such an attempt. Whereas the prescriptions for social, economic, and political change may seem long-term if not utopian, there is at least one problem which is amenable to immediate solution: the constitutional position of the police. Theoretically, the police are controlled by a tripartite system of central government, local police committees, and independent Chief Constables but the miners' strike showed this to have collapsed:

> We regard machinery for the democratic accountability of the police for decisions about the way the community is policed and for the allocation of police resources, through representatives of the local communities concerned, as an essential component of a democratic society, and a necessary precondition of the preservation of civil liberties. To all intents and purposes it no longer exists.
>
> (McCabe and Wallington, 1988, 137)

The impotence of police committees, and a complaints system which rules out questioning of policy, have effectively removed the police from any accountability at all – except to the Home Secretary, whose interests, at a time of political conflict, can never be disinterested.

Calls for the police to become accountable to the communities they serve are not, as their opponents claim, attempts to undermine police activity. They are rather attempts to wrest some control of the police back from a centralized state machinery. Public order has to be maintained, a task which ultimately but not necessarily resides with the police. The question is not whether public order should be maintained, but how and in whose interests. Jefferson and Grimshaw (1984), amongst others, have made quite specific suggestions about the form such local accountability might take. The alternative is the status quo: a *de facto* national police force, acting on behalf of the political party in power, whilst claiming that it is a devolved and independent institution interested only in enforcing the law. We therefore agree with the conclusion of McCabe and Wallington:

> Policing has an influence on the state of society, and for this reason the issues of policing policy and accountability are fundamental. But the influence of the state of society on the police is far greater. A deeply divided society cannot be policed by consent; a society whose laws unfairly restrict access to economic power will face social pressures which strain the limits of police resourcefulness. The problems of an inner-city underclass, of a legally crippled trade union movement, of groups pinned down by institutionalized racism, confront the police now, and will continue to do so, just as surely as they confront society as a whole. A society which is not vigilant in recognizing these problems, but simply leaves it to the police to maintain tranquillity through forcible control, will indeed have the police it deserves.   (McCabe and Wallington, 1988, 156)

Postscript

The main period of the research reported in this book was from 1983 to 1985. A first complete draft was submitted to our publishers in the summer of 1987, this revised version one year later. Since some of the case study material may now seem dated, it is worth emphasizing that the general problem of public order and its relationship to civil liberties has not abated. Here we note various incidents from 1987 and the early part of 1988 which indicate the continued relevance of our analysis. Lacking the necessary detailed evidence, we cannot apply our model to these instances but merely indicate the scope of events to which it could in principle be applied.

The ramifications of several incidents discussed in this book continue. In April 1988, an investigation of the policing of Wapping successfully obtained court orders requiring television companies to hand over film of events there. In May, two police officers were cleared of perjury following the Manchester University demonstration, the judge remarking that they had merely made honest mistakes. In July, the Metropolitan Police paid an out of court settlement of £75,000 plus costs to the relatives of Blair Peach, an uneasy conclusion to the events at Southall nine years before. The trials of over seventy people charged in connection with the Broadwater Farm disturbances ended. Despite a successful prosecution of the murderers of PC Blakelock, the conduct of the police investigation caused such an outcry that it was referred to the Police Complaints Authority for investigation. Lord Gifford had previously announced his intention of reopening his investigation of conditions on the estate.

Some public order situations have become recurring events. After the fatal stabbing of a street vendor at the 1987 Notting Hill Carnival, police chiefs called for it to be banned. In the same and the following year, travelling people attempting to reach Stonehenge for the summer solstice were turned away by a massive police presence, though without the disorders of previous years. Outside the South African Embassy, participants in the permanent vigil were amongst the first to feel the weight of the new Public Order legislation.

No national demonstration has recently produced significant disorder. Nor have any community disorders been headlined, though skirmishes between police and black youths were reported in 1987 from such diverse locations as High Wycombe and Wolverhampton, where the police introduced video cameras to scan the town centre. The greatest potential for industrial disorder arose during the seamen's strike of early 1988. There were several superficial similarities to the miners' strike. Management closely identified with the Conservative Party arbitrarily introduced a programme of new working practices and redundancies. The National Union of Seamen responded with mass national picketing. Sequestration of their funds followed. Eventually the strike was broken without significant disorder on the picket line. Again, the reasons for this absence would bear investigation.

In our local area of South Yorkshire, a few incidents of actual or potential disorder have occurred. Early in 1987 a march in support of Irish nationalism was attacked by skinheads and forty people were arrested. In July 1987, controversy broke out over the policing of Burngreave, a predominantly black area. Local community leaders and councillors criticized the activity of the police, who cited as justification local fears about drugs, prostitution, and street crime. In April 1988, there was no demonstration against the Cutlers' Feast, where the guest of honour was Lord Young. He was joined and acclaimed as a speaker by Clive Betts, leader of the City Council.

More troubling to the police were a series of weekend confrontations with youths in the suburbs of Sheffield. These were interpreted by the local media as a local variation of the trend identified in a report by the Association of Chief Police Officers in June 1988 on 'riots' by young men in rural areas against the police in and around public houses. In turn related to football hooliganism, surfacing once more during the European Championship in Germany, such incidents guaranteed that public disorder was once again being portrayed essentially as the problem of 'hooligans'. This image further validated existent and proposed extensions of police powers, marginalizing any questions of civil liberties and disguising the differences between issue-oriented and issue-less riots.

All these incidents testify to the continued problem of public order and the consistent refusal of those charged with upholding it to consider the issues raised in this book. It is impossible to be sanguine about the prospects for public order or civil liberties as Britain enters the 1990s.

Bibliography

Allen, V. L.(1981) *The Militancy of the Miners*, Shipley, The Moor Press.

Ardrey, R. (1967) *The Territorial Imperative*, London, Collins.

Atkinson, M. T.(1977) 'Coroners and the categorisation of deaths as suicides: changes in perspective as features of the research process', in C. Bell and H. Newby (eds) *Doing Sociological Research*, London, Allen & Unwin.

Benyon, J. (ed.) (1984) *Scarman and After: Essays Reflecting on Lord Scarman's Report, the Riots and their Aftermath*, Oxford, Pergamon.

Berk, R. A. (1974) 'A gaming approach to crowd behaviour', *American Sociological Review* 39, 355–73.

Berkowitz, L. (1972) 'Frustrations, comparison and other sources of emotion arousal as contributors to social unrest', *Journal of Social Issues* 28, 77–91.

Beynon, H. (ed.) *Digging Deeper: Issues in the Miners' Strike*, London, Verso.

Billig, M. (1976) *Social Psychology and Inter-group Relations*, London, Academic Press.

Bittner, E. (1967) 'The police on Skid-Row: a study of peace keeping', *American Sociological Review* 32 (5), 699–715.

Bowen, D. R. and Masotti, L. H. (1968) 'Civil violence: a theoretical overview', in L. H. Masotti and D. R. Bowen (eds) *Civil Violence in the Urban Community*, Beverly Hills, California, Sage.

Brewer, J. D., Guelke, A., Moxon-Browne, E., and Wilford, R. (1988) *The Police, Public Order and The State*, London, Macmillan.

Broadwater Farm Enquiry (1986) *Report of the Independent Enquiry*, London, Karia Press.

Brown, R. R. (1985) *Social Psychology*, New York, Free Press, second edition.

Brunt, R., Critcher, C., Jones, K., and Jordin, M. (forthcoming) *Representing the People: Case Studies in Media and Politics*, London, Comedia/Routledge.

Bryer, R. A., Brignall, T. J., and Maunders, A. (1982) *Accounting for British Steel*, London, Gower.

Cain, M. (1973) *Society and the Policeman's Role*, London, Routledge & Kegan Paul.

Callinicos, A. and Simons, M. (1985) *The Great Strike: The Miners'*
Strike of 1984–85 and its Lessons, London, Socialist Worker.
Cannon, T. (1982) 'Wrongful arrest', *New Statesman,* 10 November
1982.
Card, R. (1987) *Public Order: the New Law,* London, Butterworth.
Castells, M. (1976) 'Theory and ideology in urban sociology', in C.
Pickvance (ed.) *Urban Sociology: Critical Essays,* London, Tavistock.
Castells, M. (1983) *The City and the Grassroots,* London, Edward
Arnold.
Chibnall, S. (1977) *Law and Order News,* London, Tavistock.
Clutterbuck, R. (1977) *Britain in Agony,* Harmondsworth, Penguin.
Cohen, S. (1973) *Folk Devils and Moral Panics,* St Albans, Paladin.
Coulter, J., Miller, S., and Walker, M. (1984) *A State of Siege: Politics*
and Policing in the Coalfields, London, Canary Press.
Cowell, D., Jones, T., and Young, J. (1982) *Policing the Riots,* London,
Junction Books.
Crick, M. (1985) *Scargill and the Miners,* Harmondsworth, Penguin.
Critcher, C., Fielding, G., Jones, K., and Waddington, D. P. (1984)
'Report of a Survey of Attitudes to the Miners' Strike in Sheffield',
unpublished MS Sheffield, Sheffield City Polytechnic.
De Gorde Peach (1960) *The Company of Cutlers in Hallamshire in the*
County of York 1906–1956, Sheffield, The Cutlers' Company.
Dennis, M., Henriques, F., and Slaughter, C. (1956) *Coal is Our Life,*
London, Eyre & Spottiswoode.
Department of Employment (1980) *Code of Practice on Picketing,*
London, HMSO.
Di Giacomo, J. P. (1980) 'Intergroup alliance and rejections within a
protest movement (analysis of social representations)', *European*
Journal of Social Psychology 10, 329–44.
Docherty, C. (1983) *Steel and Steelmakers,* London, Heinemann.
Downes, B. (1970a) 'A critical re-examination of the social and political
characteristics of riot cities', *Social Science Quarterly* 51, 349–60.
Downes, B. (1970b) 'Black protest and urban racial violence:
confrontation politics', in J. Reidel (ed.) *State and Local Politics,*
Waltham, Blaisdell.
Dromey, J. and Taylor, G. (1978) *Grunwick: The Workers' Story,*
London, Lawrence & Wishart.
Dunning, E., Murphy, P., Newburn, T., and Waddington, I. (1987)
'Violent disorders in an English county', in G. Gaskell and R.
Benewick (eds) *The Crowd in Contemporary Britain,* London, Sage.
East, R. and Thomas, P. (1985) 'Road-Blocks: The experience in
Wales', in B. Fine and R. Millar (eds) *Policing the Miners' Strike,*
London, Lawrence & Wishart.
Evans, R. R. (ed.) (1975) *Readings in Collective Behavior,* Chicago,
Rand-McNally.
Field, S. and Southgate, P. (1982) *Public Disorder: A Review of*
Research and a Study in One Inner-City Area, London, HMSO.
Fine, B. and Millar, R. (eds) (1985) *Policing the Miners' Strike,* London,
Lawrence & Wishart.

Bibliography

Geary, R. (1985) *Policing Industrial Disputes*, Cambridge, Cambridge University Press.

Geschwender, J. (1968) 'Explorations in the theory of revolutions and social movements', *Social Forces*, 42, 127–35.

Giner, S. (1976) *Mass Society*, London, Martin Robertson.

Goodman, G. (1985) *The Miners' Strike*, London, Pluto.

Gordon, P. (1985) 'If they come back in the morning . . . The police, the miners and black people', in B. Fine and R. Millar (eds) *Policing the Miners' Strike*, London, Lawrence & Wishart.

Gurr, T. (1970) *Why Men Rebel*, Princeton, Princeton University Press.

Hall, S. and Jefferson, T. (eds) (1976) *Resistance Through Rituals*, London, Hutchinson.

Hall, S., Critcher, C., Jefferson, T., Clarke, J., and Roberts, B. (1978) *Policing the Crisis: Mugging, the State and Law and Order*, London, Macmillan.

Halloran, J. D., Elliott, P., and Murdock, G. (1970) *Demonstrations and Communication: A Case Study*, Harmondsworth, Penguin.

Harman, H. (1982) 'Civil liberties', in D. Cowell, T. Jones, and J. Young (eds) (1982) *Policing the Riots*, London, Junction Books.

Hartley, J., Kelly, J., and Nicholson, N. (1983) *Steel Strike*, London, Batsford.

Hebdige, D. (1979) *Subculture: The Meaning of Style*, London, Methuen.

Her Majesty's Government (1985) *Review of Public Order Law*, London, HMSO, Cmnd 9590.

Holdaway, S. (ed.) (1979) *The British Police*, London, Edward Arnold.

Holdaway, S. (1983) *Inside the British Police*, Oxford, Blackwell.

Home Office (1980) *Review of Arrangements for Handling Spontaneous Disorder*, London, HMSO.

House of Commons Select Committee on Home Affairs (1980) *Report on the Law Relating to Public Disorder* (Fifth Report HC 756 I and II), London, House of Commons.

Jefferson, T. and Grimshaw, R. (1984) *Controlling the Constable*, London, Frederick Muller.

Joshua, H., Wallace, T., and Booth, H. (1983) *To Ride the Storm: The 1980 Bristol 'Riot' and the State*, London, Heinemann.

Kahn, P., Lewis, M., Livock, R., and Wiles, P. (1983) *Picketing: Industrial Disputes, Tactics and the Law*, London, Routledge & Kegan Paul.

Kaye, T. (1984) ' "A Village at War": A Report to the Yorkshire Area of the National Union of Mineworkers Concerning the Policy of Policing Fitzwilliam, West Yorkshire, on Monday, 9th July, 1984', unpublished report, Coventry, University of Warwick.

Kelley, H. H. (1973) 'The processes of causal attributions', *American Psychologist* 28, 1O7–28.

Kelly, J. (1981) 'Steel: An irreversible decline?', *Marxism Today*, June, 1O–16.

Kerner Commission (1968) *Report of the National Advisory Committee on Civil Disorders*, Washington DC, Government Printing Office.

Kettle, M. (1985) 'The National Reporting Centre and the 1984 miners' strike', in B. Fine and R. Millar (eds) *Policing the Miners' Strike*, London, Lawrence & Wishart.

Kettle, M. and Hodges, L. (1982) *Uprising: the Police, the People and the Riots in Britain's Cities*, London, Pan.

Law Commission (1982) *Offences Against Public Order*, Working Paper 82, London, HMSO.

Law Commission (1983) *Report on Criminal Law: Offences Relating to Public Order*, Working Paper 123, London, HMSO.

Lea, J. and Young, J. (1982) 'The riots in Britain 1981: urban violence and political marginalisation', in D. Cowell, T. Jones, and J. Young (eds) *Policing the Riots*, London, Junction Books.

Le Bon, G. (1952) *The Crowd*, London, Ernest Benn.

Lewis, J. M. (1975) 'A study of the Kent State Incident using Smelser's theory of collective behavior', in R. R. Evans (ed.) *Readings in Collective Behavior*, Chicago, Rand-McNally.

Lieberson, S. and Silverman, A. (1965) 'The precipitants and underlying causes of race riots', *American Sociological Review* 3O, 887–98.

Litton, I. and Potter, J. (1985) 'Social representations in the ordinary explanation of a "riot" ', *European Journal of Social Psychology* 15, 371–88.

Lloyd, C. (1985) 'A national riot police: Britain's third force?' in B. Fine and R. Millar (eds) *Policing the Miners' Strike*, London, Lawrence & Wishart.

Lowe, S. (1986) *Urban Social Movements*, London, Macmillan.

McCabe, S. and Wallington, P. with J. Alderson, L. Gostin, and C. Mason (1988) *The Police, Public Order, and Civil Liberties*, London, Routledge.

Mackillop, J. (1981) *Ethnic Minorities in Sheffield*, Sheffield, Sheffield City Council.

Manning, P. K. (1977) *Police Work*, Cambridge, Mass., MIT Press.

Marsh, P. (1978) *Aggro: The Illusion of Violence*, London, J. M. Dent

Marsh, P. and Campbell, A. (eds) (1982) *Aggression and Violence*, Oxford, Blackwell.

Marsh, P., Rosser, E., and Harré, R. (1978) *The Rules of Disorder*, London, Routledge & Kegan Paul.

Marx, G. T. (1970) 'Civil disorder and the agents of social control', *Journal of Social Issues* 26 (1), 19–57.

Masotti, L. M. and Bowen, D. R. (1968) *Civil Violence in the Urban Community*, Beverly Hills, California, Sage.

Masterman, L. (1985) 'The battle of Orgreave', in L. Masterman (ed.) *Television Mythologies*, London, Comedia.

Mitchell, J. P. (ed.) (1970) *Race Riots in Black and White*, Englewood Cliffs, New Jersey, Prentice-Hall.

Moscovici, S. (1981) 'On social representations', in J. Forgas (ed.) *Social Cognition: Perspectives on Everyday Understanding*, London, Academic Press.

Moscovici, S. and Hewstone, M. (1983) 'Social representations and social explanations: from the "naive" to the "amateur" scientist', in M.

Hewstone (ed.) *Attribution theory: Social and Functional Extensions*, Oxford, Blackwell

Moscovici, S. (1985) *The Age of the Crowd*, Cambridge, Cambridge University Press.

National Council For Civil Liberties (1980) *Southall 23rd April 1979*, London, NCCL.

National Council For Civil Liberties (1984) *Civil Liberties and the Miners' Dispute*, London, NCCL.

National Council For Civil Liberties (1986) *No Way in Wapping: The Effect of the Policing of the News International Dispute on Wapping Residents*, London, NCCL.

New Society (1982) *Race and Riots '81*, A New Society Social Studies Reader, London, New Society.

Olson, M. (1965) *The Logic of Collective Action*, Cambridge, Mass., Harvard University Press.

Parsons, T. (1951) *The Social System*, London, Routledge & Kegan Paul.

Potter, J. and Reicher, S. (1987) 'Discourses of community and conflict: the organisation of social categories in accounts of a "riot"', *British Journal of Social Psychology* 25, 25–40.

Potter, J. and Wetherell, M. (1987) *Discourse and Social Psychology: Beyond Attitudes and Behaviour*, London, Sage.

Reicher, S. D. (1984) 'The St. Paul's riot: an exploration of the limits of crowd action in terms of a social identity model', *European Journal of Social Psychology* 14, 1–24.

Reicher, S. and Potter, J. (1985) 'Psychological theory as intergroup perspective: a comparative analysis of "scientific" and "lay" accounts of crowd events', *Human Relations* 30, 167–87.

Reiner, R. (1977) 'Police and picketing', *New Society*, 7 July 1977.

Reiner, R. (1985) *The Politics of the Police*, Brighton, Wheatsheaf.

Report Of The Independent Inquiry Panel (1985) *Leon Brittan's visit to Manchester University Students' Union 1st March 1985*, Manchester, Manchester City Council.

Report of the Review Panel (1986) *A Different Reality*, Birmingham, West Midlands County Council.

Rogaly, J. (1977) *Grunwick*, Harmondsworth, Penguin.

Rollo, J. (1980) 'The Special Patrol Group', in P. Harris (ed.) *Policing the Police* Vol. 2, London, John Calder.

Rudé, G. (1980) *Ideology and Popular Protest*, London, Lawrence & Wishart

Saunders, P. (1981) *Social Theory and the Urban Question*, London, Hutchinson.

Scarman, Lord (1974) *Report of Inquiry into the Red Lion Square Disorders of 15 June 1974*, London, HMSO, Cmnd 5915.

Scarman, Lord (1981) *The Brixton Disorders, 10th-12th April, 1981*, London, HMSO, Cmnd 8427.

Scranton Report (1970) *Report Of The President's Commission on Campus Unrest*, Washington DC, Government Printing Office.

Scraton, P. (1985a) 'From Saltley Gates to Orgreave: a history of the policing of recent industrial disputes', in B. Fine and R. Millar (eds) *Policing the Miners' Strike*, London, Lawrence & Wishart.

Scraton, P. (1985b) *The State of the Police*, London, Pluto Press.

Sheffield Policewatch Daily Reports, April 1984–March 1985.

Silverman, J. (1986) *Independent Inquiry into the Handsworth Disturbances*, Birmingham, Birmingham City Council.

Skolnick, J. H. (1966) *Justice without Trial: Law Enforcement in Democratic Society*, New York, John Wiley.

Skolnick, J. H. (1969) *The Politics of Protest*, New York, Simon & Schuster.

Smelser, N. (1962) *Theory of Collective Behaviour*, New York, Free Press.

Smith, A. T. H. (1985) *Public Order Law: The Government Proposals*, Public Law S33.

Smith, D. J. and Gray, J. (1985) *Police and People in London* (The PSI Report), London, Gower.

Smith, M. D. (1983) *Violence and Sport*, London, Butterworth.

Southall Rights (1980) *23rd April, 1979, A Report*, Southall, Southall Rights.

Southgate, P. (1982) *Police Probationer Training in Race Relations*, London, Home Office.

South Yorkshire Police (1980) *The National Steel Strike 1980*, unpublished report, Sheffield, South Yorkshire Police.

South Yorkshire Police (1985) *Policing the Coal Industry Dispute in South Yorkshire*, Sheffield, South Yorkshire Police.

Spencer, S. (1985) 'The eclipse of the Police Authority', in B. Fine and R. Millar (eds) *Policing the Miners' Strike*, London, Lawrence & Wishart.

Spiegel, J. P. (1969) 'Hostility, aggression and violence', in A. D. Grimshaw (ed.) *Patterns in American Racial Violence*, Chicago, Aldine.

Stark, M. J., Raime, W. J., Burbeck, S. L., and Davison, K. (1974) 'Some empirical patterns in a riot process', *American Sociological Review* 39, 865–76.

Stevenson, J. (1979) *Popular Disturbances in England 1700–1870*, London, Longman.

Sullivan, T. J. (1977) 'The "critical mass" in crowd behaviour: crowd size contagion and the evolution of riots', *Humboldt Journal of Social Relations* 42, 46–59.

Sunday Times Insight Team (1985) *Strike: A Battle of Ideologies; Thatcher, Scargill and the Miners*, London, Coronet.

Tajfel, H. (1978) 'Inter-group behaviour 1: individualistic perspectives', in H. Tajfel and C. Fraser (eds) *Introducing Social Psychology*, Harmondsworth, Penguin.

Tarde, G. (1901) *L'Opinion et la foule*, Paris, Alcan.

Thompson, E. P. (1963) *The Making of the English Working Class*, London, Gollancz.

Thompson, E. P. (1971) 'The moral economy of the English crowd in the eighteenth century', *Past and Present* 50, 76–136.

Bibliography

Thompson, E. P. (1975) *Whigs and Hunters*, Harmondsworth, Penguin.

Thornton, P. (1985) *We Protest: The Public Order Debate*, London, NCCL.

Tuck, M. and Southgate, P. (1981) *Ethnic Minorities, Crime and Policing*, London, Home Office Research Unit.

Uglow, S. (1988) *Policing Liberal Society*, Oxford, Oxford University Press.

Waddington, D., Jones, K., and Critcher, C. (1987) 'Flashpoints of public disorder', in G. Gaskell and R. Benewick (eds) *The Crowd in Contemporary Britain*, London, Sage.

Warpole, K. (1979) 'Death in Southall', *New Society*, 24 May 1979.

Weir, S. (1977) 'The police and the pickets', *New Society*, 30 June 1977.

Wright, S. (1978) *Crowds and Riots*, Beverly Hills, California, Sage.

Zimbardo, P. G. (1969) 'The human choice: reason and order versus de-individuation, impulse and chaos' in W. J. Arnold and D. Levine (eds) *Nebraska Symposium on Motivation*, Lincoln, University of Nebraska Press.

Index